ALLIGATORS, BUFFALOES, AND BUSHMASTERS

THE HISTORY OF THE DEVELOPMENT OF THE LVT THROUGH WORLD WAR II

by
Major Alfred Dunlop Bailey, USMC (Retired)

Occasional Paper

HISTORY AND MUSEUMS DIVISION
HEADQUARTERS, U.S. MARINE CORPS
WASHINGTON, D.C.

1986

This reprint edition published by Books Express Publishing
Copyright © Books Express, 2011
ISBN 978-1-780391-07-6
To purchase copies at discounted prices please contact
info@books-express.com

Foreword

The History and Museums Division, Headquarters, U.S. Marine Corps, has undertaken the publication, for limited distribution, of various non-official studies, theses, compilations, bibliographies, and monographs, as well as proceedings of selected workshops, seminars, symposia, and similar colloquia, which it considers to be of significant value for audiences interested in Marine Corps history. These "Occasional Papers," which are chosen for their intrinsic worth, must reflect structured research, present a contribution to historical knowledge not readily available in published sources, and reflect original content on the part of the author, compiler, or editor. It is the intent of the division that these occasional papers be distributed to selected institutions, such as service schools, official Department of Defense historical agencies, and directly concerned Marine Corps organizations, so that the information contained therein will be available for study and exploitation.

Alligators, Buffaloes, and Bushmasters was a master-of-arts thesis in history at the University of Utah. Its author, Major Alfred D. Bailey, USMC (Ret.), is a graduate of the U.S. Military Academy at West Point, who opted for Marine Corps service and served as a tank and amphibian vehicle officer while on active duty. In 1968-69 he commanded a company of the 1st Amphibian Tractor Battalion in Vietnam. Major Bailey currently is program manager with an aerospace company and resides in El Toro, California.

The thesis is an exact reproduction of the original submitted to the University of Utah. The illustrations, maps and photographs, are not, as a result, as clear as reproductions from originals would be. The History and Museums Division, however, has copies of all official photographs, other photographs taken by Major Bailey, and maps. These are available for further study at the Marine Corps Historical Center.

The opinion and facts presented in this thesis are those of the author and do not necessarily represent those of the Marine Corps and the Department of the Navy. In the pursuit of accuracy and objectivity, the History and Museums Division welcomes comments on this thesis from present and former amphibian tractor veterans as well as other interested individuals and activities.

E. H. SIMMONS
Brigadier General, U. S. Marine Corps (Ret.)
Director of Marine Corps History and Museums

ALLIGATORS, BUFFALOES, AND BUSHMASTERS:

THE HISTORY OF THE DEVELOPMENT OF THE LVT THROUGH WORLD WAR II

by

Alfred Dunlop Bailey

A thesis submitted to the faculty of the
University of Utah in partial fulfillment of the requirements
for the degree of

Master of Arts

in

History

Department of History

University of Utah

March 1976

ACKNOWLEDGEMENT

This thesis is dedicated to my patient wife who served as my editor-in-Chief and general source of needed encouragement during the writing of the thesis.

Special thanks are given to Mrs. Molly Sherbanee, whose attention to detail and conscientious work were vital in the typing of this paper.

A great debt is owed to the LVT Test Branch, Marine Corps Tactical Systems Support Activity, Marine Corps Base, Camp Pendleton, California for their complete support of research activity in their extensive archives.

The generous cooperation of Lieutenant Colonel R. B. Tiffany, History and Museums Branch, Headquarters, U. S. Marine Corps, Washington D.C. was instrumental in making available original combat reports used in this work.

The support, encouragement, and excellent criticism of Professor F. Alan Coombs was a key to the writing and refinement of this paper and his assistance in numerous administrative matters, which arose due to the author's non-residency in Utah was invaluable to the successful completion of this task.

And a last dedication must go to valiant men - the crews.

TABLE OF CONTENTS

ACKNOWLEDGEMENTS iv
LIST OF ILLUSTRATIONS vi
LIST OF MAPS viii
ABSTRACT ix

PART
I. BACKGROUND TO DEVELOPMENT 1
II. EARLY DEVELOPMENT 25
III. EARLY LESSONS 47
IV. TARAWA 78
V. THE MARSHALLS: THE FULL RANGE OF USE 102
VI. SAIPAN: EMPLOYMENT IN MASS 151
VII. TRACTION IN THE BLACK SAND 188
VIII. BIGGEST FOR LAST 215
IX. SUCCESSORS TO THE LEGEND 244

SELECTED BIBLIOGRAPHY 268
VITA 273

LIST OF ILLUSTRATIONS

1. Early Beetle Boat undergoing tests 18
2. The Christie Amphibious Tank 18
3. The Life Magazine article leading to discovery of the LVT . . 35
4. Side view of the Vickers-Armstrong Tank of 1931-32 36
5. Rear view of the Vickers-Armstrong 36
6. LVT(1)s coming ashore at Guadalcanal 54
7. LVT(1)s approaching the beach on a supply run 54
8. The early test version of the LVT(A)1 coming ashore 58
9. The Borg-Warner Model A 64
10. The Borg-Warner Model A with turret removed 64
11. The LVT(2) in final form 65
12. An overhead view of the cargo compartment of the LVT(2) . . 65
13. A training manual photograph of the LVT(A)2 66
14. The LVT(A)1 in final form 67
15. The LVT(A)1 in rear view 67
16. A training manual diagram on relationship of power train . . 68
17. The LVT(1) at Bougainville 73
18. Maintenance in the field 73
19. The trusty Landing Ship, Tank (LST) 87
20. A view of the beach after D-Day, Tarawa 92
21. Another grim view of the beach at Tarawa 92
22. The Landing Craft, Infantry (LCI) modified as a gunboat . . 110
23. The Landing Craft, Vehicle, Personnel (LCVP) 118
24. The long-range B-29 over Japan 152
25. The LVT(4) and LVT(2) in a floating comparison 158
26. A rear view of the first ramped LVT 158
27. Side view of the LVT(4) with a 105mm howitzer loaded . . . 160
28. Inside view of the 105mm howitzer load 160
29. Side view of the LVT(A)4 162
30. Overhead view shows open-top construction of the turret . . 162
31. The first waves of LVT(4)s head for beaches at Iwo Jima . . 203
32. LVT(4)s churning for the shoreline 203
33. Two LVTs in action during the early phases of the landing . . 205
34. Early example of terrible beach litter 205
35. The beachhead in the later stages of development 208
36. Hectic logistic activity in the beachhead 208
37. The Borg-Warner Model B 224
38. Ford Sedan mounting loading ramp of the Model B 224
39. Ford Sedan completely loaded inside the Model B 225
40. Driver's controls of the Model B 225
41. Side view of the LVT(3) 228
42. Rear view of the LVT(3) with ramp lowered 228
43. Front view of the LVT(3) 229
44. LVT(A)4s crossing the line of departure 233

45.	A platoon of LVT(A)4s waiting for orders	238
46.	The LVT(3)C	249
47.	The LVT(3)C rear view	249
48.	The LVT(P)5 front view	250
49.	The LVT(P)5 rear view	250
50.	The LVT(R)1 front view	251
51.	The LVT(R)1 rear view	251
52.	The LVT(H)6 front view	252
53.	The LVT(H)6 rear view	252
54.	The LVT(P)7 front view	257
55.	The LVT(C)7 rear view	257
56.	The LVT(R)7 rear view	258
57.	The UH-1 Iroquois helicopter	258
58.	The CH-46 Sea Knight helicopter	261
59.	The CH-53 Sea Stallion helicopter	261

LIST OF MAPS

1. Southwest Pacific Area 48
2. Solomon Islands 49
3. Landings, Central and Northern Solomons, June 1943 to
   February 1944 71
4. The Gilberts and the Marshalls 79
5. Betio Islet with Tarawa Atoll 80
6. Marshall Islands 103
7. Kwajalein Atoll 108
8. D-Day landings prior to Roi-Namur 111
9. Capture of Namur 122
10. Capture of Roi 125
11. Eniwetok Atoll 132
12. Seizure of Eniwetok 140
13. The Marianas 154
14. D-Day at Saipan 169
15. Landing plan, Iwo Jima 196
16. Nansei Shoto 216
17. Japanese Defensive Positions, 1 April 1945 219
18. ICEBERG (Invasion of Okinawa) Scheme of Maneuver 222

ABSTRACT

This thesis is concerned with the Marine Corps' actions in the discovery and development of the Land Vehicle Tracted (LVT) through World War II, and focuses on its use in the Solomon Islands and the Central Pacific. A concluding part deals with post-war development and the future of the vehicle.

In Part I, the involvement of the Marine Corps in amphibious operations is briefly traced from its early days through World War I. Between 1918 and 1940, the Marine Corps forecasted the nature of the next war in the Pacific and acted to create an organization dedicated to developing expertise in the tactical methods that eventually defeated Japan a decade later. This organization was the Fleet Marine Force.

The creation of the Fleet Marine Force stimulated landing exercises and development of amphibious doctrine and highlighted the need for an amphibious vehicle to cross shallow waters and reefs and permit attackers to choose their landing points. No satisfactory answer to this requirement had been found when by accident the Roebling Alligator was spotted in a _Life_ magazine article by a Navy admiral. This vehicle, originally intended for rescue, eventually became the LVT(1) and was intended for cargo use only.

In Part III, the early combat lessons of Guadalcanal and Bougainville showed the weaknesses in the LVT(1) suspension and track, but also illustrated the great versatility of the LVT design. Development progressed on the LVT(2), with greatly improved performance, and limited numbers were used in the landmark battle of the Central Pacific, Tarawa (Part IV).

Tarawa taught the Marine Corps bitter lessons and the subsequent changes in amphibious doctrine remained standard practice throughout the remainder of the war. The LVT(2) demonstrated its worth as a troop carrier and production moved ahead.

Part V discussed the Marshalls campaign which used the full range of the LVT including the LVT(A)1, an armored amtrac with a 37 mm tank gun, introduced to provide close-in firepower as the cargo LVTs neared the beach. The LVT(2) and the LVT(A)1, based on the proven LVT(2) chassis, together helped to capture the Marshalls far ahead of schedule, thus allowing acceleration of the timetable for the attack on Saipan.

Saipan, in Part VI, was the most massive use of the LVTs in the Central Pacific with six battalions of cargo LVT, including the new ramped LVT(4), and two battalions of armored amtracs, employing the new LVT(A)4 with a larger 75 mm howitzer. The loading ramp represented one of the greatest single design improvements in the history of the LVT.

Iwo Jima, discussed in Part VII, was the Corps' toughest battle. The LVT(4) played a crucial role both as the assault vehicle to carry troops and as the chief logistical vehicle in the battle's first days.

Part VIII examined Okinawa as the largest landing in the Central Pacific drive. The new LVT(3), a redesign of internal arrangements, was used successfully through the long campaign. The LVT(3) and the LVT(A)4 emerged as the post-war LVT for the Marine Corps.

The last part reviews progress since the end of World War II and predicts the possible successor to the LVT, the air cushion vehicle, in light of the many changes in modern warfare.

PART I

BACKGROUND TO DEVELOPMENT

"The development of the amphibian tractor, or LVT, which began in the middle 1930's provided the solution and was one of the most important modern technical contributions to ship to shore operations. Without these landing vehicles our amphibious offensive in the Pacific would have been impossible."[1]

This evaluation was provided by General Holland M. ("Howling Mad") Smith, United States Marine Corps, an amphibious pioneer and commander of the landings at Tarawa, Saipan, and Iwo Jima. This quotation summarizes the importance of the amphibian tractor in the highly complex undertaking known as amphibious warfare, an undertaking studied closely by the United States Marine Corps prior to the outbreak of World War II. The employment of the Landing Vehicle Tracked (LVT) and other tactical measures of amphibious warfare caused General J. F. C. Fuller to write,

"Though in idea these tactics were old, their novel application revolutionized amphibious warfare. In all probability, they were the most far-reaching tactical innovation of the war."[2]

Despite such praise, the role of the LVT remains largely unsung. Although the amphibian tractor and its armored, gun-carrying versions stormed the shores of Pacific Islands, North Africa, Europe, and crossed the Rhine River against the Germans, there is not one mention of it in Hanson Baldwin's well-known and comprehensive book on the great weapons of World War II.

Warfare through the centuries has been profoundly effected by technology, and many examples exist. The English Long bow, by its superior penetrating power, made the armored knight virtually obsolete in warfare after centuries of dominance. The battle of the armored gunboats Monitor and Merrimac during the American Civil War signaled the end of the era of wooden ships and the increased accuracy of rifle eventually did away with the requirement to mass troops to obtain fire power from shoulder fired weapons. Amphibious war, as practiced prior to World War II, suffered from a host of technical problems in equipment design that virtually barred it as an offensive military operation worth the risks then involved. Naval gunfire control and coordination was not perfected, communications were not reliable, and there was no specially designed landing craft for the delivery of troops on the beach. This last deficiency was perhaps the most crippling for its effect was to slow to a crawl the transport of troops to the beach and made their debarkation on the beach hazardous and costly.

The World War which faced the United States on 6 December 1941 would require the formation of an amphibious force capable of taking not just islands but islands with the ideal defensive barrier, the shallow coral reef. The Navy's Pre-War plan for war against Japan, Plan Orange called for a drive through the Central Pacific against Japan and it was this axis that was later adopted as the main attack. This required the United States to attack and seize coral atolls which were defended by the enemy at the beach and against which there was little tactical surprise possible. To successfully conduct such an attack, a highly specialized vehicle was required; one which was capable of carrying troops and cargo through rough seas, surmounting a coral reef, and moving inland with its payload.

The design that met this critical requirement was the LVT and without it the Central Pacific drive and much of our amphibious success in the Pacific generally would not have been possible. It is an outstanding example of the decisive impact of technology on the conduct of war.

The LVT record merits examination, and this thesis will study the origin of these vehicles and the role they played in amphibious warfare as it was developed prior to and during World War II. This study will focus on the Pacific Theater because this was the arena in which the vehicle found its greatest usefulness and where the doctrine governing its usage was forged.

To lay the background for such an examination, however, it is necessary first to review briefly the development of the Marine Corps up to the years preceding World War II in order to understand how the Marine Corps took the lead in the study of amphibious warfare that led to the incorporation of the LVT as a vital element of victory in World War II.

In creating its military establishment, the American colonists in many cases modeled their institutions on the British example; the United States Marine Corps was no exception. The first British Corps of Marines was created in 1664 by King Charles II in his Order in Council authorizing "The Admiral's Regiment." This directed 1200 land soldiers be raised to be distributed into the fleet and put into one regiment under one colonel.[3] This follows ancient Greek and Roman warfare practice of detaching soldiers in small groups on board fighting ships to seize other ships or objectives on land if required. These Marines came to be known as the Royal Marines, the model the Continental Congress used when, on 10 November 1775 it passed a resolution creating two battalions of Marines,

> . . . such as are good seamen, or so acquainted with maritime affairs as to be able to serve to advantage by sea, when required. . . . That they be distinguished by the names of the first and second battalions of American Marines.[4]

The first Continental Marine Unit was formed during December 1775, and put aboard the Cabot.[5] The Marines participated in numerous naval engagements during the Revolutionary War and fought as part of Washington's Army. It is significant to note that, even as early as the Revolutionary War, Marines made amphibious landings. The first significant landing was on 27 January 1778 when Marines landed and seized the forts on New Providence Island in the Bahamas.[6] Five more landings were made during the course of the war with the last landing in 1782.[7] Marine Corps involvement in amphibious operations continued into the Mexican War, where they reached a level of technical and tactical expertise not equalled until the beginning of the 1900s.[8] The most significant amphibious operation of the Mexican War involved the landing of 12,000 men of General Scott's army at Vera Cruz on 7 March 1847.[9] This early landing was notable for precise execution in waves of boats and the use of specially-designed surfboats ordered by General Scott for ferrying his troops ashore. As described by K. Jack Bauer in his book Surfboats and Horse Marines, these boats were

> . . . the first specially built American amphibious craft and were admirably suited to their purpose, their only weakness being their rather light planking. They were double-ended, broad-beamed, and flat-bottomed, with frames built of well-seasoned white oak and thwarts of pine. They were built in three sizes so that they would be stacked for transport; the largest was 40 feet long and could carry 45 or more men; the medium size was 37 feet 9 inches long and could carry 40 or more men; while the smallest was 35 feet 9 inches long and could not carry as many as 40 men. Each one carried a crew of six oarsmen, one coxswain, and a skipper.[10]

Landings during and after the Mexican War, until the advent of aircraft, featured naval gunfire as the chief weapon to gain a foothold, and were effected by surprise or in such a location so as to avoid resistance. A landing force of this period typically consisted of various ship's detachments of Marines and sailors, or in the case of Vera Cruz, where large numbers were required, specially trained Army troops. The troops were loaded on steamers or other shallow draft vessels from their transports or parent ships and were taken as close as possible to the hostile shore before debarking into ship's boats. Naval gunfire was directed against shore targets and the landing force was rowed ashore at top speed. After the initial waves, subsequent shuttling was accomplished until the entire force was ashore. Ordinary boats were most often used with the troops going over the sides with their muskets and powder, taking great care to keep their powder dry. The head-on amphibious assault that characterized the Central Pacific drive in World War II was still many years away.

Further developments in amphibious warfare occurred in the Spanish-American War, during which our involvement brought the United States into the role of a Pacific power. During this war, the Marines successfully seized Guantanamo Bay by amphibious landing with a specially organized battalion of five rifle companies and a three-inch artillery battery under the command of Lieutenant Colonel R. W. Huntington, USMC. This landing was attempted only after one month of intensive training to perfect methods of ship-to-shore movement using small boats. Its successful execution gained a vital base for advanced naval blockade operations and was instrumental in containing the Spanish Fleet in

Santiago Harbor.[11] A further indication of the growing appreciation by the United States Navy for Marine Corps capabilities in naval warfare was Admiral Dewey's letter to the Secretary of the Navy, written after the Spanish American War in which he stated,

> If there had been 5,000 Marines under my command at Manila Bay, the city would have surrendered to me on May 1, 1898, and could have been properly garrisoned. The Filipinos would have received us with open arms, and there would have been no insurrection.[12]

After the Spanish American War, the United States Navy was forced to review its ability to project its power into the far western Pacific. This was a new requirement and the need for bases along a vast line of communications leading to the Philippines became more urgent. The demonstrated ability of the Marines to conduct amphibious landings, and in particular the seizure of the base at Guantanamo Bay, directed the attention of Naval planners to what became known as advanced base operations. This involved the seizure and defense of bases that were to serve as coaling sites and supply points for naval vessels on their journey across the Pacific. A detachment of five officers and forty men was formed at the Naval Torpedo Squadron Station, at Newport, Rhode Island, as the forerunner of what would later be known as the Advanced Base Force, and their early training consisted of the proper use of mines, torpedoes, and signal communications.[13] It was envisioned that such an Advanced Base Force would be trained to operate with the Fleet to seize and defend forward bases in support of naval operations. From its small beginnings, the Advanced Base Force grew to a battalion of four rifle companies which participated in landing exercises with the Fleet at Culebra Island, in the Caribbean. These early exercises were the forerunners of a long series of landing exercises that eventually brought amphibious warfare into being as a viable offensive weapon.

Training of the Advanced Base Force, as recommended by the Navy's General Board, its war planning body, was to be in the following areas:

    (a) The construction of field fortification, gun emplacements, gun platforms and magazines;
    (b) The transportation of guns of less than 8-inch caliber from ship to point of emplacement and the mounting of same;
    (c) The construction and operating of field telegraph and telephone lines, signal, searchlight and range-finder stations;
    (d) The planting of mines, countermining and the operating of torpedoes for harbor defense.[14]

To insure mastery of these areas, the Marine Corps' Major General Commandant established the Advanced Base School in 1910 at New London, Connecticut, and later at Philadelphia.[15] In reviewing the training of the Advanced Base Force, it is important to note that the thrust of its doctrine was defensive. Landings to seize advanced bases were not envisioned as assault landings against opposition and the majority of the concern was with the defense of the base once it was secured.[16] Study of the seizure of advanced bases was theoretical only in the Advanced Base School.[17]

The first major landing exercise employing the Advanced Base Force was executed in January 1914 with the following training objectives:

    (1) Stowing material on transports;
    (2) Landing material from the transport to the beach;
    (3) Transporting the material from the beach to the various sites;
    (4) Preparation of battery sites and mounting of the guns;
    (5) Establishment of fire control and observation points;
    (6) Planting of mines;
    (7) Defense of mine fields;
    (8) Establishment and use of searchlight stations;
    (9) Exercise with guns, including target practice;
    (10) Covering the site selected against attacks from the land, including transportation necessary for supply and handling of materials.[18]

The exercise was carried out according to plan, complete with landings against defenses by Marines and sailors of the fleet. Umpires on the scene ruled that the defenses held.[19] The valuable experience gained from this exercise caused the Secretary of the Navy to approve recommendations that such exercises be held once a year.[20] Expeditionary tasks followed which interrupted the annual landing exercises until 1922. For example, the landings at Vera Cruz to seize the customhouse in 1914 absorbed the Advanced Base Force for most of that year. Marines also landed in June 1915 at Cap-Haitien in Haiti to begin what amounted to a twenty year occupation when civil war and revolt led to a virtual collapse of order in that country. Under State Department orders, Colonel Waller assumed command of 88 officers and 1,941 men of the 1st Marine Brigade and commenced the long work of restoring a permanent peace.[21] In May 1916 with the bulk of the Advanced Base Force now committed in Haiti, civil war in Santo Domingo required further efforts to restore peace using Marines from the Advanced Base Force and detachments from Marine Barracks, Guantanamo Bay.[22] Then, World War I caused a major effort on the part of the Marine Corps bringing with it important changes for the future of the Corps.

At the time of declaration of war on 6 April 1917 the Marine Corps numbered 511 officers and 13,214 enlisted. During the course of the war, the Corps expanded to a peak of 2,462 officers and 72,639 enlisted just after Armistice.[23] Marines fought as part of major United States Army formations and one Marine General Commanded an Army division. There was no amphibious warfare for the Marines, instead they fought hard on the continent executing the same missions as those given to the Army. No landings were required because units were transported to friendly ports in France and from there to training areas before going into combat on the Western Front. When the war ended, the Marine Corps rapidly demobilized to a strength of 1,104 officers and 16,061 enlisted by 30 June 1920.[24] Although the Corps shrank to near pre-World War I size, it was to be forever changed by the aftermath of the War.

As a result of the War, Japan received as a mandate from the League of Nations all the islands in the Pacific formerly governed by Germany, which included the Marianas (less Guam), the Marshalls, and the Carolines. Japan was instructed not to fortify these islands but secretly did so as tension grew against the United States. In particular, the Marianas became the anchor of Japan's inner defenses in the Pacific.[25] Even prior to World War I, United States military planners had viewed Japan as a probable adversary of the United States as periods of tension came and went between the two countries. Color-coded plans had been drafted prior to World War I for action against all of the United States' possible enemies, and one of these, Plan Orange, was the plan for war against Japan. Plan Orange required substantial revision as a result of the new situation in the Pacific After World War I and the need for advanced bases of operation was accepted if the United States was to fight its way across the Pacific to reinforce the garrisons of the Philippines and Guam, now surrounded by Japanese territory.[26] In view of the Marine Corps experience in advanced base operations and amphibious landings, the conclusion might be drawn that the mission of seizing and defending the needed advanced bases for the Navy would be a logical one for the Marine Corps. This was not always the case and many Marine Corps officers remained oriented toward World War I doctrines even as late as 1926. General Holland M. Smith described the officers with whom he attended school at the field officer's course at Quantico, Virginia as

"...still floundering among the outdated doctrines of World War I."[27]
He further noted that,

> From the first day of the course, I found myself deep in difficulties because I objected to the emphasis placed upon defensive tactics. The Mission of the Marine Corps is primarily offensive. Any other role deprives us of our effectiveness.[28]

Fortunately for the development of the Marine Corps, there were perceptive men in the Corps who agreed with General Smith's views and were already taking steps to orient the Marine Corps towards an offensive, amphibious future. During and after World War I, Major Earl H. Ellis, stationed at Headquarters, Marine Corps, lectured and wrote concerning plans necessary to execute advanced base seizure and defense. During the World War I period, his work was directed more towards the defensive aspects of advanced base operations, but as a result of the Japanese mandates in the Pacific, he rewrote his studies with a greater offensive emphasis.[29] His new study was titled "Advanced Base Operations in Micronesia", and was approved by the Major General Commandant John A. Lejeune on 23 July 1921 as Operation Plan 712H. This plan examined the steps necessary to seize advanced bases in the Pacific, and was so detailed in its examples that it predicted nearly the exact number of Marines which were required later to seize Eniwetok in the Marshall Islands on 17 February 1944.[30] This operations plan became the basis for Marine Corps planning between the world wars. It is fortunate for the United States that Ellis completed his principal work prior to his untimely death in 1923 on the Japanese mandated Island of Palau in the Pacific. His death occurred under mysterious circumstances and the Japanese put out the unlikely story that Ellis drank himself to death. A young chief pharmacist's mate from the U. S. Naval Hospital in

Yokahama volunteered to go to Palau and recover the body. He cremated the body but returned a mental case, unable to give a consistent, coherent account of his trip or of the manner of Ellis' death. His condition began to improve but both he and his wife died in the 1923 Japanese earthquake which destroyed the hospital.[31]

The importance of Ellis' work merits a brief look at the contents and direction it gave to Marine Corps planing during that period. The complete operations plan contained a War Portfolio, a work sheet to accompany the war portfolio, and Ellis' study. As stated in the introduction to the War Portfolio section, the overall purpose of the document was:

(a) To set forth for the information and guidance of those concerned:
    (1) War Plans based upon existing conditions which can be put into effect immediately.
    (2) Development Plans, i.e., plans for development of the Marine Corps beyond that now authorized as may be required to insure a satisfactory condition of readiness for the presentation of effective and economical war against our most probable enemies.

(b) To serve as a guide for the coordination of all the peace activities and training of the Marine Corps towards reaching and maintaining the prescribed condition of readiness to execute the War Plans.[32]

Ellis began the plan by describing the then current (1921) posture of the Marine Corps and the detailed action necessary to mobilize it in case of war. This included preparation of orders, movements of supplies, and assignment of ships to ports for embarkation. After mobilization, Ellis named the Marshalls, Carolines, and the Marianas Islands the strategic groups which had to be attacked, seized, and denied to the enemy and on which bases were to be constructed for exerting pressure on Japan and bringing her fleet to decisive battle.[33] He then launched into his detailed study, "Advanced Base Operations in Micronesia",

which covered the following subjects:

    (a) Description of the theater of operations to include sea, air, land, economic, and population factors.
    (b) Description of the enemy in the area, and the strategy, tactics, and forces needed to defeat him.
    (c) Discussion of the details necessary to conduct a successful defense of such bases from enemy attacks, whose characteristics are described.
    (d) Summary of strategy, tactics, and organization with supporting tables.

Ellis summarized strategic situation facing the United States in his

introduction:

> In order to impose our will upon Japan, it will be necessary for us to project our fleet and our forces across the Pacific and wage war in Japanese waters. To effect this requires that we have sufficient bases to support the fleet, both during its projection and afterwards. As the matter stands at present, we cannot count upon the use of any bases west of Hawaii except those which we may seize from the enemy after the opening of hostilities. Moreover, the continued occupation of the Marshall, Carolines, and Palau Islands by the Japanese (now holding them under mandate of the League of Nations) invests them with a series of emergency bases flanking any line of communications across the Pacific throughout a distance of 2200 miles. The reduction and occupation of these islands and the establishment of the necessary bases therein, as a preliminary phase of the hostilities, is practically imperative.[34]

The study then touched on the key point with respect to Marine Corps

development:

> The extent to which the Marine Advanced Base Force will participate in these operations will very likely depend upon the number of Marines available - <u>and their military worth in advanced base operations</u>. If skilled in ship-to-shore operations and inculcated with a high morale and offensive spirit, they will doubtless be used to the limit - if only for the sake of general economy of lives.[35] (Emphasis Ellis')

It is important to realize that at this stage of development the offensive nature of amphibious warfare was only beginning to take shape. Emphasis was shifting from preoccupation with the defense of bases to the seizure of bases because of the loss of so many strategic bases in the Pacific to Japan after World War I. With Operation Plan 712H signed and approved by the Commandant, the Marine Corps had its marching orders. Although the course had been charted, there were to be many intervening steps before anything resembling modern amphibious readiness was to be achieved.

A period of training, education, and discussion now began, led by the Major General Commandant. Amphibious exercises were resumed in April 1922 and in 1923 the name of "Advanced Base Force" was changed to "Expeditionary Force". General Lejeune lectured on this subject at the Naval War College on 14 December 1923 clearly expressing his views when he stated:

> It has been recognized by the Joint Board and by the War Plans Division of Naval Operations, and is so recorded, that a large force of Marines for expeditionary work is essential to the furtherance of the naval plans, and that this force should be an integral part of the Fleet. The Joint Board has laid down that "The most important function of the Marine Corps (in relation to War Plans) is to seize and hold temporary advance bases in cooperation with the Fleet and to defend such bases until relieved by the Army."[36]

Lejeune emphasized the value of fleet exercises with debarkation under conditions closely resembling that of combat, and then went on to stress the great advantage that the Marine Corps enjoys with respect to the key issue of unity of command in amphibious operations by being part of the Naval service and able to achieve mutual understanding through familiarity with amphibious problems.[37] He concluded his discussion of expeditionary duty by stating,

> The maintenance, equipping, and training of its expeditionary force so that it will be in instant readiness to support the Fleet in the event of war, I deem to be the most important Marine Corps duty in time of peace.[38]

General Lejeune's lecture touched upon a key factor that should be examined during this important period in Marine Corps and amphibious warfare development. This factor was the attitude of the United States Army towards the developing specialization of the Marine Corps in the amphibious role. Even in the early days of the Advanced Base Force, the Navy had considered the suitability of the Army for the mission of advanced base defense but decided that the Marine Corps presented fewer problems because it was already part of the Navy Department. As stated by Admiral Dewey, President of the General Board:

> In the opinion of the General Board the requirements of the naval establishment of the United States include a military organization of sufficient strength in numbers and efficiency to enable the Navy to meet all demands upon it for services within its own sphere of operations, without dependance upon the corporation of the Army for troops and military supplies, for such a force of the Army may not always be available.[39]

The Navy's preference for a service within its own department seems natural enough in 1975, but in 1900 the amphibious capabilities of the Marine Corps were far from developed. It is also true that the preference of the Navy for the Marine Corps was not seriously disputed by the Army at that time or even until World War II. The United States Army, having as its mission sustained combat on continental land masses, tended to be preoccupied with its own internal problems and commitments and disputes over the ownership of the amphibious mission did not arise. The Army's inattention to amphibious warfare prior to World War II is eloquently summarized in a statement attributed to General George C. Marshall, who in conversation with Marshal Voroshilov during the Tehran Conference of 1943, stated,

> My military education and experience in the First World War has all been based on roads, rivers, and railroads. During the last two years, however, I have been acquiring an education based on oceans and I've had to learn all over again. Prior to the present war I never heard of any landing-craft except a rubber boat. Now I think about little else.[40]

A further deterrent to Army acceptance of amphibious responsibility was the negative interpretation of the World War I lessons of Gallipoli. The Gallipoli Landings by the British during February and March 1915 were considered by many to be the first modern attempt at amphibious warfare. These major amphibious landings were to support Russia's request for a British diversion against Turkey by forcing the Dardanelles and attacking towards Constantinople using only Royal Navy units. Although nearly successful, the first attempt was cancelled when two ships struck mines in an area the British thought they had cleared. Four weeks later British, Australian, and New Zealand troops landed on Gallipoli Peninsula, but the Turks had used the interim time to good advantage by heavily reinforcing their position. The landings on 25 April 1915 took place at six separate beaches and there was great confusion and loss of life. Of the 60,000 troops initially put ashore, casualties had reached 20,000 by May 8. Reinforcements were sent and effected two promising landings in the Turkish rear; these both failed due to confusion over conflicting orders. After this fiasco, the British decided to evacuate the troops, which they did in a brilliant night withdrawal without losing a single life. Throughout the operation lack of amphibious expertise had caused major problems. For example, the original loading was done in Alexandria without regard to the sequence in which the supplies would be needed. Reloading was required and was conducted on an island in the immediate area of the objective thus thoroughly compromising any hope of surprise. In addition, there were at all times critical shortages of landing craft and Naval ships. Communications failed nearly completely and there was little emphasis on the essential element of speed. Troops sat on the beach and did nothing while their commanders worried about further orders.[41] This disaster led many to feel that amphibious landings were still not feasible, particularly in daylight. Admiral of the Fleet, Lord Keyes, who commanded naval support elements in the Gallipoli Campaign, wrote:

> Among the most valuable lessons we learnt from the original landings was the folly of attempting to storm a defended beach in daylight. All our amphibious operations after this, whether attacking or evacuating, were carried out with as many hours of darkness in hand as was possible, and also, having regard to the vital importance of surprise, done nothing to disclose our intention before dark.[42]

It is also true that writings dating far back into military history have painted gloomy pictures of the chances for success of landings from the sea. One of the military classics on strategy, The Art of War by Baron De Jomini, states:

> These are operations of rare occurrence, and may be classed as among the most difficult in war when effected in presence of a well prepared enemy... A great difficulty in such an operation is found in the fact that the transports can never get near the beach, and the troops must be landed in boats and rafts, which takes time and gives the enemy great advantages. If the sea is rough, the men to be landed are exposed to great risks; for what can a body of infantry do, crowded in boats, tossed about by the waves, and ordinarily rendered unfit by sea-sickness for the proper use of their arms?[43]

Thus, the failure of the Gallipoli landing tended to reinforce the pessimistic view held by Army military strategists with regard to the value of amphibious operations on a major scale. In contrast, Marine Corps Schools, Quantico, adopted the study of the Gallipoli Landing as a model for lessons to be learned.[44] This basic difference in outlook between the Army and the Marine Corps allowed the Marine Corps to move ahead alone in the development of amphibious strategies between the wars. As stated by Russell F. Weigley,

> ... it was the Marine Corps that did most to follow up these lines of thought and, in fact, made ship-to-shore landing operations a particular specialty.[45]

Experimentation continued between 1922 and 1925 with landing exercises at Culebra and Hawaii, where the Army was part of the landing force. It is during this period that the Christie Tank, a forerunner of the LVT, was tested. The enterprising inventor and manufacturer, Walter Christie, won permission from the Marine Corps and the Navy to test his amphibious tank as part of the exercises at Culebra in February 1924. This was a test of Christie's third modification since he first started work on the vehicle in 1921. The vehicle used could be operated on tracks, wheels, or in the water and had a barge-shaped hull, open at the top and constructed of one-fourth inch armor plate. In the water it was driven by two propellers and steered by varying the speed of the propellers and/or the tracks. The entire tank was sixteen feet, eight inches long, weighed seven tons, was powered by ninety horsepower, six cylinder engine, and had a remarkable suspension system consisting of rubber tires on coil springs. The vehicle could travel at 18.5 miles per hour on tracks, thirty mph on wheels, and move at 7.5 mph in the water, faster than many later LVTs. Although tested successfully in the Hudson and Potomac, this promising design did not impress the Naval observers at Culebra as being sufficiently seaworthy. It was subsequently rejected, scrapped, and the design later sold to Japan.[46] It is helpful to realize at this point that interest in amphibious vehicles focused on making tanks amphibious rather than on the development of cargo or personnel carriers that were amphibious because of the concern over the lack of firepower in the leading waves as they approached the beach. Naval gunfire of the day was not sufficiently accurate to work in close to the troops and aviation was in its infancy. Therefore, ways were sought to incorporate maximum firepower into the approaching landing waves themselves to pin down the enemy after the naval gunfire had lifted from

Figure 1. The early Beetle Boat undergoing tests during landings in 1924.

Figure 2. The Christie Amphibious Tank tested and rejected in 1924.

the immediate landing area. No further testing of this type of vehicle was conducted until the discovery of the Roebling Tractor in 1937.

In addition to the Christie Tank, attention and concern also focused on the clear deficiencies in existing landing craft of the mid-1920's. A derivation of a British designed boat, nicknamed the "Beetle Boat", was tested during the Culebra exercises in 1924 and found to be awkward and too large for the limited load it carried (75 mm gun and 60 to 100 troops).[47] The landing craft of the day continued to be basic whale boats and Navy launches, which were round bottomed, wood constructed, and limited in carrying capacity. Because these boats had a round bottom, they drew too much water to be easily retracted after beaching and unloading troops and their handling in surf was also tricky. The search for proper landing craft was to be more continuous than the attention paid to amphibious vehicles and many types of craft were tested between 1924 and 1940 before a successful design emerged.

After 1925, landing exercises ceased due to the heavy demands placed on the Marine Corps by expeditionary duty in Nicaragua and China. In China, for example, Marines settled down to a routine of drills and demonstrations under the command of General Smedley D. Butler, one of the Corps' most colorful figures. The point of the productions was to show the flag conspicuously and display American ability and competency to foreign nationals abroad. One such event had an unexpected climax:

> During an exhibition of stunting, Captain James T. Moore zoomed over the crowds, went into a spectacular climbing roll, lost both wings off his plane and parachuted into a moat in front of the stands. "Trust Smedley," a lady spectator commented, "he always puts on a wonderful show."[48]

Despite the frivolity in China, both commitments, China and Nicaragua, were more than enough to drain the Marine Corps of every man who could carry a rifle and amphibious exercises were halted until 1935. In the interval however, momentous events were occurring in the Corps-events that would be turning points in the history of amphibious warfare.

During the 1920's and 1930's, as Marine expeditionary forces were being dispatched to Nicaragua and China, the concept crystallized of assigning a portion of the Marine Corps on a permanent basis to the Naval Fleet primarily to make landings. This idea had long been held by the Assistant Commandant of the Marine Corps, Major General John H. Russell, who suggested it to the Commandant, Major General Ben H. Fuller. Fuller approved a letter to Chief of Naval Operations on 17 August 1933 which recommended that the name of the expeditionary forces be changed to Fleet Marine Force and that such a force be incorporated as a permanent and integral part of the Fleet. This recommendation intended to alleviate the constant manpower drain imposed by peacetime garrison duties and would dedicate a body of Marines to the full-time study, development, and practice of amphibious war. This historic letter was fully endorsed by Chief of Naval Operations, Director of War Plans (Navy), and Commander in Chief U. S. Fleet, in four weeks, a remarkably short period of time considering the scope of the letter and the levels of endorsement it required. The entire concept drew relatively little comment in view of its future impacts. With one decision to implement the concept of the letter, the Secretary of the Navy, Claude A. Swanson, created the force that would fight its way across the Pacific during World War II using a new form of warfare.

At the suggestion of the Director of War Plans for the Navy, Swanson chose the term "Fleet Marine Force" to describe the new attachment and requested that the Major General Commandant draw up recommended doctrinal guidelines for implementation.[50] These guidelines were embodied in Navy General Order Number 241 of 7 December 1933 which was the charter for the Fleet Marine Force of today. Certain portions of that Order clarify the new status of the Marine Corps:

> 1. The force of Marines maintained by the Major General Commandant in a state of readiness for operations with the Fleet is hereby designated as Fleet Marine Force (F.M.F.), and as such shall constitute a part of the organization of the United States Fleet and be included in the Operating Force Plan for each fiscal year.
>
> 2. The Fleet Marine Force shall consist of such units as may be designated by the Major General Commandant and shall be maintained at such strength as is warranted by the general personnel situation of the Marine Corps.
>
> 3. The Fleet Marine Force shall be available to the Commander in Chief for operations with the Fleet or for exercises either afloat or ashore in connection with Fleet problems. The Commander in Chief shall make timely recommendations to the Chief of Naval Operations regarding such service in order that the necessary arrangements may be made.
>
> 4. The Commander in Chief shall exercise command of the Fleet Marine Force when embarked on board vessels of the Fleet or when engaged in Fleet exercises either afloat or ashore. When otherwise engaged, command shall be as directed by the Major General Commandant.
>
> 5. The Major General Commandant shall detail the Commanding General of the Fleet Marine Force and maintain an appropriate staff for him.[51]

Paragraphs 6, 7, 8, and 9 treated the basic administrative arrangements of this new force. With respect to the development of amphibious warfare and the future of the LVT, this event was the starting point for serious and continuous experimentation in all aspects of amphibious war and doctrine. The practical effect was to set aside a body of Marines available for amphibious exercises, and to provide for the development of special equipment to meet new tactical needs. The FMF was to be isolated to the maximum extent possible from expeditionary demands for troops which had previously halted landing exercises for years at a time. The Marine Corps now entered an era of accelerated training for amphibious war.

Notes

[1] Holland M. Smith, "Amphibious Tactics," *Marine Corps Gazette*, October, 1946, p. 22.

[2] J. F. C. Fuller, *The Second World War* (New York: Duell, Sloan, and Pearce, 1949), p. 207.

[3] Robert Debs Heinl, Jr., *Soldiers of the Sea* (Annapolis: United States Naval Institute, 1962), pp. 3-4.

[4] Worthington Chauncey Ford, ed., *The Journals of the Continental Congress, 1774-1789* (34 vols., Washington, D.C.: Government Printing Office, 1904-1937), III, p. 348.

[5] William M. Miller and John H. Johnstone, *A Chronology of the United States Marine Corps, 1775-1934* (Washington, D.C.: Historical Branch, G-3 Division, Headquarters, U.S. Marine Corps, 1965), p. 8.

[6] Ibid., p. 21.

[7] Ibid., p. 30.

[8] Holland M. Smith, "Amphibious Tactics," *Marine Corps Gazette*, July 1946, p. 46.

[9] Ibid., p. 29.

[10] K. Jack Bauer, *Surfboats and Horse Marines* (Annapolis: United States Naval Institute, 1969), p. 66.

[11] Smith, "Amphibious Tactics," July 1946, p. 46.

[12] Kenneth J. Clifford, *Progress and Purpose: A Developmental History of the United States Marine Corps 1900-1970* (Washington, D.C.: History and Museum Division, Headquarters, U.S. Marine Corps, 1973), pp. 3-4.

[13] Smith, "Amphibious Tactics," July 1946, p. 46.

[14] Clifford, *Progress and Purpose*, p. 10.

[15] Ibid., p. 13.

[16] Smith, "Amphibious Tactics," July 1946, p. 47.

[17] Ibid.

[18] Clifford, *Progress and Purpose*, p. 18.

[19] Ibid., p. 19.

[20] Ibid., p. 21

[21] Heinl, Soldiers of the Sea, p. 173.

[22] Ibid., p. 180.

[23] Clifford, Progress and Purpose, p. 22.

[24] Ibid.

[25] John Toland, The Rising Sun (2 vols., New York: Random House, 1970), vol. 2, p. 594.

[26] Russell F. Weigley, The American Way of War (New York: Macmillan Publishing Co., 1973), p. 254.

[27] Holland M. Smith, Coral and Brass (New York: Charles Scribner's Sons, 1949), p. 57.

[28] Ibid.

[29] Earl H. Ellis, "Advanced Base Defense During the Present War," (Unpublished and undated report, Headquarters, Marine Corps), p. 1.

[30] United States Marine Corps, Operations Plan 712H (Washington, D.C.: Headquarters, Marine Corps, 1921), p. 33.

[31] Smith, Coral and Brass, p. 56.

[32] Operations Plan 712H, p. 1.

[33] Ibid., p. 8.

[34] United States Marine Corps, "Advanced Base Operations in Micronesia," in Operations Plan 712H (Washington, D.C.: Headquarters, U.S. Marine Corps, 1921), p. 1.

[35] Ibid., p. 2.

[36] John A. Lejeune, "The United States Marine Corps," The Marine Corps Gazette, December 1923, p. 250.

[37] Ibid., p. 252.

[38] Ibid., p. 253.

[39] Clifford, Progress and Purpose, p. 10.

[40] Robert E. Sherwood, Roosevelt and Hopkins: An Intimate History (New York: Harper Brothers, 1948), pp. 555-556.

[41] Vincent J. Esposito, ed., *The West Point Atlas of American Wars* (2 vols., New York: Frederick A. Praeger, 1953), pp. 28-32.

[42] Lord Keyes, *Amphibious Warfare and Combined Operations* (New York: Macmillan Company, 1943), p. 149.

[43] Baron De Jomini, *The Art of War* (Philadelphia: J. B. Lippincott & Co., 1862; reprint ed., Westport, Conn.: Greenwood Press, Publishers, 1974), pp. 226-29.

[44] Clifford, *Progress and Purpose*, p. 45.

[45] Weigley, *The American Way of War*, p. 254.

[46] Borg-Warner Corporation, *Research, Investigation, and Experimentation in the Field of Amphibious Vehicles* (Kalamazoo: Ingersoll Kalamazoo Division, 1957), pp. 40-42.

[47] Clifford, *Progress and Purpose*, p. 33.

[48] Heinl, *Soldiers of the Sea*, p. 292.

[49] Major General Commandant Letter of 17 August 1933 to the Secretary of the Navy.

[50] Director of War Plans, United States Navy, Letter of 23 August 1933 to the Secretary of the Navy.

[51] United States Navy, *Navy Department General Order 241* (Washington, D.C.: Navy Department, 1933), pp. 1-2.

PART II

EARLY DEVELOPMENT

With the creation of the FMF, a full-time organization of Marines could now begin to perfect the art of amphibious war. First, however, there was a significant deficiency that had to be corrected before landing exercises could be productively resumed, and that deficiency was the lack of a comprehensive doctrine on amphibious operations. Surprisingly, there had been no coordinated attempt to collect amphibious experiences until 1933. Although there were several manuals published by the Navy and the Joint Board (an agency created for service cooperation and the predecessor of the Joint Chiefs of Staff) during the pre-war period, for service dealing with joint overseas expeditions, none actually addressed the mechanics of an amphibious operation. The best attempt was titled Joint Overseas Expeditions, and appeared in January 1933 after approval by both the Secretary of the Navy and the Secretary of War. The stated purpose for this Joint Board manual was ". . . . to present a set of general principles for the planning and conduct of joint overseas expeditions . . ."; its total length was only 43 pages.[1] Although it dealt soundly with the subject, even at the late date of 1933 it did not mention the Marine Corps and discussed amphibious operations with the assumption that the United States Army would be the landing force. The manual's contents were derived from comments from all services, including the Marine Corps, and it did serve as a basis for further study when the Corps started drafting its own amphibious doctrine.

Despite its generality, this manual recognized that special equipment was necessary to conduct a successful, large-scale amphibious landing:

> Because of the special nature of the operations required in the transfer of troops, equipment, and supplies from ship to shore against enemy opposition and under supporting fire from friendly ships, special equipment must be provided by the Navy. This includes special boats for landing the assault troops, including installation of machine guns therein, and the provision of protection as far as practicable against small arms fire from shore; special boats, barges, and motor lighters for landing all other troops and their equipment, including artillery tanks, airplanes, and motor and animal transport, and supplies; provision of special ammunition required for the artillery support; and special communications equipment.[2]

With the creation of the FMF, the Commandant saw the need for a detailed document showing how to conduct amphibious landings. To develop "The book" on the subject, the Commandant used the wealth of experience in the student body at Marine Corps Schools at Quantico. Routinely, the Marine Corps ordered its top officers to refresher courses at Marine Corps School, Quantico, as preparation for assumption of greater responsibilities in the future. The students at the Schools in 1933 represented some of the most experienced officers in amphibious operations at that time. He directed that classes be suspended and work begun on writing the manual no later 15 November 1933.[3] This may seem delayed because ideally the doctrine should precede the creation of the organization of the FMF, however, a majority of the student body had been mobilized for duty in Cuba in a false alarm which resulted in no landing.[4] The student body, after initial meetings and development of an outline, formed separate committees dealing with Tactics, Staff Functions, and Training, which were the bulk of the manual, and smaller groups worked on aviation and naval matters. The Commandant approved this landmark document on 13 June 1934 and its initial title was <u>The Tentative Manual for Landing</u>

Operations.[5] The manual was used in mineograph form at Marine Corps Schools through the winter of 1934-1935 and was not given outside publication until July 1934 when the Navy Department retitled it <u>Manual for Naval Overseas Operations</u>. A revised version, now titled <u>Tentative Landing Operations Manual</u>, was published in July 1935, with photos and sketches and was widely distributed.[6] All versions were published with a "Restricted" Classification which was the lowest order of classification below "confidential" and the highest rating of "secret". Although changed in 1941, 1942, and 1943, this manual's contents at the outset substantially created amphibious doctrine as it would be practiced throughout World War II.[7]

The manual established the Amphibious Task Force as divided into two main parts, the Landing Force and the naval support groups consisting of the Transport Group, Covering Group, Air Group, and Fire Support Group.[8] The overall commander was to be the Naval Commander, with the commander of the Landing Force responsible to the Naval Commander for employment of the forces ashore.[9] It discussed the critical area of ship-to-shore movement and assigned responsibility for this phase to the Naval Commander.[10] The important area of fire support was explained and the first beginnings of an effective air support doctrine were included as a supplement to the use of naval gunfire. In words which almost exactly describe the later practices of close air support during World War II, the manual states,

> When the ship's fire lifts, attack aviation and dive bombers take over the neutralization of strong points in the beach defenses by attacking machine guns, antiboat guns, artillery searchlights and reserves whose movements or location constitutes an immediate threat.[11]

This doctrine was an indirect outgrowth of early tests with naval gunfire which demonstrated a characteristic flat trajectory and a large range error despite good accuracy in deflection. The large range errors required the early halt of naval gunfire on the beach area to insure the safety of the approaching troops. Aircraft had demonstrated acceptable accuracy with bombs when working in the proximity of troops, and aviation became the chief weapon for the task of hammering the beach. The manual also discussed the logistics of the amphibious operation including a wealth of detail on the loading data for standard Marine Corps equipment and boat capacities, and it stressed the fundamental relationships of the landing force scheme of maneuver on the beach to the combat loading of transports carrying the assault troop units. This was one of the great failings at Gallipoli. In amphibious war, after the mission has been assigned, the manual described what could be called a backwards planning process, that is, the first decision made is the scheme of ground maneuver that is to be employed by the Landing Force to secure the objectives. From this decision, it could be determined what unit will land first and this in turn decided the sequence in which the transports are to be loaded. This sequential loading to support the tactical scheme of maneuver ashore is called combat loading and is detailed in the manual because the combat loading of ships is a science which occupies the attention of many logistic planners early in the amphibious planning process.

The Tentative Manual for Landing Operations included an overall description of the state of the art in landing craft design to 1934. Progress remained limited and the boats listed for use in landing troops and supplies were ship's lifeboats and launches modified for use in landing operations. Three types were listed and described in detail:

1. A squad of "X" Boats was listed as desirable for assault waves. These were self-propelled, seaworthy, with a speed of twelve knots when loaded; they had a capacity of ten men, fully equipped, lying prone on the bottom, with a crew of three men - a coxswain, a gunner, and an engineer. They were armored from the turn of the bilge to about one foot above the waterline at the sides, with an armored, removable shield forward, high enough to protect the coxswain and gunner from shrapnel and small arms fire. A large number of boats of this type would be required and there was no overhead cover. Armament was a double machine gun in the bow and/or shoulder-fired automatic weapons.

2. A section of "Y" Boats was listed as desirable for assault waves. This was an enlarged "X" boat with a capacity of 25 men in addition to the crew, and was suitable for the transportation of a rifle section or a machine gun section, less one machine gun cart. It's speed of twelve knots and general characteristics, other than size, were similar to the "X" boat. It was noted that this boat facilitated "nesting" or stacking of boats if both "X" and "Y" boats were used together.

3. The 45 foot Artillery Lighter or "W" Boat was the third type described. It was efficient for landing artillery, tractors, and tanks. It had shallow draft, square stern, and was not self-propelled. Its capacity was listed as two "light" tanks.

The detailed description of these special boats was followed by a comment which illustrated the tentative nature of research in this vital area:

Although the above special type boats are shown here in detail with their characteristics and capacities, it should be noted in passing that they are to date still subject to further experiment, development, and improvement; that in their present development, they have not been constructed in any quantity. Provisions, therefore, must be made in case of boats in volume to use the Standard Navy Types now generally distributed throughout the Fleet.[12]

Concern was expressed throughout the manual over the difficulty of bringing fire to bear on the beach from the landing waves themselves. If this could be done, then the defenders on the beach would be pinned down right to the last second before the leading waves touched shore. Many types of arrangements were mentioned including beaching specially built ships with artillery lashed to their decks, landing boats with mortars mounted in them, and mounting machine guns on the bows of landing boats. None of these measures were thoroughly tested and at one point the manual even spoke in a gloomy tone on the subject:

> Attempts to employ field artillery materiel fastened to the decks of vessels are of doubtful value due to the sights and elevating and traversing mechanism ordinarily installed on field artillery.[13]

The manual concludes one part:

> Thus, in order to keep the hostile machine-gun fire reduced to a minimum, a great deal will depend upon the supporting fire of accompaning ships and the guns mounted in the bows of landing boats.[14]

The qualities of protection and firepower for the leading waves were not to be incorporated into amphibious warfare for many years, and these same critical factors would be supplied by the advent of the LVT.

After the publication of the manual, landing exercises resumed on an annual basis with the objective of measuring the progress of amphibious tactics and techniques. Fleet Landing Exercise Number 1, sometimes abbreviated Flex 1, took place between 24 January and 8 March 1935 and consisted of daily troop landings at Culebra Island and tactical landings of a reinforced regiment with artillery and aviation to establish the defense of a fleet base. This exercise used regular ship's boats of up to 50 feet in length which could carry 110 Marines. The exercise was considered to be a success despite an insufficient number of landing craft which hampered realistic landing practice. From 29 April through 12 June 1935 the FMF also participated in United States Fleet Exercise XVI by landing a battalion of infantry and a battalion of artillery at Midway Island in the Pacific.[15] Fleet Landing Exercise Number 2 was staged between 4 January and 24 February 1936 and placed more emphasis on ship-to-shore operations, although training ashore was also performed. During this exercise a recommendation was made that the Marine Corps FMF be provided with assault transport ships, configured to carry troops. This critical shortage was not met until 1941.[16] The deficiencies in landing craft continued to attract concern and General Holland Smith noted, "The need was also recognized for a fast, maneuverable, well protected landing boat."[17] Fleet Landing Exercise Number 3, 24 January through 10 March 1937 was notable for the first actual live firing of naval guns in support of troops landing on San Clemente Island, and included the 1st United States Army Expeditionary Brigade, under Marine Corps overall command, within the landing force. Three experimental landing craft were thoroughly tested by the bad weather experienced during the landings. A forty foot standard ship's boat proved to be the best available ship's launch, but recommendations for a maneuverable, surf-capable landing craft were still renewed.[18]

The Marine Corps was well aware of the unsuitability of existing craft for landings and in 1933 formed the Marine Corps Equipment Board composed of eleven members who served on a part-time basis to discover and recommend types of equipment for amphibious operations. The Board gained in importance as the years passed and by 1937 was expanded to twenty officers assigned full-time.[19] The corresponding Navy department responsible for design, construction, and purchase of all boats and ships was the Bureau of Construction and Repair, renamed the Bureau of Ships in 1940. During the mid-1930s there was little money to spare and procurement of landing craft remained a low priority item on the Navy's list. Curiously, despite the obvious strategic importance of amphibious equipment, particularly landing craft, the Navy's reluctance to spend money on this vital area, which they viewed as Army and Marine operations, persisted until 1942. Presidential pressure, generated by concern over the upcoming North African landings, caused the Navy to move construction of landing craft from tenth position on the list in March 1942 to second position, only behind aircraft carriers, by October 1942.[20] Any progress made before this time was due primarily to the tenacity of Marine officers on the Equipment Board and a few sympathetic Naval officers in Washington. However, the Navy did recognize enough importance in the issue to establish the Continuing Board for the Development of Landing Boats for Training Operations, in January 1937. This board had representatives from the Chief of Naval Operations, the Commandant of the Marine Corps, Bureau of Construction and Repair, and the Army Bureau of Ordnance.[21] The driving force among all these agencies, however, remained the Marine Corps Equipment Board.

At the conclusion of Fleet Landing Exercise Number 3, there still remained no suitable American amphibian vehicle for testing. With the rejection of the Christie Tank in 1924, the void remained unfilled. The Borg-Warner Report of 1957 supplied a well-informed opinion as to the reasons for this lag:

> It should not be concluded that this lack of interest was due solely to particular weaknesses of the first amphibian tanks or of their designers, rather, the dormant period in military amphibian, and to a large extent all military vehicle development, was largely the result of a lack of available funds for research and development caused by the reduction in military expenditures which normally accompany periods of peace. Further, the perfecting of ferrying and bridging equipment for tanks rather than adapting them for water travel, slowed the development of a true amphibian.[22]

The most successful amphibian of the times appeared to be the British Vicker-Armstrong Light Amphibious Tank, a design not imported by the United States. Two experimental tanks were developed for testing by the British War Office in 1931-1932. They were not accepted by the British but enjoyed considerable success as a foreign sales item, particularly to Russia, which later developed its successful T-37 design from this model. The Vicker Tank used a mounted Caliber 30 machine gun, had a crew of two, weighed 2.17 tons, and was powered by a 90 horsepower six-cylinder engine. Like the Christie in 1924, the British attached balsa wood mudguards, covered with sheet metal, to the watertight hull to give the tank added bouyancy. It moved 20 to 27 mph on land but was capable only of 3.72 mph in water, thus making its usefulness to the leading waves contingent upon a tricky feat of coordination by sending it ahead of the leading waves which were catch up near the beach to take advantage of its machine gun firepower as they neared the beach.[23] Such feats were not feasible at this stage in amphibious development. The chief difficulty with the vehicle lay in its floatation with decks awash, making it susceptible to complete submersion in rough water or surf. Despite the dearth of seemingly effective amphibious designs, a chance event was to occur that would provide the Marine Corps with a pilot model for the design of a successful amphibian vehicle.

The 4 October 1937 issue of Life Magazine ran an article entitled "Roebling's Alligator for Florida Rescue", with the following lead:

> Shocked by the great Florida hurricane of September, 1935, John A. Roebling of New Jersey's bridge building family, told his 28 year old son, Donald, that some sort of amphibian vehicle might have saved many lives by transporting victims through the swamps, over drowned roads, across debris filled bayous. Donald agreed, went to work, after many expensive months produced the "Alligator" shown in operation on his Florida estate.[24]

The article contained pictures of the tracked amphibian moving through swamp, in water, and climbing a steep embankment. During this period, Major General Louis McCarthy Little, Commanding General of the FMF, and his Chief of Staff, Colonel E. P. Moses, were conferring with Admiral Edward C. Kalbfus, Commander, Battleships, Battle Force, United States Fleet, concerning upcoming landing exercises. At a dinner, the Admiral remarked on the Life article and the possible value of the "Alligator" to the Marine Corps. General Little was quick to see the possible significance of the Roebling amphibian and forwarded the article to the Commandant of the Marine Corps.[25] The Commandant in turn forwarded the information on to the Marine Corps Equipment Board and asked them to look into the usefulness of the amphibian for military purposes. In March 1938 Major John Kaluf, the Secretary to the Equipment Board, visited Mr. Roebling at his shop in Clearwater, Florida, at the direction of the President of the Equipment Board, Brigadier General Frederick I. Bradman, USMC. Major Kaluf took about 400 feet of movie film of the Alligator, which was fully operational, and returned to Quantico to give a favorable endorsement of the utility of this vehicle.[26] Kaluf wrote in his official report, ". . . subject boat has possibilities for use in landing troops and supplies at points not accessible to other types of small boats."[27] The Commandant concurred with Major Kaluf's observations

Figure 3. The actual Life magazine article which led to the discovery of the LVT(1).

Figure 4. Side view of the Vickers-Armstrong Tank of 1931-32 which was the most successful amphibious tank design of the era.

Figure 5. Rear view of the Vickers-Armstrong. Note the propeller-rudder apparatus.

and in May 1938, recommended to the Navy's Continuing Board for Development of Landing Craft that "steps be taken to procure a pilot model of this type of amphibious boat for further tests under service conditions and during Fleet Landing Exercise Number 5."[28] Though attached comments on the Commandant's letter, the Continuing Board, the Bureau of Construction and Repair, and finally the Chief of Naval Operations reacted negatively citing lack of funds (much of the available money had been absorbed by ongoing landing craft development) for such a purely experimental project.[29] To classify the Roebling Alligator as a purely experimental project was perhaps an injustice and a closer look at this remarkable private development project will be valuable.

The model viewed by Major Kaluf in March 1938 was actually the third modification of the original vehicle completed in 1935. The engineering on the vehicle featured two decisive refinements over previous attempts at amphibian design. The first was the incorporation of aluminum into the hull of the vehicle to reduce weight. At this time aluminum was not well known and methods to work it had to be devised by Mr. Roebling at his shop. Weight reduction resulted in less immersion of the hull and higher water speeds are obtained. The second feature of the Roebling design was the use of paddle-like cleats bolted to the track to derive propulsion from the track in the water as well as on land. The first model had these cleats set straight across the track, but water speed was a disappointing 2.3 mph despite an impressive twenty-five mph on land. The original vehicle was twenty-four feet long, weighed 14,350 pounds, and was powered by a ninety-two horsepower Chrysler engine. A second modification was completed in April 1936 with the cleats now set diagonally across the track, weight reduced by 2,240 pounds, and an eighty-five horsepower Ford V-8 engine used for power. Land speed dropped to eighteen mph but the water speed increased to 5.45 mph. Further interim work was done on this vehicle and the weight decreased by 310 more pounds, with a slight increase in land and water speeds. A third modification, completed in 1937, resulted in the most significant advances. The length of the Alligator was reduced by four feet, which cut weight by 3,100 pounds, and the cleats were changed to a curved shape, set diagonally across the track. Roebling also redesigned his track away from the traditional bogie and idler wheels used in tanks, which caused considerable drag in the water. His new track was a chain with built-in roller bearings sliding on a smooth steel channel which encircled the track contour. Idler blocks actuated by hydraulic jacks kept track tension rather than the old idler wheels. The net result of all these improvements was a new low vehicle weight of 8,700 pounds, increased maneuverability, a water speed up to 8.6 mph, and a land speed between eighteen and twenty mph.[30] This third modification was the design featured in the *Life* article and later viewed by Major Kaluf.

Despite Navy disapproval of the Marine Corps request for purchase of a pilot model, interest continued. Major Kaluf returned to Florida in January 1939 and viewed further operations of the Roebling Alligator. His favorable comments were reviewed by Brigadier General E. P. Moses, the new President of the Equipment Board, whose reaction was summarized by Lt. Colonel Croizat, "The General agreed with Kaluf that the vehicle as it stood was not suited to hard military use but that it was of potential value and that necessary modification could be made."[31] In September General Moses and Major Linsert, the new Secretary of the Equipment Board, visited Mr. Roebling and witnessed further trials. The most significant development of this visit was that General Moses finally persuaded Mr. Roebling on the military value of his vehicle and Mr. Roebling agreed to design an Alligator with military characteristics.[32] Roebling completed this new design by May 1940 incorporating all experience gained up to that time. The vehicle was twenty feet, eight inches long, eight feet wide, eight feet high at the driver's cab, and weighed about 8,000 pounds. Its speeds were fifteen to twenty-five mph on land and eight to ten mph in water. It had a nineteen inch ground clearance which was a great advantage in overland travel and precluded becoming "high-centered" or stuck on obstacles between its tracks. It could push down an eight inch Yellow Pine tree without difficulty and climb a fifty-five degree slope. It would not sink, even with its open hold full of water, and it drew less than three feet of water empty. The Alligator was powered by a ninety-five horsepower Mercury engine, and steered by two vertical levers between the driver's knees.[33] The $20,000. for this vehicle was procured from the Navy's Bureau of Ships (formerly Bureau of Construction and Repair) from funds allocated for landing craft development. It is interesting to note that Mr. Roebling only used $16,000. to build his model and spent considerable time and effort attempting to return the unused $4,000 (he was eventually successful).[34] At this point, with more money becoming available as the European military situation worsened, the Navy contracted with Mr. Roebling to build a vehicle based on the May 1940 design but powered by a 120 horsepower Lincoln-Zephyr engine. This work was inspected by General Moses and a party of Marine and Navy officers on 26-27 August 1940. The results were highly satisfactory with some minor modification being agreed on within the terms of the contract. This model was completed and given its final tests by 14 October 1940.[35] Speeds were twenty-nine mph on land and 9.72 mph in water.[36] It was shipped to Quantico during the first week in November for tests and on the day of its arrival at the Equipment Board, a call was received indicating that the Commandant was going to personally inspect the vehicle. He arrived two days later with an unexpected party of high ranking Army and Navy officers to observe the tests. The demonstrations were a success with the admirals and generals being taken for rides without incident, although later the Alligator did get stuck in the mud.[37]

This test won acceptance by the Navy, but they had modifications in mind. The test models during this time had been constructed of aluminum and Marine observers were convinced that this would not withstand hard military use. Aluminum during this period was not completely exploited as a construction material and methods for its shaping and attachment were not well-suited to LVT construction. Mr. Roebling had to devise original methods of construction in order to incorporate aluminum. This primitive state of affairs accounts for much of the reluctance on the part of Marine Corps observors to accept aluminum for combat use. In retrospect, the desire of steel construction appears justified in view of the pummeling the vehicles received pushing through jungles, scraping over coral, and bouncing against landing craft during troop transfer operations.

The Quantico tests were on a Thursday, and the following Saturday the Navy negotiated a contract with Mr. Roebling for delivery of 100 Landing Vehicles Tracked (LVT) of all-steel construction, based on Marine Corps recommendations.[38] The Food Machinery Corporation had a plant at Dunedin, Florida, near Mr. Roebling's Clearwater shop and had constructed some parts for him previously. Mr. Roebling now turned to FMC for assistance in production and redesign necessary for an all-steel amphibian. Mr. James M. Hait, Chief Engineer of the Peerless Division of FMC, organized an engineering team for redesign using all-steel construction and welding vice rivets, which until this period were a common method of constructing steel vehicles. Two prototypes were built at the Riverside FMC plant. This successful effort was followed by the Navy awarding FMC the contract for further official design of the vehicle, now officially known as LVT(1), and a contract for further delivery of 200 more LVT(1)s. The first vehicle came off the assembly line in July 1941.[39]

Aluminum test vehicles received their sea test as part of Fleet Landing Exercise Number 7, which was the last in the series of Landing Exercises before World War II. It took place between 4-14 February 1941, under the overall command of General Holland M. Smith, Commanding General of the newly organized (1 February 1941) 1st Marine Division. This exercise involved units of the Army and was a successful test of the amphibian's worth at sea.[40] Following this test a small amphibian tractor detachment was formed at Quantico and moved to a site at Dunedin, Florida, on 2 May 1941. It was commanded by Major W. W. Davies and included four other officers and thirty-three enlisted. This detachment established a training center for drivers and mechanics and received the new LVT(1)s as they came off FMC assembly lines at Lakeland, Florida, and Riverside, California. After training, personnel were sent to newly forming units of the 1st Amphibian Tractor Battalion (AmTrac is the official abbreviation today). This battalion was part of the new 1st Marine Division and its organization was to consist of a Headquarters and

Service Company and four letter companies (A, B, C, and D) which contained the tractors and crewmen. The Battalion was complete by 16 February 1942.[41]

Even during the initial design stages of the LVT(1), a turreted model had been envisioned by Mr. Roebling. Such an amphibian, armored and mounting a gun, would be the practical answer to the problem of incorporating firepower into the leading waves of the landing force to keep the beach defenders pinned down until the last second. Initial sketches were made in January 1940 by Mr. Roebling and later completed by Major Linsert, but no further action was taken. During June 1941 the Commandant of the Marine Corps recommended that a turreted LVT be developed mounting a 37 mm gun and three machine guns, with enough armor protection to withstand Caliber 50 machine guns, in order to overrun beach defenses. The Chief of Naval Operations approved these specifications and directed the Bureau of Ships to perfect a design. Bureau engineers began development in cooperation with Mr. Roebling and FMC, but their plans were not finished until December 1941.[42] The Bureau of Ships called in the Morse Chain Company Division of Borg-Warner to assist in redesign of the Roebling Track. As the United States entered the War, it was felt that a complete redesign was necessary and Borg-Warner thus launched a design project in cooperation with the Navy for a turreted LVT. These efforts were to lead to an invaluable addition to the LVT family of vehicles as the War progressed.

At the opening of World War II, the only available LVT was the military version of the Roebling Alligator, the LVT(1) which had the following characteristics:

Construction: Hull constructed of arc-welded steel from 14 gauge to 3/16 inch thickness. Bottom plate is 3/16 inch sheet steel running from stern to forward bumper. Sponsons (sides) of the vehicle were 12 gauge, and cab was from 14 gauge sheet steel. Hull was divided into three compartments: cab, cargo, and engine compartment in the rear.

Suspension: Suspension was rigid with rollers built into track riding on steel channels which acted as guides around the sponson. Drive sprockets were rigidly attached to the hull in the rear and slack in the track was reduced by an idler block in the front of the sponson. Each track weighed 650 pounds.

Maneuverability/Mobility: Ground pressure with the cleats fully sunk into the ground (4 inch penetration) was 7.8 pounds per square inch. The LVT(1) could turn in the water in its own length by reversing one track and going ahead with the other, both at full speed.[43]

Weights: The LVT(1) weighed 17,500 pounds empty with maximum gross weight of 22,000 pounds (full of fuel, fully loaded, with full crew). Cargo capacity was 4,500 pounds.

Dimensions: The Alligator was 21 feet long, 9 feet 10 inches wide, 7 feet 8 inches high, and had a ground clearance of 19 inches.

Speeds: Powered by a 150 horsepower Hercules engine, speed on land was 12 mph (far slower than previous models due to the weight increase from all-steel construction) and between 6 and 7 mph in water.[44]

As the Marines entered World War II with this vehicle, much potential could be seen, yet the specific tasks for its use were to be developed from the lessons of battle. Such lessons were not long in coming.

NOTES

[1] Holland M. Smith, "Amphibious Tactics," *Marine Corps Gazette*, October, 1946, p. 22.

[2] J. F. C. Fuller, *The Second World War* (New York: Duell, Sloan, and Pearce, 1949), p. 207.

[3] Robert Debs Heinl, Jr., *Soldiers of the Sea* (Annapolis: United States Naval Institute, 1962), pp. 3-4.

[4] Worthington Chauncey Ford, ed., *The Journals of the Continental Congress, 1774-1789* (34 vols., Washington: Government Printing Office, 1904-1937), III, p. 348.

[5] William M. Miller and John H. Johnstone, *A Chronology of the United States Marine Corps, 1775-1934* (Washington: Historical Branch, G-3 Division, Headquarters, U.S. Marine Corps, 1965), p. 8.

[6] Ibid., p. 21

[7] Ibid., p. 30.

[8] Holland M. Smith, "Amphibious Tactics," *Marine Corps Gazette*, July, 1946, p. 46.

[9] Ibid., p. 29.

[10] K. Jack Bauer, *Surfboats and Horse Marines* (Annapolis: United States Naval Institute, 1969), p. 66.

[11] Smith, "Amphibious Tactics," July, 1946, p. 46.

[12] Kenneth J. Clifford, *Progress and Purpose: A Developmental History of the United States Marine Corps 1900-1970* (Washington: History and Museum Division, Headquarters, United States Marine Corps, 1973), pp. 3-4.

[13] Smith, "Amphibious Tactics," July, 1946, p. 46.

[14] Clifford, *Progress and Purpose*, p. 10.

[15] Ibid., p. 13.

[16] Smith, "Amphibious Tactics," July, 1946, p. 47.

[17] Ibid.

[18] Clifford, *Progress and Purpose*, p. 18.

[20] Robert E. Sherwood, *Roosevelt and Hopkins: An Intimate History* (New York: Harper Brothers, 1948), p. 554

[21] Clifford, *Progress and Purpose*, p. 48.

[22] Borg-Warner Corporation, *Research, Investigation, and Experimentation in the Field of Amphibious Vehicles* (Kalamazoo: Ingersoll Kalamazoo Division, 1957), p. 45.

[23] Peter Chamberlin and Chris Ellis, *Tanks of the World*, 1915-1945 (New York: Galahad Books, 1972), p. 84.

[24] Roebling's Alligator for Florida Rescues," *Life*, October 4, 1937, pp. 94-95.

[25] Victor J. Croizat, "The Marine's Amphibian," *Marine Corps Gazette*, June, 1953, p. 41.

[26] John Kaluf, "Selling the Amphibian," *Marine Corps Gazette*, September, 1953, p. 8.

[27] Frank O. Hough, Verle E. Ludwig, and Henry I. Shaw, *Pearl Harbor to Guadalcanal*, Vol. I of *History of the United States Marine Corps Operations in World War II* (5 vols.; Washington: Historical Branch, G-3 Division, Headquarters, United States Marine Corps, 1958), p. 32.

[28] Ibid.

[29] Ibid., p. 33.

[30] Borg-Warner Corporation, *Research, Investigation, and Experimentation*, pp. 45-46.

[31] Croizat, "Marine's Amphibian", p. 41.

[32] Ibid., p. 42.

[33] *The Alligator*, Sales pamphlet (Clearwater: Donald Roebling, 1940).

[34] Croizat, "Marine's Amphibian," p. 42.

[35] Clifford, *Progress and Purpose*, p. 56.

[36] Borg-Warner Corporation, *Research, Investigation, and Experimentation*, p. 49.

[37] Croizat, "Marine's Amphibian," p. 42.

[38] Ibid.

[39] Clifford, *Progress and Purpose*, pp. 56-57.

[40]Holland M. Smith, Coral and Brass (New York: Charles Scribner's Sons, 1949), p. 97.

[41]Clifford, Progress and Purpose, p. 57.

[42]Hough, Ludwig, and Shaw, Pearl Harbor to Guadalcanal, p. 34.

[43]Borg-Warner Corporation, Research, Investigation, and Experimentation, pp. 65-66.

[44]Food Machinery Corporation, Amphibians (San Jose: Food Machinery Corp., 1942), p. 16.

PART III

EARLY LESSONS

The Japanese attack at Pearl Harbor shocked America and galvanized the country into action, although at the time of the attack there were shortages of needed war materiel and few trained men. This situation generally applied to all the armed services, yet the Marine Corps was the first ordered to take the offensive against the enemy. The time for testing of the Corps' new amphibious doctrine and equipment was at hand.

Notwithstanding President Roosevelt's decision to give priority attention to Germany's defeat, the tactical opportunity to take an offensive first developed in the southwest Pacific where the Japanese had landed on Guadalcanal and Tulagi in the Solomons and were constructing an airfield which would threaten United States forward bases at Efate in the New Hebrides and at Espiritu Santo. Japan's extended position on the tip of the Lower Solomon Islands offered the United States a chance to isolate the area and conduct an amphibious landing to seize the initiative, an act badly needed for public morale following setbacks including the loss of Guam, the Philippines, and Wake Island in the first days after Pearl Harbor. On 25 June 1942, the Joint Chiefs of Staff advised Admiral Nimitz and Vice Admiral Ghormley to prepare for an offensive into the lower Solomons to seize the Tulagi-Santa Cruz-Guadalcanal area, with a D-Day set for 1 August 1942.[1] The planning phase began immediately in an atmosphere of urgency.

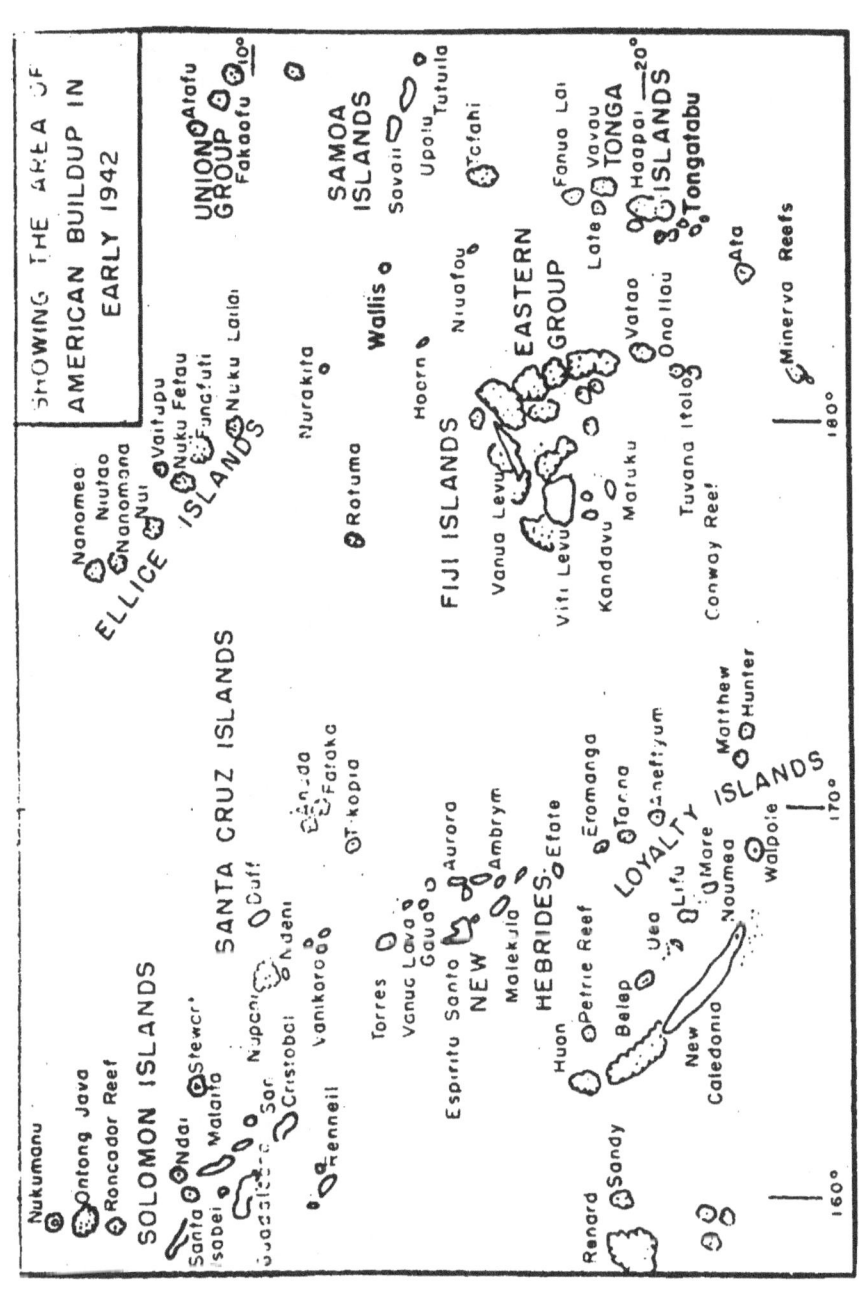

Map 1. Southwest Pacific area.

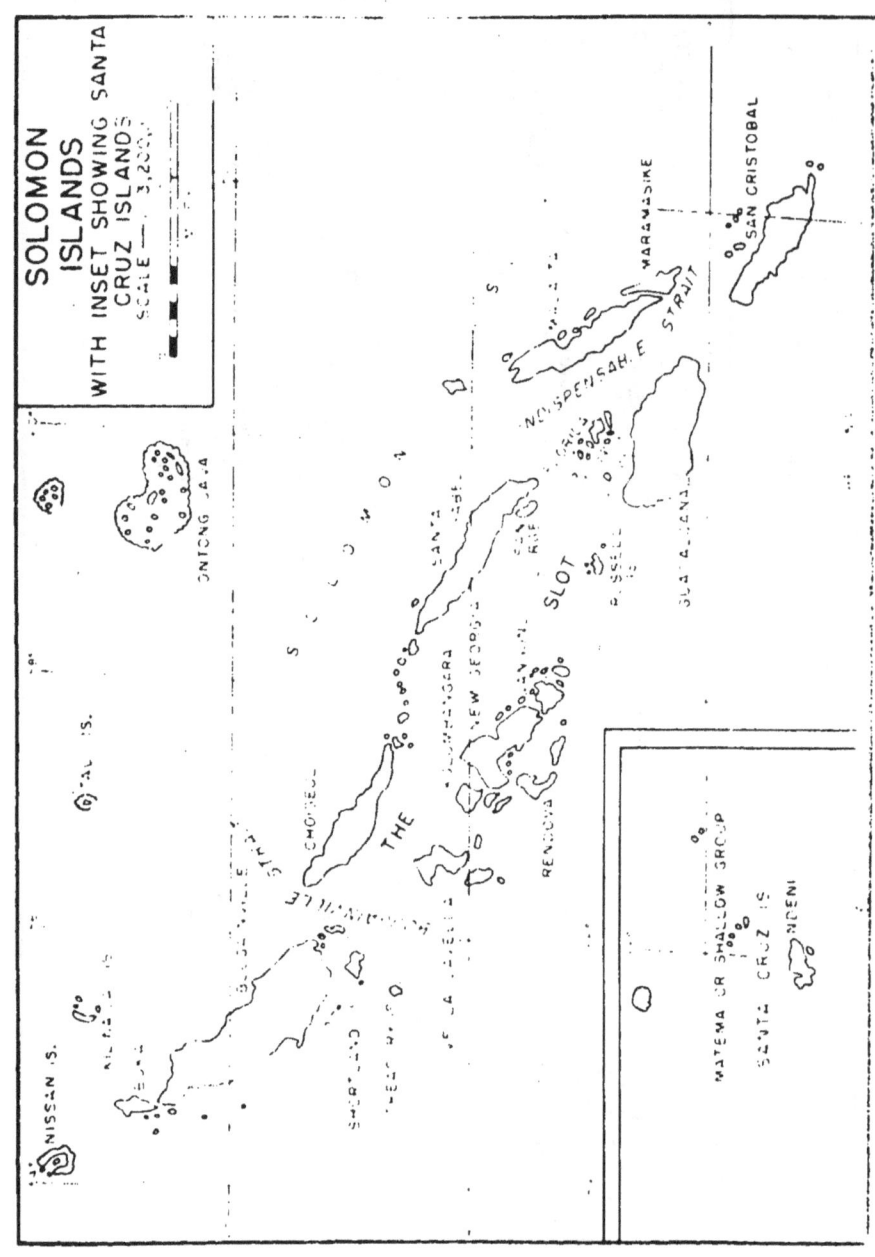

Map 2. Solomon Islands.

At the outset, the LVT(1) was assigned exclusively a supply role. Amphibious planning during this time was guided by Change Number 1 to Fleet Training Publication (FTP) 167, issued 2 May 1941. This document was based on the Marine Corps <u>Tentative Landing Operations Manual</u> of 1935, and its pages contained the latest thinking on the use of landing craft and amphibians. FTP 167 listed the desirable characteristics of leading wave landing boats as:

    1. Armament: Should mount suitable weapons capable of producing heavy volume of fire.

    2. Speed: Should be fast. Boats for leading waves should have a speed of not less than 12 knots; a greater speed is desirable.

    3. Shallow Draft: Should be able to run well up on any type of beach override or overwater obstacles and ground on a fully even keel.

    4. Good Surfboat: Should be seaworthy and easily handled in surf.

    5. Armor: Should have armor protection against small arms fire. This is particularly necessary for coxswain, gunner, engine and gasoline tank.

    6. Rugged: Not easily damaged by pounding in the surf.

    7. Nesting: It is desirable that the boats be suitable for nesting or stowing in tiers aboard ship.[2]

FTP 167 also contains a section on Special Navy Landing Boats that gives guidance on the LVT:

    . . . vehicle may be employed tactically in groups to effect landings of entire combat teams or they may be distributed to combat teams as small groups for landing of equipment, ammunition, and supplies required in the initial stages of a landing. They should be particularly useful in landing artillery and transporting their weapons and ammunition to their firing positions.[3]

The manual included pictures of current landing craft and had a picture of the Roebling design of May 1940 which was the first military oriented aluminum design. From the above it appears that information on the basic capabilities of the Roebling amphibian was available even though the date of Change 1 to FTP 167 was May 1941 a period during which the Roebling had just entered mass production and before the first model rolled off the assembly lines. With the exception of speed, an important factor, the LVT(1) met the requirements of a desirable landing craft for a leading wave, but was never given this mission at Guadalcanal. Leading waves were to be landed in the standard boat-type landing craft then available. There is no evidence that suggests that the LVT(1) was ever considered for anything other than cargo transportation. This thinking seems to have originated through an early reputation of mechanical unreliability and inefficiency. As described by its manufacturer, Food Machinery Corporation, the LVT(1) held fifty gallons of gasoline for a land cruising range of 120 miles, or 2.4 miles per gallon.[4] Although this was an expensive method of transporting supplies, it appeared to be the more prudent use of the vehicle instead of use as an assault vehicle where mechanical break-downs could strand part of the leading waves at sea. The vehicle was not planned for a continual shuttle of supplies, but only until wheeled vehicles were landed to assume the transport of supplies inland.[5] Further, at Guadalcanal there were only a few hydrographic charts with just enough information to prevent a trading schooner from grounding, and this minimal intelligence did not indicate off-shore reefs or other obstacles that required the use of the amphibian's land-water capabilities. (In fact, the coral reefs around the island of Tulagi forced early debarkation of the troops from their landing boats on D-Day when they ran aground on coral reefs thirty to hundred yards from shore. Fortunately for the men, waist to armpit-deep in water, there was no initial opposition to the landings because the Japanese were caught by surprise.[6])

The planning period was incredibly short considering the complexity of the unknowns, the strategic significance of the operation, and the enormous distances involved. The 1st Marine Division was enroute to Wellington, New Zealand, when the warning order for the Guadalcanal operation was delivered on 25 June 1942. Mount out (departure) for the 1st Division, from Wellington, was set for 22 July. The three infantry regiments and the artillery regiment of the division were scattered across half the globe on 25 June: the 5th Marine Regiment was at Wellington, the 1st Marine Regiment was enroute at sea, the 7th Marine Regiment was at Samoa on garrison duty and was not released until late in the operation, and the Division's artillery regiment, the 11th Marines, was at sea enroute also to Wellington. Units at sea were loaded administratively for maximum usage of space and as the landing plan developed, these units required reloading at Wellington to support the scheme of maneuver. This later reloading was accomplished under severe handicaps of wet weather which ruined non-waterproofed foodstuffs, lack of civilian help - because the highly unionized stevedores at New Zealand could not agree on terms, and inadequate dock space - which stopped trucks from moving among the piles of gear and forced man-handling where possible. The net result was loss of supplies that were badly needed, and significantly for the LVT, seventy-five per cent of the heavier wheeled vehicles had to be left behind with the rear echelon when the division sailed.[7] This meant there would be more use of LVTs than originally planned.

Company A, 1st Amphibian Tractor Battalion, was the first unit to leave the United States, when it went overseas with the 5th Marine Regiment to Wellington in May 1942. The entire 1st Amtrac Battalion, less one platoon, was assigned to support the Guadalcanal landings, now rescheduled for 7 August, with Company A, 2nd Amtrac Battalion plus the one platoon from 1st Amtracs assigned to support the Gavutu-Tulagi landings across Sealark Channel from the main island of Guadalcanal.[8] This detached assignment of one platoon created some hardship initially because maintenance facilities were concentrated in the headquarters company of the battalion which was landing at Guadalcanal, thereby leaving the detached units capable of performing only the most basic type of maintenance such as tightening, cleaning, and lubricating.[9] Under the then-existing tables of the organization, the number of tractors assigned to support the Guadalcanal landing was about 86, and those assigned to the Gavutu-Tulagi landings totalled about 42. Each of the three letter companies in an Amtrac Battalion contained 3 platoons with approximately 10 tractors per platoon with 2 tractors in company headquarters. Headquarters and Service Company of the Amtrac Battalion contained mechanics, clerks, cook, and command facilities.[10]

Surprisingly, considering the haste with which the operation was planned, things went like clockwork on D-Day, 7 August. The Line of Departure was crossed on time by the 5th Marines and they hit the beach after the 5,000 yard approach at 9:10 A.M. On its first day of action, amphibian versatility was demonstrated. Warned that the rivers of the area would be deep, engineers had constructed a rough wooden bridge from scrap available on ships. This bridge was carried to the beach on D-Day by two LVTs which drove into the Tenaru River, a stream on the flank of the landing area, and became the supporting pontoons for it during the crossing of early assault elements of the landing force.[11]

The 5th Marines pushed inland against no resistance. The reserve regiment, the 1st Marines, came ashore at 9:30 A.M. Artillery arrived

Figure 6. LVT(1)s coming ashore somewhere in Guadalcanal. Note the machine guns manned and ready.

Figure 7. LVT(1)s approaching the beach on a supply run from anchored transports in the background.

next and generated one of the first of many improvised missions for the LVT. As the LVTs unloaded heavy cargo on the shore, they also towed artillery into position because there was an inadequate supply of wheeled vehicles which normally did this.[12] The perimeter continued to expand throughout the day and next two days, against no resistance. Although the landings at Tulagi were a surprise, the island required two days of fighting to clear. The Guvutu-Tanambogo Islands were tiny fragments hooked together by a causeway and the landings there were heavily opposed but successful with fighting through the first day and on into the second. Two tanks were used on Tanambogo with one set afire by oil-soaked rags hand-carried by Japanese soldiers. Forty-two Japanese bodies were counted stacked around the burned-out tank after combat.[13] Five LVT(1)s of Company A, 2d Amtrac Battalion, proved to be versatile pieces of equipment in this fight:

> They carried water, supplies, ammunition, and personnel to shore and evacuated wounded on the return trips. On one occasion a tractor moved some distance inland to attack a Japanese position that had pinned down and wounded a number of Marines. Using their two machine guns, one .30 and one .50 caliber, the tractor's crew neutralized the enemy fire and then evacuated the wounded Marines.[14]

The 1st Marine Division's Final Report noted, however, that:

> . . . This was an emergency undertaking only as it is not considered that the tractor is a tactical combat vehicle.[15]

The perimeter that stabilized at Guadalcanal was comprised of a 9,600 yard main line of resistance facing seaward and a 9,000 yard inland stretch running through dense jungles. The inland stretch could not be covered by position defenses and a critical need developed for all available personnel to cover these extensive lines. For the remainder of the long struggle for Guadalcanal, the 1st Amphibian Tractor Battalion held an inland sector with machine guns dismounted from their vehicles while performing foot patrols. The need for the men was more critical than the need for the vehicle. The 1st Marine Division was relieved by fresh Army and Marine units on 9 December 1942 and sailed for Australia for a well-earned rest and re-training period. With it went the LVTs of the 1st Amtrac Battalion.

There is a scarcity of records concerning the use of the LVT in the Guadalcanal Campaign, but there are only positive reports where the vehicle is mentioned. The keynote to its first debut was the discovery of the vehicle's great versatility through its mobility. Nowhere in the reports are the mechanical problems of the tractor emphasized but rather the focus is on its ability to get the job done. The Marine Corps' official history of the campaign summarizes it concisely, ". . . the amphibian tractor emerged as a versatile piece of equipment whose importance and utility could hardly be overestimated."[16]

As versatile as it was, the LVT(1) was also the first of its kind, and, as with all initial designs, needed improvements became apparent as time passed. The chief weakness of the LVT(1) was its track and suspension system. Before the War, this weakness had been observed by Borg-Warner engineers who visited Clearwater, Florida, at the request of the Navy during October 1941, to observe the Roebling Alligator in action:

> It was quite evident from examination of the tracks that there is a tremendous amount of friction, because the roller bearings cease to function as bearings after a short period of operation and have to be dragged around the track guides. Rapid wear of the bearings is the result of excessive overloading, together with entry of sand and water which soon destroys rolling action.[17]

The Borg-Warner engineering team further observed:

> There does not seem to be however, any method by which the track life can be substantially improved without a complete re-design. It was the consensus of opinion that a track running on bogey wheels of suitable design would be superior to any track which carried its own wheels.[18]

Further testing was performed by the United States Army at Aberdeen Proving Grounds in Maryland between 30 April to 20 July 1942 and conclusions drawn, while critical of the track design, also address other areas of design:

> The outstanding deficiency of the Roebling Amphibian is its propulsive inefficiency on land and on the water. The speed of the Vehicle in water is less than half that of screw-propelled boats with streamlined hulls of the same power and displacement. This comparative inefficiency of the Amphibian is due to (1) inefficient means of propulsion; (2) high towing resistance of the hull. The high towing resistance may be attributed to: (1) high friction loss due to excessive wetted surface; (2) bad wave-making and eddy-making qualities of the hull. Maximum water speed - 6.1 mph.[19]

The Army report represents early interest in the program and they monitored development of the LVT from November 1940 when high ranking Army officers observed the Quantico tests of the vehicle.

The problems noted in the Roebling design pointed to a complete redesign in order to overcome unreliability and improve vehicle performance. Although Borg-Warner was consulted by the Navy on design problems, the Navy chose to continue with Food Machinery for development of an improved amphibian design. FMC's designs were completed during December 1941 and they began tests on prototypes of not only a cargo-carrying LVT, but also concurrently an armored amphibian design. These design efforts were once again under the direction of Mr. J. M. Hait, and included assistance from the faculties of the California Institute of Technology and the University of California. Tests were conducted using models in tanks, and over 100 different shapes of grousers (track cleats) were tested before the best all-around "W" shape grouser was adopted.[20]

The Navy specified certain broad design criteria for these re-design efforts. For both the armored and the cargo versions of the LVT, the Navy

Figure 8. The early test version of the LVT(A)1 coming ashore. The armored canopy eventually became a tank turret, based on the Borg-Warner designed Model A.

indicated a desired land speed of at least 15 mph and a water speed of approximately 8 mph. The armored amphibian was not to weigh more than 27,000 pounds.[21] Early test results were encouraging with the armored design weighing 26,730 pounds with full fuel and oil and attaining speeds of 23 mph on firm land in fourth gear and 7.75 mph in water. The cargo design, weighing 25,400 pounds, attained a speed of 8.03 mph in water.[22] The heart of the new designs lay in the new suspension and track which in contrast to the rigid, no springs suspension of the LVT(1), featured eleven rubber-tired bogie wheels on torsional rubber springs mounted on each side of the vehicle to give a smoother and more stable ride on land. The track had hermetically sealed bearings to prevent entry of sand and water and extra-high track guides to keep the track from being thrown off the suspension in tight turns. The new grouser design on the track did not develop lateral pressure and wear in water like the Roebling design. FMC selected front drive using tested components of the M3 light tank, stating, ". . . a front drive is very advantageous, as it permits the chains to unload mud and debris before the links engage the drive sprockets."[23] Four universal joints were used between the engine and transmission and flexible couplings between the transmission and final drive to permit hull distortion without power loss or damage to the drive line components.[24]

While FMC was developing an armored amphibian and cargo carrying LVT, a simultaneous effort was underway at Borg-Warner as a result of their October 1941 visit to observe the Roebling Tractor in operation. Borg-Warner felt that re-design was the only way to overcome the problems of the Roebling Alligator and immediately launched into construction of a pilot model.[25] The Borg-Warner effort moved at a fast pace and a vehicle was completed and tested within six months, thus gaining for Borg-Warner the honor of completing the first modern armored amphibian, called the Model A. The Borg-Warner approach, while a comprehensive re-design, more closely approximated some of the engineering used in the Roebling LVT. The basic track cleat designed by Roebling was retained, but the rollers were removed from the track, increased in size, and incorporated into the bottom of the sponsons. These were large Timken bearings, protected by double neoprene and rawhide seals, turning on chrome-plated shafts.[26] Larger idler wheels and drive sprockets were used, coupled to a fully automatic transmission, which allowed transition from water to land without hesitation for shifting. Borg-Warner used a high-tensil strength, corrosion-resistant steel which they corrugated to obtain high strength combined with lighter weight. A unique feature of the Model A was the convertability of the basic vehicle. Borg-Warner designed a basic cargo-carrying vehicle of 17,000 pounds to carry a load of 5,000 pounds. To convert the cargo-carrier to an armored amphibian, the turret and decking was lowered into the open cargo space and it became a 22,000 pound combat vehicle with speeds of 17 mph on land and 8 mph in the water. An important engineering feature was the use of the standard M3 light tank turret which allowed the combat version to coaxially mount a 37 mm gun and a caliber .30 machine gun in the turret, which represented heavier gun power than the FMC design using only machine guns. The vehicle mounted in the bow, for use both in the combat and cargo configuration, one caliber .30 machine gun with vertical and horizontal movement and one caliber .30 machine gun with only vertical movement. The limited movement appears to have been intended to permit one gun to fire straight ahead of the vehicle. The vehicle was powered by a 141 horsepower, eight cylinder engine.[27]

While Borg-Warner perfected many engineering changes with their pilot Model A, their approach remained basically closer to the Roebling design and did not represent as great an improvement as the FMC approach. Borg-Warner's suspension did not give the smooth ride of the torsion suspension of FMC, and FMC's track design eliminated lateral forces in the water while Borg-Warner retained the basic Roebling cleat. Speeds of the vehicles were close in the water, but FMC's early designs moved faster (23 mph versus 17 mph) on land. Also, FMC's early designs in the cargo-carrier had a 7,000 pound capacity versus Borg-Warner's 5,000 pounds for the Model A. Despite Borg-Warner's failure to win design competition over FMC, they contributed a significant feature to future armored amphibian design with their use of the standard M3 light tank turret. This feature was incorporated into the official design of the new armored amphibian designated the LVT(A)1 (A for armored).

In their final form, entering production in April 1943 the LVT(A)1 and its cargo version, the LVT(2), named "The Water Buffalo", were derived from the same FMC basic design sharing all components except the additional armor, turret, and armament of the LVT(A)1. The turret on the armored amphibian was power operated and the gun gyro-stabilized to increase accuracy while shooting on the move. A comparison of the performances of the LVT(1), LVT(2), and the LVT(A)1 is instructive:

	LVT(1)	LVT(2)	LVT(A)1
Length	21'6"	26'1"	26'1"
Width	9'10"	10'8"	10'8"
Height (Overall)	8'2"	8'1"	10'1"
Weight (Unloaded)	18,500 lbs.	24,250 lbs.	30,000 lbs.
Cargo	4,500 lbs.	5,950 lbs.	950 lbs.
Fuel Capacity	50 gallons	110 gallons	104 gallons
Cruising Range			
(land)	120 miles	150 miles	150 miles
(water)	50 miles	50 miles	50 miles
Armament	Provision for 1 Cal. 50 MG up to 4 Cal. 30 MG	Provision for 1 Cal. 50 MG up to 4 Cal. 30 MG	1 37 mm gun (turret) 1 Cal. 30 MG (turret) 2 Cal. 30 MG external
Engine	150 HP Hercules	Continental W-690-9A, 250 HP	Continental W-690-9A, 250 HP
Speeds			
(land)	12 mph	20 mph	20 mph
(water)	6-7 mph	7.5 mph	7.5 mph
Armor Thickness			
(cab)	none	1/2"	1/2"
(hull)	none	1/4"	1/4"
(turret)			
sides, front	--	--	1/2"
rear	--	--	1/2"
top	--	--	1/4"

Source: Instruction Book for Tracked Landing Vehicles, 1943, pages 12-13.

A further development of the Water Buffalo family of vehicles was the LVT(A)2. This was an armored version of the cargo carrying, unarmored, LVT(2). The LVT(A)2 did not have a turret and was the only LVT to carry the (A) designation (for armor) that did not have a turret with a large-caliber gun. Its external appearance was nearly identical to that of the LVT(2) except instead of clear plexiglass windows for driving, the LVT(A)2 was fitted with an armored hatch that opened to permit direct viewing or closed to protect the driver. The LVT(A)2 also was equipped with two rotating periscopes on top of the cab to permit the driver to see with the direct-view hatch closed for protection. The armor was one-half inch on the cab and one-quarter inch on the hull adding a total of 2,400 pounds to the unloaded weight of the vehicle and reducing its cargo capacity from 5,950 pounds for the unarmored version to 4,550 pounds for the LVT(A)2. A further significant refinement in the LVT(A)2 was the addition of self-sealing gasoline tanks.[28] All other performance and characteristics of the LVT(A)2 remained the same as the LVT(2).

As production commenced on the new family of vehicles, the Secretary of the Navy formed the Continued Board for the Development of the Landing Vehicle Tracked on 30 October 1943. This board was to be the chief agency for supervising the improvement of the growing variety of LVTs, based on the recommendations of the users.

The LVT(A)1 and the armored cargo carrier, LVT(A)2, were designed to resist heavy machine gun fire and thus were able to function as troop carrying and assault vehicles in the lead waves of a landing against a defended shore. This capability was cited as vital when in 1941 the Commandant of the Marine Corps recommended construction of armored, heavily armed LVTs to overrun beach defenses. FTP-167 had further endorsed the use of the vehicles in the assault role. The production of the Water Buffaloes in 1943 was therefore a logical continuation of this approach, yet the next major campaign in the Pacific again used the LVT as a logistical vehicle.

The central objective of the Solomons Campaign was the isolation of the Japanese stronghold of Rabaul on New Britain Island, with its numerous airfields and naval bases. Rabaul functioned as the Japanese anchor for their Solomons operations and its destruction or neutralization would undermine Japanese strength in the area and make their position

Figure 9. The Borg-Warner Model A with its tank turret and 37mm gun in place.

Figure 10. The Borg-Warner Model A with the tank turret removed, ready to haul cargo.

Figure 11. The LVT(2) in final form. Notice the "w" shaped grousers on the track. This shape remained standard throughout the war. Photos from the War Department traning manual on the vehicle.

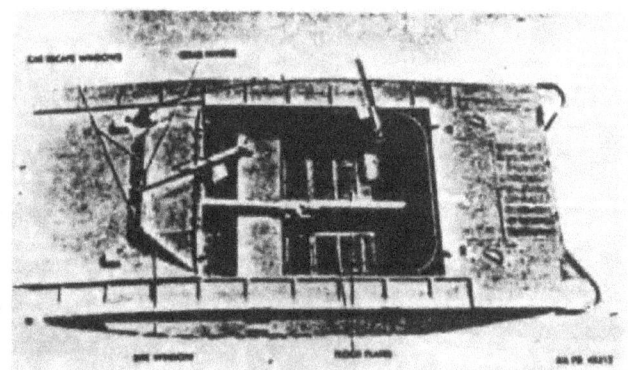

Figure 12. An overhead view of the interior of the cargo compartment of the LVT(2). Note the driveshaft splitting the compartment.

Figure 13. A training manual photograph of the LVT(A)2. This was identical to the LVT(2) except that it was constructed of heavy metal sheet amounting to armor protection from one-quarter to one-half inch thick.

Figure 14. The LVT(A)1 in final form. Note the turret is identical to that used on the Borg-Warner Model A.

Figure 15. The LVT(A)1 in rear view. Note the provision for two externally mounted caliber .30 machine guns. There are no statistics on the casualties suffered by the operators of these machine guns, but they were clearly vulnerable in comparison to the more fortunate crew housed inside the vehicle operating the main gun.

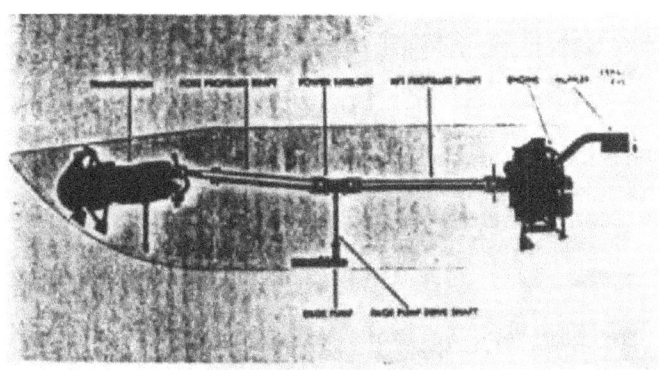

Figure 16. A training manual diagram showing the relationship of the power train components. The rear engine mounting required a long drive shaft through the middle of the vehicle.

untenable. A direct leap from Guadalcanal was not possible for numerous reasons, but the major consideration was the inability of carrier aviation to furnish sufficient air power. It was necessary to secure intermediate islands along the Solomons chain to provide air bases for land based aircraft of the United States Army Air Corps to augment the air effort against Rabaul. Also, there were sufficient Japanese bases in the Solomons to make the establishment of any supply line up the Solomons a difficult matter without first securing these enemy concentrations. Thus, after the termination of the Guadalcanal Campaign in February 1943 the United States embarked on its "island hopping" strategy up the Solomons chain. First captured were the Russell Islands, followed by a difficult and drawn-out campaign against the Japanese complex in New Georgia, completed on 29 August 1943. The New Georgia campaign used twelve LVTs as artillery prime movers.[29] The next move would be into the Northern Solomons to secure a site for an airfield to bring land based bombers and fighters within range of New Britain. After considerable deliberation, the large island of Bouganville was chosen, and the 3rd Marine Division, new and not yet combat tested, was selected as the landing force.

Considerations affecting the choice of Bouganville had bearing on the planned use of the LVTs. After the difficult struggle to take New Georgia, commanders were reluctant to undertake another head-on fight with the Japanese in the Northern Solomons area, which was closer to Rabaul and with large formations of Japanese stationed on the island of Bouganville itself. To avoid a direct confrontation, Allied planners utilized the large size of the island, 125 miles long by 30 miles wide, and searched for and found a spot relatively undefended and away from air and land forces of the Japanese. This was the Cape Torokina area of Empress Augusta Bay, where intelligence estimated only 300 defenders were present. The landing site was a wet, swampy, run-off area for mountain streams running down from the island's central mountain chains. Thick jungle and bamboo choked this region and the beaches were seldom more than 15 yards wide. This unlikely location was also roughly in the middle of the west coast of the island, and a maximum distance away from the two major airfields and concentrations of Japanese, which were 15,000 in the north and 6,800 in the south.[30] The landing was therefore a planned surprise, but there was no intention of capturing the entire island and only enough beachhead would be established to defend the planned airfield to be constructed on Cape Torokina.

This plan dodged a head-on assault against a heavily defended beach and therefore eliminated the requirement for armored LVTs to blast their way onto the beach as part of the leading waves and emphasized LVT logistical capabilities, similar to the Guadalcanal landings. D-Day was set for 1 November 1943.

With the landing site within air attack range from airfields on Bouganville and New Britain, an intensive air campaign was conducted to reduce any Japanese air retaliation to zero. In September, one month prior to the landings, the Japanese air strength was estimated at 154 planes in the Northern Solomons area compared with 476 planes of all types for the Japanese in the overall Bouganville-Rabaul area.[31] The air command for the Bouganville could muster 728 planes of all types and were assisted by the Army Air Force bombers of General Kenney. Air operations during October were intensive with U.S. aircraft in the air almost daily. One Japanese airfield on Bouganville was hit 23 times and resembled a

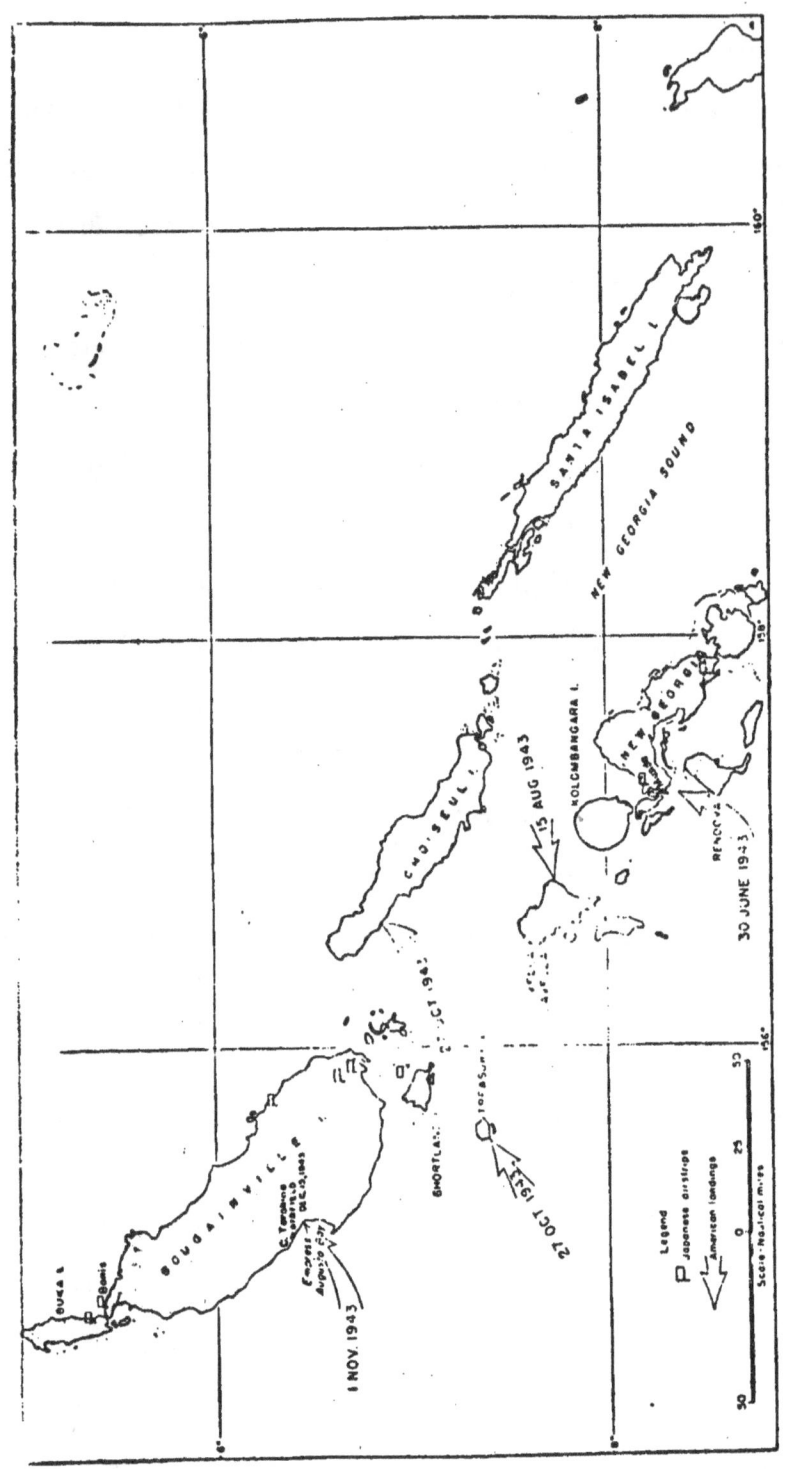

Map 3. Landings, Central and Northern Solomons, June 1943 to February 1944.

moonscape after the treatment from Marine, Navy, and Army fliers.[32] Rabaul was also hurt by high level bomber attacks during October. The net result of this air campaign was to eliminate Japanese air interference when the landings were executed on 1 November 1943.

The element of surprise was retained and the landing force moved ashore largely without opposition. Only in the area of Purata Island and Cape Torokina was resistance significant due to a troublesome 75 mm anti-boat gun and defensive works on the beach. The landing force moved inland and reorganized, opening the beach for logistical activity, even though along the northern beaches many landing craft had been damaged by unexpectedly high surf and were cluttering the beach. The congestion of the northern beaches caused a decision to switch cargo deliveries to the southern beaches that remained uncluttered from damaged landing craft, and this in turn caused some congestion because the narrow beaches could not accomodate increased dumps and there was no room in the thick jungle to transport supplies inland. Despite this problem, the supplies were moved due to increased emphasis on the unloading process which initially entailed using fully forty per cent of the landing force strength in logistical duties to avoid the congestion and pile-up that occurred at Guadalcanal. Some soldiers were not released back to their parent units for several days. Ammunition and gasoline were dangerously close to each other and to troop areas and a vulnerable build-up of supplies did occur during the early days of the Bouganville landing despite the best efforts of the large working party. Fortunately, the devastating blows dealt to the Japanese air power in the area reduced the size of Japanese air retaliation. There were air attacks during the peak periods of supply congestion on the beach but fighter cover and the anti-aircraft fire of

Figure 17. The LVT(1) at Bougainville working in its primary role for that campaign. Note the requirement to hoist everything over the side due to the lack of a loading ramp.

Figure 18. Maintenance in the field took place under difficult circumstances. The engine is being removed from the forward vehicle.

the destroyer screen drove off the attackers. The largest attack occurred at 1:00 P.M. and consisted of 70 Japanese planes. They were driven away with no significant damage to U.S. forces but valuable time was consumed due to the need for evasive tactics by transports that were required to stop unloading and put to sea.[33] The congestion was further aggravated by the lack of exits from the beach and non-existent roads. It was under these circumstances that the LVT once again demonstrated itself as the machine of the hour. According to the official history:

> Already these lumbering land-sea vehicles had proven their worth in carrying cargo, ferrying guns, and evacuating wounded men through the marsh lands and the lagoons, and the variations of their capabilities under such extreme circumstances were just beginning to be realized and appreciated.[34]

A total of 124 LVTs were landed at Bouganville, all being the Roebling designed LVT(1). Twenty-nine landed early with the assault echelons on D-Day with later increments bringing the 3rd Amtrac Battalion up to its total strength.[35] As the perimeter expanded, the LVT was frequently the only vehicle that could carry supplies forward through the knee-deep mud. This continuous strain on the vehicles created a maintenance problem of significant proportions and the largest number of vehicles available at any one time was sixty-four, with the number once dropping to twenty-nine.[36] Nevertheless, the official history pays further tribute to the LVTs during the expansion of the perimeter:

> Without the 3rd Amphibian Tractor Battalion, the operation as planned could not have been carried beyond the initial beachhead stages; and it was the work of the LVT companies and the skill of the amtrac operators that made possible the rapid advance of the IMAC forces during the first two weeks.[37]

After 24 March 1944 significant Japanese attacks against the perimeter, now reinforced with United States Army units of the 37th Division, ceased and departure of the Marine units commenced with the last Marine units departing on 21 June 1944. It had been a protracted campaign, in difficult terrain, against a determined enemy, and it also marked a high point for the reputation of the LVT. The official history states flatly, "Had it not been for the amtracs, the supply problem would have been insurmountable."[38] The amtracs hauled 22,992 tons of rations, ammunition, weapons, organizational gear, medical supplies, packs, gasoline, and vehicles, as well as reinforcements and casualties.[39] Another quotation from a Marine captain who served on Bouganville summarizes the appreciation felt by the Marine riflemen in the foxholes:

> Not once but all through the campaign the amphibian tractor bridged the vital gap between life and death, available rations and gnawing hunger, victory and defeat. They roamed their triumphant way over the beachhead. They ruined roads, tore down communications lines, revealed our combat positions to the enemy - but everywhere they were welcome.[40]

With such a complete demonstration of its logistical value to its credit, the LVT was next to be called on to lead the assault as well. The new model LVT(A)1 and the LVT(2)s were coming off the production lines and the LVT(2) would be ready for the next major operation planned for the Central Pacific theater. It was to be a severe test at a place called Tarawa.

NOTES

[1] Frank O. Hough, Verle E. Ludwig, and Henry I. Shaw, Pearl Harbor to Guadalcanal, Vol. I of History of the United States Marine Corps Operations in World War II (5 vols.; Washington: Historical Branch, G-3 Division, Headquarters, United States Marine Corps, 1958), p. 236.

[2] United States Navy, Fleet Training Publication - 167, Change No. 1 (Washington: U.S. Navy Department, 1941), p. 44.

[3] Ibid., p. 56.

[4] Food Machinery Corporation, Amphibians (San Jose: Food Machinery Corp., 1942), p. 16.

[5] Borg-Warner Corporation, Research, Investigation, and Experimentation in the Field of Amphibious Vehicles (Kalamazoo: Ingersoll Kalamazoo Division, 1957), p. 66.

[6] Hough, Ludwig, and Shaw, Pearl Harbor to Guadalcanal, pp. 263-264.

[7] Ibid., p. 250.

[8] Ibid., p. 261.

[9] Victor J. Croizat, "The Marine's Amphibian," Marine Corps Gazette, June, 1953, p. 43.

[10] 1st Amtrac Battalion, Muster Rolls (In the Field: 1st Amtrac Battalion, 1943).

[11] John L. Zimmerman, The Guadalcanal Campaign (Washington: Historical Division, Headquarters, United States Marine Corps, 1949), p. 45.

[12] Hough, Ludwig, and Shaw, Pearl Harbor to Guadalcanal, p. 256.

[13] Ibid., p. 269.

[14] Ibid., p. 270.

[15] Ibid.

[16] Ibid., p. 270.

[17] Harold Nutt, "Amphibian Tank Report," (Borg-Warner Memorandum, 1941), p. 1.

[18] Ibid., p. 2.

[19] United States Army, *First Report on Amphibian Tractor (Roebling)* (Aberdeen: Aberdeen Proving Grounds, 1942), p. 1.

[20] Food Machinery Corporation, *Amphibians*, p. 4.

[21] Ibid., p. 3.

[22] Ibid.

[23] Ibid., p. 5.

[24] Ibid.

[25] Nutt, "Amphibian Tank Reports," p. 6.

[26] Borg-Warner Corporation, "Borg-Warner Amphibian," (Undated Information Brochure), p. 3.

[27] Ibid., pp. 1-6.

[28] War Department, *Instruction Book For Tracked Landing Vehicles* (Washington, D.C.: War Department, 1943), p. 13.

[29] Douglas T. Kane and Henry I. Shaw, *Isolation of Rabaul*, Vol. II of *History of United States Marine Corps Operations in World War II* (5 vols.; Washington: Historical Branch, G-3 Division, Headquarters, United States Marine Corps, 1958), p. 56.

[30] Ibid., pp. 171-176.

[31] Shaw and Kane, *Isolation of Rabaul*, p. 185.

[32] Ibid., p. 186.

[33] Shaw and Kane, *Isolation of Rabaul*, p. 217.

[34] Ibid., p. 229.

[35] Ibid., p. 292.

[36] Ibid., pp. 252-253.

[37] Ibid.

[38] Ibid., p. 292.

[39] Ibid.

[40] John Monks, Jr., *A Ribbon and A Star* (New York: Henry Holt and Company, 1945), p. 65.

PART IV

TARAWA

The battle for Tarawa would be the first major engagement in the opening of a new American offensive route in the Pacific War, through the Central Pacific. The United States position in the Solomons, which surrounded and contained the key strongpoint of Rabaul, now permitted the opening of the Central Pacific drive, an avenue of approach long-favored in pre-war plans including the Navy's Plan Orange. The Japanese had been hurt severely by American air raids against Rabaul and were now unable to mount serious airstrikes against United States offensive moves because Japanese bases in the Solomons, which would have posed a flank threat to American lines of communications in a Central Pacific drive, had been captured for allied use. Navy thinking favored a Central Pacific route which aimed directly for Japan via capture of the Marshalls and the Marianas Island groups and culminated with the seizure of a major staging base near Japan for the final assault. General MacArthur, Commanding General of the Southwest Pacific Theater, favored a longer route via New Guinea and the Philippines which would provide better security for successive allied moves due to the greater amount of land available for bases. It would also allow for an early return to the Philippines in fulfillment of his pledge to return, and would provide security for Australia. The debate was resolved during May 1943 at a meeting of the Combined Chiefs of Staff in Washington. The Combined Chiefs, the highest

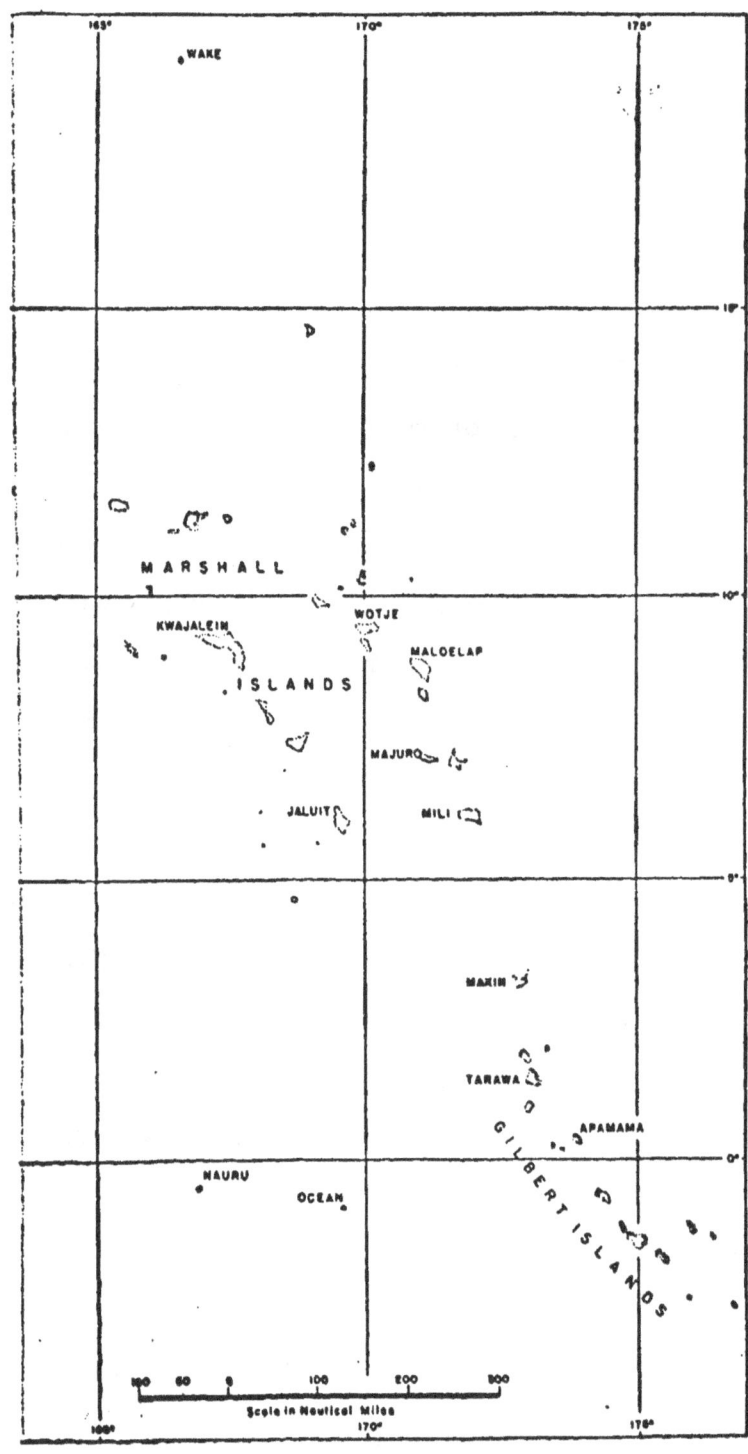

Map 4. The Gilberts and Marshalls.

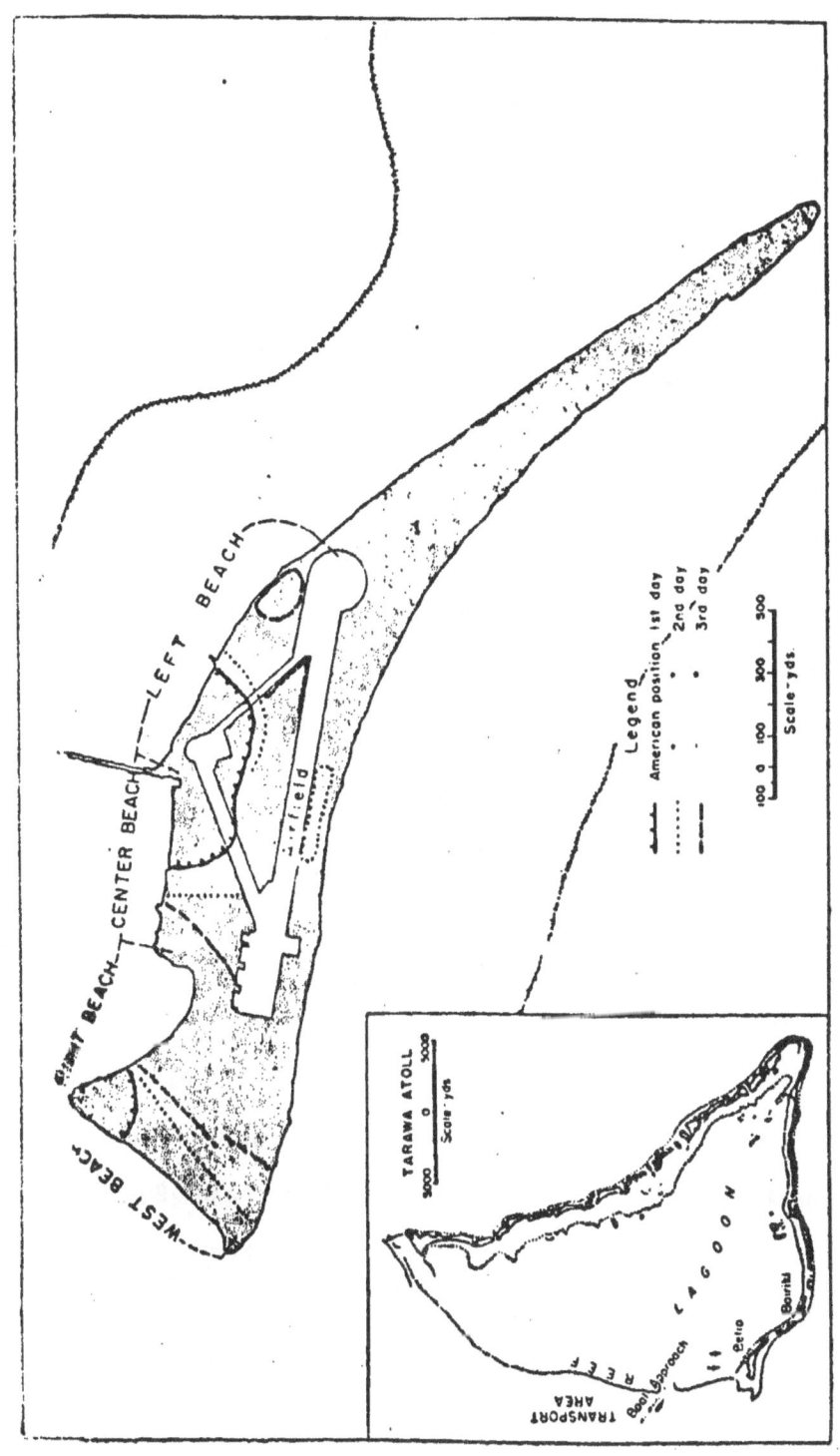

Map 5. Betio Islet with insert of Tarawa Atoll.

military planning council comprised of British and American Chiefs of Staff, favored the Navy's Central Pacific thrust, yet also maintained MacArthur's drive through the New Guinea-Phillipines to neutralize the Japanese in that area and provide security for the main drive through the middle Pacific.

The Navy's direct-approach plan was feasible because of the new strength of carrier aviation and the ability of the Navy to support itself at sea with its own army (Marines), air arm, sea force, and mobile service facilities. The Navy was to cut free of the cramped waters of the Solomons and make long-distance leaps between islands through the Central Pacific towards Japan. The increase in speed was promising and the prize was worth seeking. The stage was set for Tarawa.

There was little intelligence available on the main island group, the Marshalls, and the Joint Chiefs of Staff selected the Gilbert Islands as the first objective for the Central Pacific Drive. Capture of the Gilberts would give valuable bases for air reconnaissance of the Marshalls and defenses in the Gilberts appeared weaker than those in the Marshalls.

The Joint Chiefs directive on invasion of the Gilberts was dated 20 July 1943 and an organization for the invasion was established by Admiral Nimitz on 24 August 1943. The Landing Force included the Fifth (V) Marine Amphibious Corps under the command of Major General Holland M. Smith and major ground components were the 2d Marine Division under General Julian C. Smith, and the 27th Army Division commended by Major General Ralph C. Smith. (None of these Smiths were related.) D-Day was initially set for 1 November but later moved to 20 November 1943 allowing only two months for the newly established organization to develop plans and organize the teamwork so essential in an amphibious landing.

The key to the defenses on the Gilberts was the island of Betio in the Tarawa atoll. Here the Japanese had constructed one of the few usable airfields in the Gilberts and had fortified the island. The island of Makin was selected as the target for the landing of the 27th Army Division due to its weak defenses and its nearness to the Marshalls, while the tougher objective of Betio was given to the 2d Marine Division with its greater amphibious experience.

Planning was based on intelligence information gathered from old charts and aerial photos and little was initially available. The Tarawa Atoll, and the target island of Betio within it, were poorly charted and even Navy Hydrographic Office charts proved unreliable. Interviews were conducted with former residents and aerial and submarine photos were taken. One photo of Betio was particularly valuable because it allowed analysts to estimate the size of the enemy force from shoreline latrines visible in the photo.[1] As intelligence accumulated, critical differences from past experiences grew obvious. It became clearer that the island was heavily fortified on the beach, whereas previous landings frequently avoided opposition there. The island of Betio, about the size of New York's Central Park, was three miles long by 1,500 yards wide at its widest point, and therefore the element of surprise was very difficult to achieve because the defenders would never be far from their positions. On this tiny island there were estimated between 2,500 and 3,100 defenders crammed into bunkers, log emplacements, and foxholes.[2] Numerous large caliber guns, anti-aircraft guns, and machine guns were noted in photographs. In contrast to previous landings, Betio in the Tarawa Atoll presented a coral reef with no discernible gaps. Regardless of direction, the reef would have to be crossed in order to land.

Water depths over the reef became a critical point of intelligence and one difficult to assess with accuracy. Fully loaded landing craft drew four feet of water; the LVT could cross the reef regardless of water depth. Little was known of the tides over the reefs at Betio. Some who had sailed in the area reported freak tides that ebbed and flowed irregularly over the reef and initial estimates of two feet of water were predicted for 20 November 1943. Later discussions with other sailors of the area gave hope for as much as five feet of water over the reef and it was this larger figure that was finally accepted. A former resident of the island, Major F. L. G. Holland, a New Zealander, took strong exception to this optimistic figure but could not disprove the tables prepared by intelligence analysts.[3] The strong defense at the beach and the shallow waters of the reef dictated that assault waves of the landing force be embarked in the LVTs to insure an early foothold. This point, however, was hotly disputed between General Holland M. Smith, the landing force commander, and Admiral Kelly Turner, the Amphibious Force Commander, before it was accepted. General Smith finally took a flat stand, "No amtracs, no operations."[4] Admiral Turner saw no need for the vehicles due to the accepted five-foot figure for depths of water over the reefs, but nevertheless relented at this point and the vehicles were included in plans.

The inclusion of LVTs in the operation raised another point of considerable importance to planners. The 2d Amtrac Battalion was to support the 2d Marine Division, but it had only seventy-five combat-worthy LVT(1)s after much work and preparation in New Zealand.[5] More tractors were needed to boat the first three waves, the minimum number of waves considered acceptable for a chance of success by General Smith.[6]

Fifty additional LVT(2)s were located and shipped to Samoa, where they were met by a newly formed company of the 2d Amtrac Battalion during October 1943. Unfortunately, the new vehicles were in poor mechanical condition because they were left unattended for four to five months in San Diego. Three of the four weeks available in Samoa prior to embarking for the target area were required for maintenance and combat preparation of the vehicles. Combat preparation of these LVT(2)s included the mounting of a twenty-six inch by forty inch piece of three-eighths inch boiler plate on the front of the cab. Further plating was not possible due to lack of materials. Also, one caliber 50 machine gun and a caliber 30 machine gun were mounted forward and a caliber 30 machine gun mounted aft, to be operated by the embarked troops as they moved towards the beach. Five days of training were conducted after these preparations prior to embarkation of the LVT(2)s on 8 November. One rehearsal was conducted by the Battalion Commander, Major Drewes, on 12 November, on the way to the target area. The new company with its fifty LVT(2)s arrived in the transport area off Betio at 3:30 A.M. on 20 November.[7]

The LVT(1)s of the 2d Amtrac Battalion underwent a similar preparation in New Zealand prior to embarkation. An additional one-quarter inch of armor plating was mounted on the front and sides of the cab and a 1 1/2 foot square piece of armor plating was mounted inside the cab to protect the driver. Two caliber 50 machine guns were mounted forward and one caliber 30 was mounted aft. Two large grappling hooks were attached to the rear to pull up defensive wire laid down by the Japanese on the beaches.[8] The net effect of these combat modifications was to add weight which would result in a slower water speed of the vehicles. While tests were run to determine the extent of the reduction, the full impacts of the slower speeds were not appreciated until the vehicles were on their way against the beaches on D-Day.

Planning for Tarawa utilized some standardized control measures developed from previous campaigns and refinement of amphibious doctrine to organize the movement of landing craft. Amphibious assaults adopted the "Line of Departure" as the start line for the dispatch of waves to the beach. This line was located 6,000 yards from the beach at Tarawa, is marked by an anchored control vessel, and runs parallel to the beach to permit a straight run. The 6,000 yard distance allowed formation of the waves beyond range of small arms and effective machine gun fire, and all unloading, forming, and organization of the assault takes place seaward of this line. The line of departure allows the Naval Commander, through his control vessel, to control the dispatch of landing craft in waves to the beach and thus coordinate their movement with the firing of naval gunfire and air support attacking the beaches. Once dispatched across the line of departure, landing craft proceed in designated boat lanes to the beach. The width of the boat lane is determined by the width of the beach being attacked; a boat lane is normally assigned to each battalion. The number of waves varies with the size of the unit landing. As the leading waves approach the beach, close coordination is important to insure that the ongoing friendly gunfire does not hit the landing forces. At Tarawa this coordination was attempted using a time schedule. The LVTs were scheduled to hit the beach at H-Hour, a term standardized to designate the particular time, to the nearest minute, that the landing force was to touch sand. If the waves of landing craft fell behind schedule or got ahead of schedule, it was necessary to establish a new H-Hour to adjust schedules of fire. Naval gunfire and air support schedules were normally expressed in times of H Plus or minus so many minutes. Thus, if the scheduled time of H-Hour was changed, all air support and naval gunfire would shift also. As the leading waves neared the beach, naval gunfire was to shift inland or to the flanks and air support was to make a last minute strafing run over the beach. If time schedules were accurate, all fire support would shift or cease just as the leading waves hit the beach.

Planning called for 42 LVT(1)s in the first wave, each carrying 18 combat-equipped Marines, 24 LVT(2)s in the second wave, each carrying 20 combat-equipped Marines, and 21 LVT(2)s in the third wave. There were therefore a total of 1,656 Marines designated for the first three waves. There were also to be eight empty LVT(1)s following the first wave and five empty LVT(2)s following the third wave to act as reserve vehicles for those that might become disabled on the 6,000 yard run from the line of departure to the beach.[9]

Differences in ship design necessitated a complex procedure for embarkation of troops into the LVTs. Troop transports were deep draft vessels and were equipped to carry only the LCVP (Landing Craft, Vehicle, Personnel), the standard landing boat with bow ramp. LVTs were too heavy to be carried by the lifting arms of the troop transports, so they were carried to the area by LSTs (Landing Ship, Tank) which were seagoing shallow draft vessels with large bow doors and ramps designed to permit beaching. Due to their shallow draft, the LSTs were capable of stationing themselves much closer to the line of departure in the shallow waters. This procedure was desirable because LVTs were slow and long runs to the line of departure invited increased mechanical failures. With the LSTs in the shallow water near the line of departure, and the transports

Figure 19. The trusty Landing Ship, Tank (LST) beached at Bougainville. This photograph shows the bow doors through which the LVTs entered the water.

dropping anchor further out to sea in the deeper waters, troops had to climb down cargo nets to the LCVPs of the transports and be carried to the waiting LVTs which had left their LSTs. The troops then entered the LVTs from the small LCVPs in a designated transfer area seaward of the line of departure prior to the tractors forming into waves for crossing the line of departure. This involved procedure took the better part of two hours, but surprise by this time was already lost due to the pounding by ships and aircraft being delivered. The Japanese were well aware of the impending attack before the waves ever reached the line of departure. Minesweepers were to proceed ahead of the waves, clearing the boat lanes and marking the lanes with bouys. They were then to take station at the line of departure. Later waves were to be landed in the LCVPs which drew three feet of water fully loaded. Because the Commanding General of the 2d Marine Division, Major General Julian Smith, viewed chances for enough water as only 50-50, the troops were briefed to be prepared to debark from the LCVPs if they were unable to cross the reef due to insufficient water over the reef.[10]

Estimates of the enemy were accurate. The Japanese force, commanded by Rear Admiral Keiji Shibasaki, consisted of 1,122 men of the 3rd Special Base Force, and 1,497 men of the elite Sasebo Special Naval Landing Force. In addition, there were 2,217 laborers from construction units. Since many of these were untrained, the Admiral's effective force was about 3,000 men, with twenty coastal defense guns, ranging in size from 80 mm to 8 inch, ten 75 mm howitzers, five light tanks mounted 37 mm guns, and numerous other smaller weapons. Concrete tetrahedron obstacles had been placed to force landing craft into lanes where the smaller coastal defense guns could destroy them. Inland, the command posts, communications, and ammunition dumps had been housed in massive concrete bunkers that would withstand even direct hits from large caliber naval guns. Not all the concrete bunkers were integrated into the defense system, many were built simply as shelters and had areas not covered by fire; the Marines were later able to find shelter in these blind spots.[11]

Against this formidable target the 2d Marine Division was to land with but one regiment, the 2d Marines, with the 2d Battalion, 8th Marines reinforcing, or a total of approximately 6,000 men. The 6th Marine Regiment was retained under Corps control as the reserve, and General Julian Smith retained the other two battalions of the 8th Marines as division reserve. Thus, there was barely a two-to-one numerical advantage to the attacker; normal combat doctrine called for a three-to-one advantage to the attacker in offensive operations. This ratio was barely enough to permit the Marines to carry the beach.

Before the Marines arrived, preliminary bombardment featured the heavy use of 7th Air Force B-24s in addition to carrier aviation of the Navy. The preliminary air strikes began as early as 17 September with carrier aircraft striking targets in the Gilberts including the Tarawa Atoll. B-24s began their strikes on 13 November with 18 bombers against the Tarawa Atoll. This attack pace varied but continued until 19 November combining both the high-level attacks of the B-24s with the lower level work of the carrier aircraft.[12] It should be noted at this point, however, that the impressive figures for tonnage of bombs and naval gunfire thrown against Betio did not yield impressive results. The general approach taken was that of area neutralization. While this produced some casualties and did extensive damage to the Japanese communications system on the island, it did not destroy many of the concrete fighting structures or kill a significant portion of the dug-in garrison. One of the hard lessons that was to come out of this fight was that preliminary bombardment, particularly by naval gunfire, had to be registered on individual targets and each destroyed in turn to produce a true softening of the beach. The Japanese were building substantial, tough pill boxes and bunkers and only direct hits would knock them out of action. Direct hits are not achieved by area fire but by painstaking one-round-at-time adjustment.

Dawn of D-Day found the LSTs opening their huge bow doors and lowering their ramps into the sea. The LVTs rumbled out and wallowed into the ocean to move to rendezvous points to receive troops. The troops, embarked in assault transports, clambered down large rope nets and entered LCVPs, which were also carried by the assault transport. They were then carried to the waiting amtracs where the transfer was made into the LVTs prior to the run into the beach. Little difficulty was encountered at this stage although the water was turbulent. Some enemy fire was landing in and near the transport area where the transfer operations were taking place, but no interference was experienced and the amtracs formed up in lines and headed for the line of departure, preceded by a guide boat. The LVTs were delayed approximately fifteen minutes to permit last minute shelling of the beach, but then they crossed the line of departure and headed for shore at top speed. There was some initial difficulty with wave formation, but at the half-way point all was in proper formation.[13]

Due to the late start over the line of departure, H-Hour (the hour that the troops were to hit the beach) at 8:30 A.M. could not be met and was postponed until 8:45 A.M. This was followed by another postponment due to the slow progress of the tractors towards the beach caused because the leading wave consisted of slower LVT(1)s which forced the faster LVT(2)s in wave 2 to slow down to keep the 300 yard interval assigned between the waves. H-Hour was finally set at 9:00 A.M. as the tractors neared the beach, but due to the poor communications of the day, not all fire support agencies were aware of this new time. Dust and smoke concealed the progress of the tractors, so the naval gunfire ceased fire at 8:55 A.M. to allow aircraft to make their close-in runs just ahead of the approaching amtracs. The aircraft complied but the amtracs were even behind the new scheduled H-Hour of 9:00 A.M. Most of the first wave hit the beach at 9:10 A.M. with movement during the last ten minutes unsupported by naval gunfire or aircraft.[14] At distances between 500 to 800 yards the tractors encountered the reef and climbed over it with no difficulty. Machine gun fire was received from this point into the beach with increasing severity. During the last 200 yards to the beach, eight tractors were put out of action by this type of fire.[15] LVT machine guns were operated by the embarked troops and assisted in putting down some of the fire that swelled from the beach as friendly supporting fire diminished and died away prematurely. Four LVTs negotiated the log wall at the beach and moved inland to the middle of the island before discharging their Marines. Offloaded LVTs backed off the beach to take advantage of their frontal armor, and most returned out to sea to attempt to pick up troops from the later waves embarked in LCVPs. There was not enough water over the reef to float the LCVPs, only a few inches in some places, and these troops were forced to wade ashore, exposed from the waist up to withering cross-fire, unless they were fortunate enough to be collected by the returning LVTs. On the first return trip to the

Figure 20. A view of the beach after D-Day. The horrible aftermath is evident and this and other Marine Corps photographs shocked America. The attrition among the LVTs is clear.

Figure 21. Another grim view of the beach at Tarawa. LVT number twenty-seven may be the mine casualty mentioned in 2d Amtrac Battalion Special Action Reports. The pier, which figured in the action during D-Day and after is in the background.

edge of the reef, about fifteen tractors sank in deep water due to the many holes in their hulls from machine gun and rifle fire.[16] The tractors had power driven bilge pumps, but these were not enough to handle the flood of water coming into the hulls and the later common practice of carrying wooden plugs to drive into bullet holes had not been adopted. Major Henry J. Drewes, the Battalion Commander, was killed by anti-boat fire in an LVT(2) about 9:30 A.M. on D-Day and Captain Henry G. Lawrence assumed command for the remainder of the operation. LVTs returning to the beach after landing the initial waves used a route covered from fire along a pier jutting out into the reef. This single route was used by the LVTs to return troops from the boats at the edge of the reef to the beach. There were never enough LVTs, however, to handle all the troops and most had to wade to shore, over 500 to 800 yards of fire swept, blood stained water. Casualties among this group were grim with companies sustaining thirty-five to seventy per cent losses just to reach the beach.[17] It was only through the outstanding combat leadership and initiative of young officers and NCOs that Marines reached the shore at all. In such a terrifying atmosphere, one man retreating to the rear would have started a stampede; none did. The amtrac's mechanical cousin, the tank, did not fare well. Only seven tanks out of fourteen landed on D-Day managed to cross the reef and gain the beach. All others suffered from drowned engines when they sank into deep potholes.[18] Once the tanks went into battle, they gave good service, although most were disabled by the end of D-Day. General Julian Smith committed his division's reserves and asked for permission to commit the Corps reserve before D-Day had ended. This permission was granted but the 6th Marines were not landed until the next day when the situation clarified and General Julian Smith was able to piece together the positions of his units and their situations.

After the initial movement of troops to the beaches, LVTs immediately assumed logistical roles by bringing supplies in from boats at the edge of the reef and evacuating casualties out to boats at the reef, or in some cases, directly to ships at sea. For the most part, however, the dwindling number of LVTs were badly needed to carry supplies across the reef as only the LVTs and very small boats were able to move in the shallow water. Much of this activity was done at night due to heavy enemy fire during the day. LVTs pulled sleds, rubber boats with cargo, trucks, and caterpiller tractors across the reefs. Many other tasks were assigned by the Division's Shore Party organization which had the responsibility of moving the incoming supplies across the beach into dumps, and moving supplies inland to the troops.

After the main landings against Betio's lagoon side, heavy congestion developed on the narrow beaches because troops were unable to penetrate far inland. As night fell on the first day, some assault companies had lost more than half their men to effect a penetration of only 300 yards. The night was surprisingly quiet and the fire discipline of the Marines was good considering this was the first combat for many. The following day reserves landed from LCVPs and took severe casualties as they waded towards shore. They were badly needed because many rifle companies were now down to fifty to seventy-five men from their normal strength of 235.[19] Gradually, despite the losses, combat power of the Marine units grew as machine guns were put back into action that had been lost during the fury of the landing and tanks were repaired that had been damaged during D-Day. LVTs continued to perform logistic runs and aided in evacuation of the wounded. Progress continued to be slow as all battalions forged straight ahead; by nightfall positions were as far as 750 yards inland across the 1,500 yard width of the island. The fighting was marked by small groups of Marines, together with engineers with blocks of TNT, attacking the heavy fortifications. The Engineer would tie the blocks of TNT together and throw this makeshift charge through the gun ports of the pill boxes. After the explosion, a flame-thrower man would direct a stream of flaming fuel through the gun port and riflemen would then mop up any remaining resistance. Gains were a yard or two at a time.[20] During the third night the Japanese conducted three night attacks which resulted in heavy casualties to them and thus speeded American victory. The biggest was at about 4:00 A.M. in the morning of 23 November, and consisted of about 300 Japanese. Dawn revealed the bodies of 200 Japanese 50 yards in front of Marine positions. The last day's fighting secured the last of the island around 1:00 P.M.[21]

Additional mop up was required and conducted by a contingent of troops and LVTs left behind to garrison the island. For the landing force of Marines, it was the bloodiest fight in the history of the Corps with total casualties of 3,149.[22] This amounted to 12 per cent of the overall force but a much higher percentage with respect to the fighting troops. The 2d Amtrac Battalion was no exception to this trend. For the assault on Tarawa they were shock troops rather than logistics personnel and their casualties were high. Out of 500 personnel of the battalion, 323 were killed, wounded, or missing.[23] The high casualties shocked America, but out of this cauldron came the lessons that were to be the final refinement of amphibious doctrine and they were to be used throughout the remainder of the war.

The assault on Tarawa was the first assault against a defended coral atoll. Coral atolls were to be the most frequent type of island that the Marines would face until late in the war and the techniques used to take such an island were tested at Tarawa. The most important tactical lesson of the operation was the new role of the LVT as an assault vehicle.[24] General Holland M. Smith, the overall commander and the future commander of the landings at Saipan and Iwo Jima, felt that the vehicles had stood the test and stated:

> After Tarawa, I made up my mind that all future landings would be spearheaded by amphibious vehicle, either the open-decked amtrac, of which a new improved model was already being made available, or amphibian tanks, carrying heavier guns, which were in production.[25]

The official Fifth Amphibious Corps recommendation was for an increase from one to two battalions of cargo amtracs supporting a division in future landings and it also recommended the additional support of a battalion of armored amphibians, the LVT(A)1, which was becoming available.[26]

The most graphic illustration of the value of the LVT in an assault across a shallow reef is the study of the casualty pattern at Betio. There, the first three waves were in amtracs and their casualties were described as light on reaching the beach. The heaviest casualties, between thirty-five and seventy per cent in some companies, were suffered by the men that had to wade in to the beach from the edge of the reef when their LCVPs could not navigate the shallow water.[27] Water depth varied from a few inches to three feet and most landing craft were unable to move across. Although the amtracs attempted to return to save troops wading across the reef, the number of LVTs rapidly began to dwindle and there were never enough to lift even a small portion of the succeeding waves.

Because of the high mortality of amtrac vehicles, the need was highlighted to embark as many waves as possible in amtracs at the outset, because their later capability to return from the beach for later waves could not be predicted. At Tarawa, the attrition among the vehicles was particularly high among the old LVT(1)s that had outlived their usefulness even before going ashore at Tarawa. General Holland Smith noted in his book that the average mechanical life of the LVT was 200 hours and some used at Tarawa had been run 400 hours before the landing.[28] At the end of the operation at Tarawa (that is after the first three days when the island was declared secured) there were only nineteen LVT(1)s functioning out of seventy-five, and only sixteen LVT(2)s out of the original fifty. An examination of the losses shows that only four LVT(1)s were disabled from mechanical failure, while the remaining fifty-two LVT(1)s were lost as a direct result of enemy fire by sinking, burning, or in one case, hitting a mine. This same picture applies to the newer LVT(2)s with only four out of action from mechanical failures while the remaining thirty vehicles were lost as a direct result of gunfire causing them to sink at sea, explode from igniting fuel tanks, or in the case of one, hitting a mine. The Battalion Commander, Captain Lawrence, stated in his recommendations a future need for 300 tractors to support a Marine Division with a replenishment rate of seventy-five per cent for the LVT(1)s and about thirty per cent for the LVT(2).[29] With respect to this critical need for sufficient LVTs in a reef assault, the outstanding analysis of Professors Isely and Crowl pinpoints the basic problem: "The critical failure at Tarawa was the lack of momentum in the assault. . . . Blame, if there be any, should rest on the lack of amphibian tractors. . . ."[30]

Fire support from the cargo carrying LVT(1)s and (2)s as they closed on the beach consisted of embarked troops firing the machine guns mounted on the tractors. Approximately 10,000 rounds were fired by the eighty-four machine guns mounted forward on the forty-two assault tractors, or an average of about 100 rounds per machine gun. Since preparation fire lifted prematurely at Tarawa by some ten minutes, it was these machine guns that provided the only close-in suppressive fire for the assault waves.[31] The mounting of machine guns was to continue on cargo LVTs, although the mission of providing firepower in the leading waves was to shift to the LVT(A)1s then just leaving production lines. The Battalion Commander recommended the forward mounting of two caliber 30 machine guns instead of the use of a caliber 50 and a caliber 30 to simplify ammunition requirements and allow more rounds to be available - caliber 50 ammunition is bulky, and many felt the gun was unreliable.[32]

The vehicle losses at Tarawa also caused recommendations by the Battalion Commander for additional armor on the front of the cab, bow, belly, and sides. Such additional armor was incorporated in the new LVT(A)2 and was applied to later models of LVTs in the form of portable armor that could be attached to conduct an assault landing then detached to allow the vehicle to carry more cargo in the later stages of the operation when the beach was not under fire and cargo capacity, rather than armor protection, was the capability most needed. Along with armor protection, a recommendation was made for future models to use periscopes rather than direct vision through an opening which endangered the driver.[33] For many models of the later LVTs, this type of vision was incorporated.

Many LVTs were lost as a result of fire from igniting fuel tanks pierced by enemy bullets. The two main fuel tanks in both the LVT(1) and

(2) were located in the rear, one on each side of the engine. These areas were not armor protected and the tanks were steel with no self-sealing capability. Their vulnerability proved to be costly at Tarawa. Later models incorporated Goodrich self-sealing tanks for a higher measure of protection.[34]

In an overall review of Tarawa, differences from previous Marine campaigns are numerous. The emphasis completely shifted from the earlier use of LVTs in logistics to application in the main assault, with the surviving vehicles then employed for logistical missions. The critical need for the LVT in assaults across the reefs of the Central Pacific was emphasized at Tarawa by the high casualties suffered by the men wading ashore from landing craft unable to cross the reef. Although the LVTs at Tarawa were depleted heavily by enemy action, the models in production would provide the design improvements in armor, armament, and durability to make the LVT more survivable and reliable. Success hung in the balance at Tarawa during the first hours using eighty-four LVTs in the assault waves. Without any LVTs at all, the assault on Tarawa would have failed, and it is this fact that was apparent to General Holland M. Smith when he had insisted that unless LVTs were used, there would be no assault at all. As he stated flatly in his book, ". . . for impassable reefs the solution was the amphibious vehicle."[35]

NOTES

[1] Henry I. Shaw, Jr., Bernard C. Nalty, and Edwin T. Turnbladh, Central Pacific Drive, Vol. III of The History of the United States Marine Corps Operations in World War II (5 vols.; Washington, D.C.: Historical Branch, G-3 Division, Headquarters, United States Marine Corps, 1966), p. 29.

[2] Ibid., p. 30.

[3] Ibid., p. 31.

[4] Holland M. Smith, Coral and Brass (New York: Charles Scribner's Sons, 1949), p. 120.

[5] 2d Amtrac Battalion, Special Action Report (In the field: 2d Amtrac Battalion, 1943), p. 2.

[6] Smith, Coral and Brass, p. 120.

[7] 2d Amtrac Battalion, Special Action Report, p. 1.

[8] Ibid., p. 2.

[9] Ibid., p. 3.

[10] Shaw, Nalty, and Turnbladh, Central Pacific Drive, p. 31.

[11] Shaw, Nalty, and Turnbladh, Central Pacific Drive, p. 48.

[12] 2d Amtrac Battalion, Special Action Report, p. 3.

[13] Ibid.

[14] Shaw, Nalty, and Turnbladh, Central Pacific Drive, pp. 58-59.

[15] 2d Amtrac Battalion, Special Action Report, p. 4.

[16] Ibid.

[17] Shaw, Nalty, and Turnbladh, Central Pacific Drive, pp. 59-62.

[18] Ibid., pp. 65-66.

[19] Ibid., p. 74.

[20] Ibid., p. 79.

[21] Ibid., p. 89.

[22] Ibid., p. 636.

[23] Ibid., p. 108.

[24] Ibid.

[25] Smith, Coral and Brass, p. 133.

[26] Shaw, Kane, and Turnbladh, Central Pacific Drive, p. 109.

[27] Ibid., p. 60.

[28] Smith, Coral and Brass, p. 133.

[29] 2d Amtrac Battalion, Report of Galvanic Operations (In the field: 2d Amtrac Battalion, 1943), pp. 1-4.

[30] Jeter A. Isely and Philip A. Crowl, The United States Marine and Amphibious War (Princeton: Princeton University Press, 1951), p. 233.

[31] 2d Amtrac Battalion, Special Action Report, p. 8.

[32] Ibid., p. 6.

[33] 2d Amtrac Battalion, Special Action Report, p. 6.

[34] United States War Department, TM 9-775, Landing Vehicle Tracked, MK I and MK II (Washington: United States War Department, 1944), p. 170.

[35] Smith, Coral and Brass, p. 134.

PART V

THE MARSHALLS: THE FULL RANGE OF USE

The capture of the Gilberts accomplished the seizure of airfields which permitted long-range air reconnaissance against the Marshalls. Three airfields were in operation immediately after the capture of the Gilberts and aerial photos provided badly needed intelligence for staffs who had started planning the conquest of the Marshalls even before the capture of Tarawa. The Marshalls were mandated to Japan after the defeat of Germany in World War I and represented the first penetration of the inner defenses of Japan in the Pacific. The attack of these islands was expected to be as difficult as that of Tarawa, but the lessons of Betio were available and it was assumed the same mistakes were not to be repeated.

The Marshall Islands occupy a vast stretch of ocean and include the world's largest coral atoll, Kwajalein, which encloses 655 square miles in its lagoon. This group of islands also contained a larger number of major Japanese bases than had been faced in the Gilbert attack. To prevent the Japanese from concentrating against a single United States operation from their bases in the Marshalls which included Mille, Maloelap, Wotje, Jaluit, and Eniwetok Atolls - many of which had airfields, plans were developed calling for simultaneous landings at Kwajalein and Majuro atolls. The Majuro Atoll was selected as a target due to its light defenses and the excellent anchorage it would afford the fleet for later

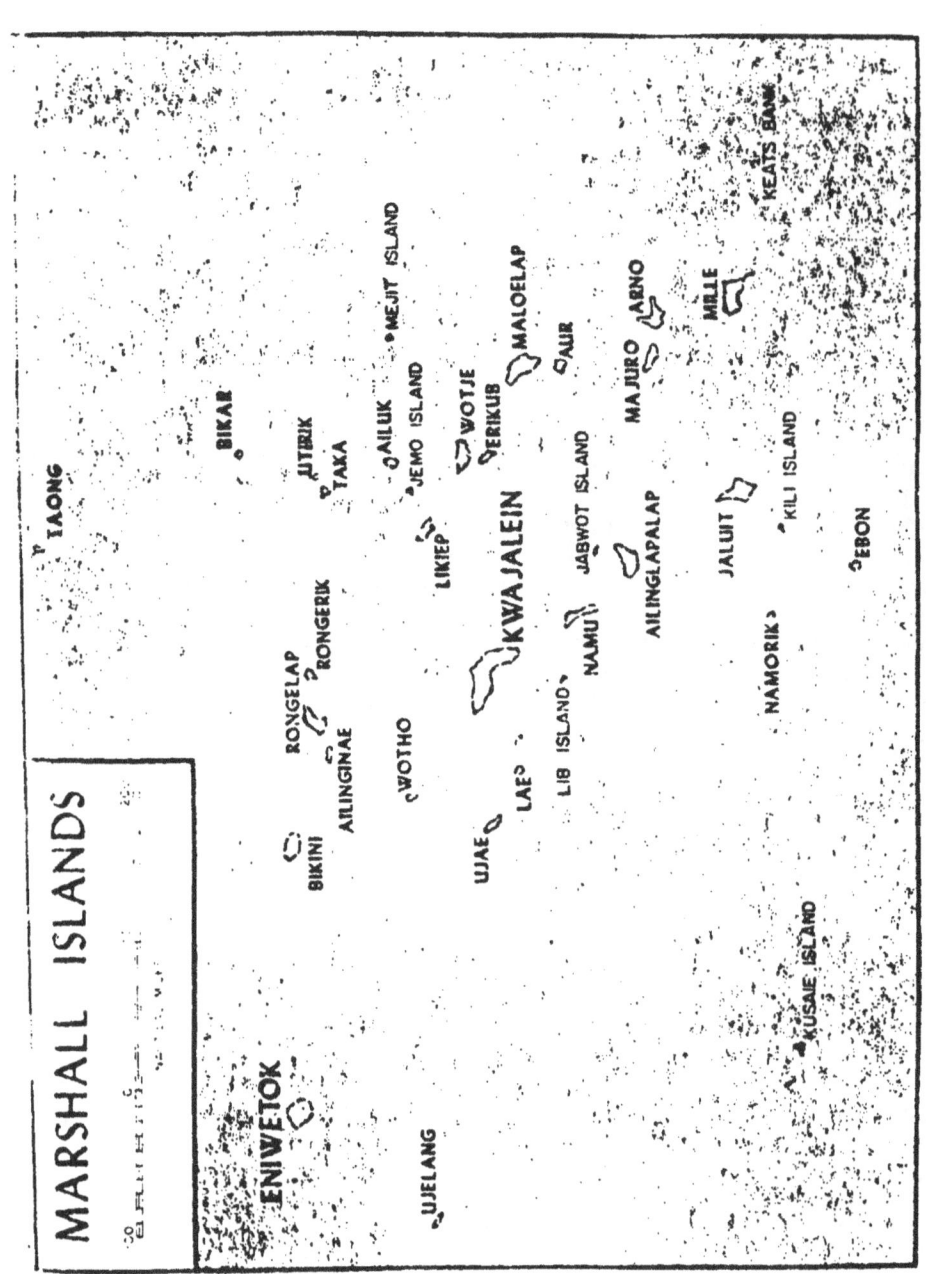

Map 6. Marshall Islands.

staging against the Marianas. Kwajelein Atoll would also be a future fleet anchorage and contained principal airfields at the islands of Roi-Namur and Kwajalein. The other major bases in the Marshalls were to be neutralized by heavy air raids prior to and during the landing operations.[1]

The Joint Chiefs of Staff designated the 4th Marine Division, in training in the United States at Camp Pendleton, California, the experienced 7th Infantry, which had landed in the Aleutians, and the 22d Marine Regiment, then on duty in Samoa, as the landing forces for the Marshalls Campaign under overall command of Major General Holland M. Smith, USMC. Another reinforced regiment, the 106th Regimental Combat Team (RCT) was added from the 27th Infantry Division as the final plans for the assault on the Marshalls took shape. The Joint Chiefs exerted pressure to strike at the earliest moment and after several delays to allow more training and ship repair, fixed 31 January 1944 as the latest that the operation could be executed. This early date put considerable pressure on the green 4th Marine Division, still in the San Diego area, to complete its training, rehearsals, and organization in time to embark and sail for a rendezvous at the Marshalls. Division exercises were held on 14-15 December and 2-3 January 1944 with the last virtually a rehearsal because this landing included the actual Naval transports which were to carry them to the target area.[2] The Naval group was green as the 4th Division and this combination of inexperienced forces would produce unfortunate results later. The 4th Division departed between 6-13 January 1944 without ever having incorporated the final operation orders into their training or rehearsals.[3] The 7th Division, by contrast, was stationed in the Hawaiian Islands during the planning phase of the

Marshalls and was able to review and utilize the final operation plans in their training and final rehearsals between 12 and 17 January 1944. The 22d Marines was shipped to the Hawaiian Islands for training and joined the 7th Division in final landings.

The inexperienced 4th Marine Division was assigned to capture the islands of Roi-Namur and adjacent small islets, while the 7th Infantry Division was assigned the island of Kwajalein and its surrounding small islands. The Majuro Atoll was to be secured by the Fifth (V) Amphibious Corps Reconnaissance Company since little or no opposition was expected.

Intelligence showed that Roi-Namur was the headquarters of the 24th Air Flotilla which controlled air operations in the Marshalls and was commanded by Vice Admiral Michiyuki Yamada. The garrison was composed of 1,500 to 2,000 aviation mechanics, ground personnel, and pilots. The only trained ground combat troops were 300 to 600 members of the 61st Guard Force and about 1,000 laborers. Kwajalein totaled about 1,750 men from various sources including 1,000 soldiers from the Army's 1st Amphibious Brigade, 500 men from the Navy's 61st Guard Force, and 250 men from the 4th Special Naval Landing Force. To avoid a repitition of Tarawa, great pains were taken to determine the accurate hydrographic characteristics of the target islands and Underwater Demolition Teams, highly skilled Navy swimmers trained to reconnoiter beaches and destroy underwater obstacles to amphibious landings, were employed for the first time with excellent results. All islands were completely surrounded by coral reefs, as had been the case at Tarawa. The strongest enemy defenses were oriented towards the sea, so United States landings were to be executed from within the lagoon.[4]

The defenses of Roi-Namur included ten pillboxes scattered over the intended landing beaches of the 4th Division housing 7.7 mm machine guns, Armored Amphibian Tractor Battalion. These units contained almost 350 tractors including LVT(2)s of the cargo type and LVT(A)1s of the armored amphibian type.[7]

Training conducted prior to departure for the Marshalls had not completely prepared the crews for the coming operation. The root cause appears to be the rapid build-up in amphibian tractor battalions after the Tarawa landing which emphasized the utility of the LVT in attacking across coral reefs. The 1st Armored Amphibian Battalion, prior to taking delivery of its new LVT(A)1s, had furnished one officer and fifty men to pilot LVT(2)s for the 2d Marine Division at Tarawa. This experienced cadre became the core for that battalion's expansion to four companies, but the 4th Marine Division's 4th Amphibian Tractor Battalion was split on 5 December 1943 to form the 10th Amphibian Tractor Battalion composed of B and C Companies, and both battalions were diluted with recruits to bring them up to strength. This dilution was continued when yet another reinforcing tractor unit, Company A of the 11th Amphibian Tractor Battalion, was formed. In addition to the serious effects of the overall lack of experienced personnel caused by the expansion, about thirty percent of the officers had never had duty with troops. Less than thirty days were available for training the newly formed battalions, but the time was also needed for embarkation and a myriad of other activities required to form and then move a heavy equipment battalion such as an LVT battalion. A partial list of the activities of the newly formed 10th Amtrac Battalion prior to departure from Camp Pendleton serves as an illustration:

1. Constructing a temporary camp during rainy weather.
2. Requisition and moving battalion supplies, followed crating for

embarkation aboard ship - this totaled eighty tons of equipment not counting the LVTs.

    3. Assimilating and training new troops.

    4. Collaborating with infantry unit leaders during planning - which consumed much of the officer's time and was aggravated by changes in plans.

    5. Training of naval boat officers in guiding LVTs to the beach.

    6. Armoring both the 4th and the 10th Battalion's LVTs - a task performed by the 10th Amtrac Battalion.[8]

The net result was to produce an undertrained LVT organization for an operation that was tactically more complex than any previous landings attempted in the Central Pacific.

The detail plans for the capture of the Roi-Namur islands required preliminary landings from the seaward side of the islands of Mellu and Ennuebing to the southwest of Roi-Namur to secure the northern pass into the lagoon. The landing force was then to move inside the lagoon for Ennugarret Island was to be seized by crossing from Ennumennet Island. These islands were to be used for artillery positions for the next day's assault. The LVTs were brought into the area by LSTs which were to be stationed about 3,000 yards off the target islands. The landing troops would be brought over to the LSTs from transports in LCVPs, then climb the cargo nets up the side of the LSTs and move down inside where they would board the tractors. This was a complex plan but was an improvement over the procedure used at Tarawa involving the tricky business of transferring troops between the LVT and a bouncing small boat in the open sea. At the line of departure, General Schmidt, commander of the 4th Marine Division, planned to organize his waves with new techniques for a powerful

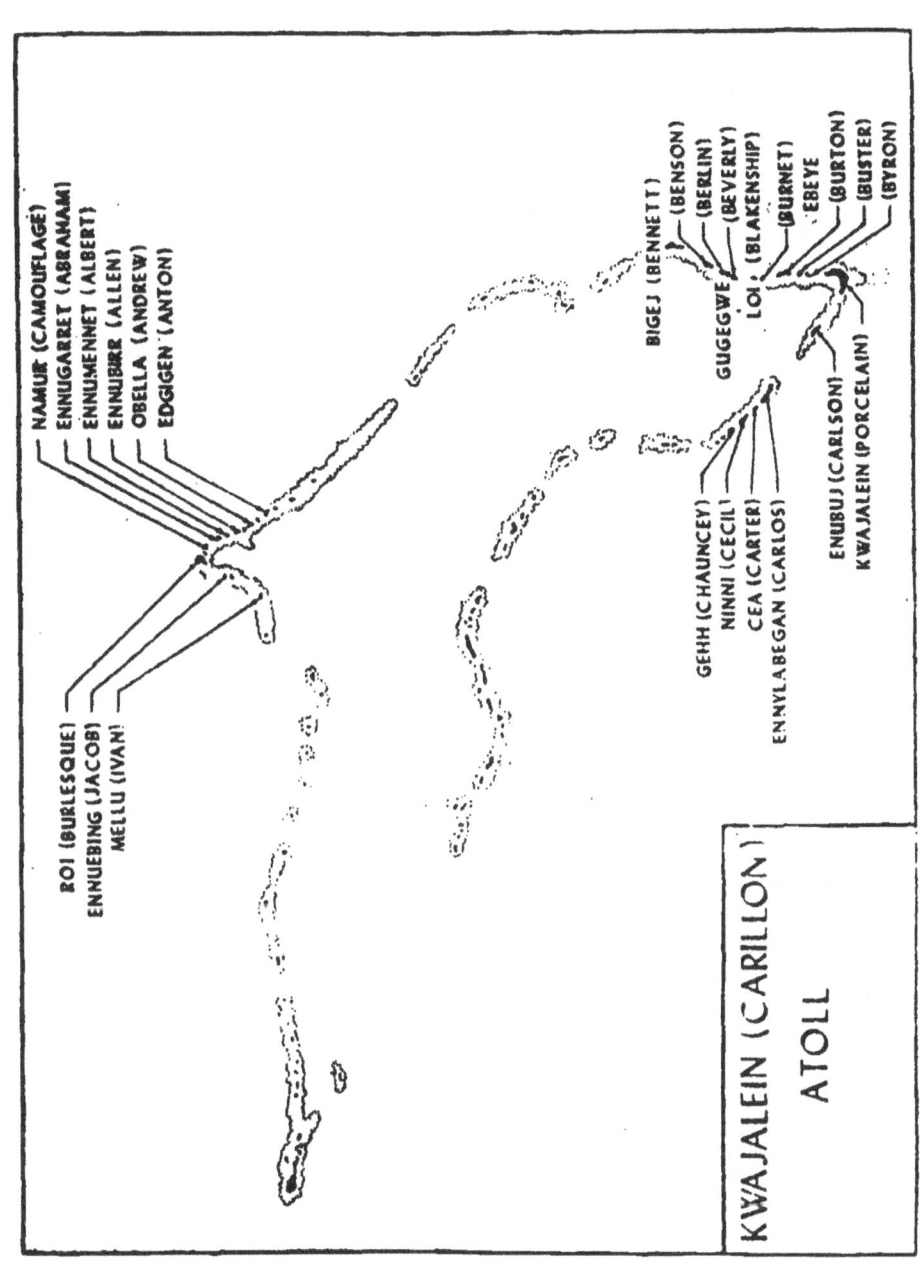

Map 7. Kwajalein Atoll.

neutralization of the beach just ahead of the leading waves of LVT(1)s. Landing Craft, Infantry (LCI), a small craft used to land infantry directly on beaches from gangways, was modified to mount caliber .50 machine guns, 40 mm and 20 mm guns, and 4.5 inch rockets. These gunboats would lead the way until about 1,000 yards off the beach, where they were to halt, fire their rockets, and then continue to support the landing with their automatic weapons by moving to the flank of the boat lanes. The LVT(A)1s were to pass through the LCIs and open fire with their 37 mm cannon and three caliber .30 machine guns. They would continue this surpressing fire right up to the beach. The troop carrying LVT(2)s were to pass through the LVT(A)1s and move to the beach before the defenders could recover. LVT(A)1s were to cease fire as their fires became too dangerous to the friendly troops. They were then to continue to support the landing by firing from the flanks of the boat lane or by leading the troops inland in the role of tanks.[9]

Supporting arms coordination had improved as a result of a valuable lesson from Tarawa, both naval gunfire and close air support would key on the position of the landing craft as they approached the beach rather than attempt to adhere to a fixed time schedule as at Tarawa. This flexibility was to be a key factor in the success of the operation when the LVTs fell behind schedule.

Preliminary softening operations against the Marshalls had commenced in November with air strikes from carriers in the area, with the heaviest tonnages dropped after the airfields were completed in the Gilberts. Land based aircraft was used extensively for neutralization of the Marshalls until 29 January 1944 when carrier aviation returned to the Marshalls in support of the landings. Aerial bombing was longer and more

Figure 22. The Landing Craft Infantry (LCI), modified as a gunboat, was capable of launching hundreds of 4.5-inch rockets and later also mounted mortars.

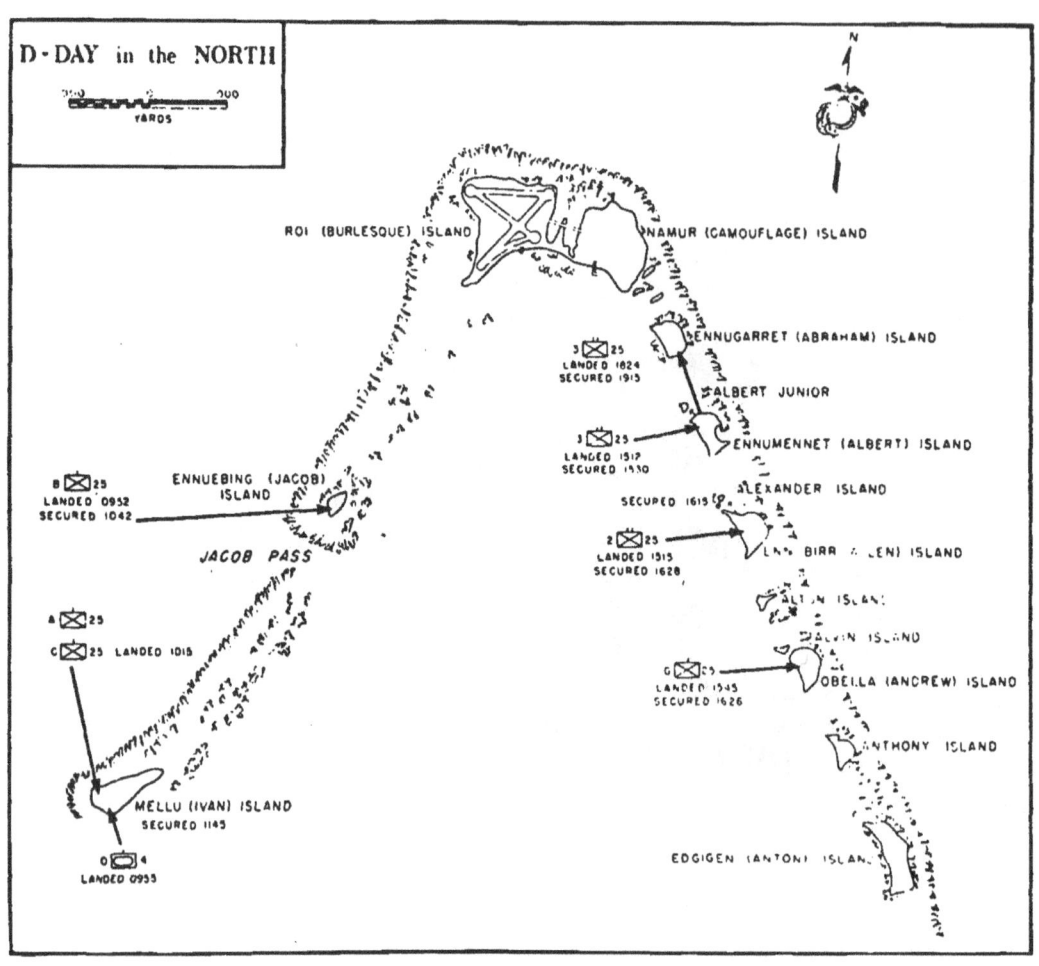

Map 8. D-Day landings prior to Roi-Namur.

intense than at Tarawa and specific targets identified through photos were attacked rather than dropping bombs on "area" targets.[10] Surface ship bombardment of the outlying islands began on D-Day, 31 January 1944, during the early morning hours. Bombardment also started at this time against the islands of Roi-Namur in preparation for the landing on the morning of February 1.

The first landings against Mellu and Ennuebing islands were scheduled at 9:00 A.M. with the first battalion of the 25th Marine Regiment scheduled as the landing force. The landings on D-Day were to be supported by the 10th Amtrac Battalion and Company A, 11th Amtrac Battalion. The 4th Amtrac Battalion was withheld entirely to ensure that there would be enough tractors to land the 24th Marine Regiment on Roi Island the next day.[11] Fire support for the D-Day landings was also provided by a provisional platoon from the 1st Armored Amtrac Battalion. Company B, 10th Amtrac Battalion, was to carry troops into beaches on Mellu and Ennuebing islands using fifty tractors organized into four platoons. Each platoon had twelve tractors except the 4th, which had ten. Company headquarters used four tractors. Within the 1st Platoon of Company B, six specially modified tractors were included which mounted rocket launchers for added fire support.[12]

Problems arose almost from the beginning for the landings at Mellu and Ennuebing. Due to the inexperience of both the Marines and Naval personnel, few were present who knew anything about debarkation of LVTs within the LSTs. The elevators which lowered the LVTs from the upper "weather" deck to the lower deck, sometimes called the tank deck, were too small. To position an LVT on the elevator successfully, it had to be driven up a makeshift ramp at an extreme angle which caused wear on the clutch and required skill from the driver, often not available.[13] Despite this, the tractors were eventually unloaded, but problems did not stop. Once debarked, the tractors were to proceed to transfer areas to receive troops from LCVPs. This is a repeat of the Tarawa procedure, which was used only during the first two landings. (Subsequent landings the following day within the lagoon would bring troops to the LSTs to load aboard the LVTs.) The tractors entered rough seas whipped by winds up to twenty miles per hour, seasonal for the Marshalls at that time of year, which slowed not only their progress to the transfer areas but the progress of the troops in their LCVPs also. Radios became soaked and inoperative so that last-minute changes in the detailed landing plans were received by the tractor company informally from the troops boarding the tractors.

The line of departure was marked by the anchored destroyer Phelps which acted as the control vessel for the landings. The Control Officer aboard the Phelps could see that the original H-Hour of 9:00 A.M. would not be met and signaled first a fifteen-minute and then a few minutes later an estimated twenty-minute delay before the troops would hit the beaches. General Schmidt and Admiral Conolly, the Naval Commander, both aboard the task force flagship, realized that a delay was required and at 9:03 A.M. signaled for a new H-Hour of 9:30 A.M.[14] As this was being done, the Phelps gave the signal for the waves to cross the line of departure to allow the troops to start the run to the beach to arrive at the new H-Hour of 9:30 A.M. The waves were not organized and, as one LVT platoon commander described it, amounted to ". . . . three waves jockeying around as one headed for Jacob Island (code name for Ennuebing Island)."[15] The waves were preceded by the LCI gunboats and the armored amphibians.

Thanks to the lessons of Tarawa, fire support schedules were adjusted to the position of the waves as they approached the beach. Aerial observers radioed the progress of the waves and naval gunfire and air support, informed of the delay, extended their coverages of Mellu and Ennuebing islands.

The LCIs released their rocket payload with the unholy roar that 4.5 inch rockets emit when fired and moved to the outside of the boat lanes for further support. The LVT(A)1s passed through the gunboats firing their 37 mm cannon on the move. The rocket-loaded LVT(2)s were unable to fire their rockets because assault troops, who were to assist in firing the rockets, were not qualified and the launching racks, burdened with the weight of the rockets, were almost all torn from their mountings as the tractors hit the rough coral reef.[16] The LVT(A)1s continued to lead until about 200 yards from the beach where they sheered off and lay to the outside of the line of the advancing troop tractors. Fire coordination at this point was tricky since it is desirable to keep cannon fire on the beach up to the last minute. One troop tractor sustained minor damage when it was riddled by an LVT(A)1 that continued to fire just a little too long.[17] The troop carrying tractors hit the beach at Ennuebing and Mellu at 9:52 A.M. and 10:15 A.M. respectively, meeting little opposition, and both islands were secured after about one hour's fighting. A total of thirty enemy dead was counted between the two islands.[18] Artillery landed immediately following the seizure of the islands, carried by the tractors of Company A, 11th Amtrac Battalion. Tractors which had carried the first waves reorganized and assisted in further transport of troops and supplies to Mellu and Ennuebing.

The scene of action shifted rapidly to inside the lagoon for landings against the islands of Obella, Ennubirr, and Ennumennet islands, all of which were to be secured by the end of D-Day for artillery positions to support the main landings the following day. The Second and Third Battalions of the 25th Marines were scheduled as the landing force, although only the 2nd Battalion was to be carried by LVTs of Company C, 10th Amtrac Battalion, still aboard the LSTs. There were not enough LVTs to boat units at Obella and Ennumennet and these landings were conducted with LCVPs. Tractors were discharged from their LSTs west of Mellu Island and waited for Mellu and Ennuebing to be secured. These LVTs then received troops from LCVPs and moved through the passage south of Ennuebing to the line of departure for Ennubirr Island. Some loss of control occurred as Company C's radio malfunctioned when soaked by the spray from the sea's heavy swells. The primary control vessel, the destroyer Phelps, due to a Navy decision, reverted to fire support and thus left control to a secondary control vessel equipped with the plans and radios for the job. However, this vessel was not aware of the change in plans and failed to assume control, leaving the Assistant Division Commander, General Underhill, embarked in a small sub-chaser, holding the proverbial bag. The first he knew of the situation was when the Phelps swung by and announced by bull horn, "Am going to support minesweepers. Take Over!"[19] By aggressive action and with the aid of the Naval Boat Control Officers and personnel of the infantry battalions making the landings, control was restored. The loss of control caused a delay in the planned hour for landing from 11:30 A.M. to 2:30 P.M. This also could not be met and a further delay to 3:00 P.M. was authorized by Admiral Conolly. The Phelps, free of her duties as fire support for the minesweepers, returned to her duties as control ship and took station on the new line of departure for the afternoon assaults. During the time that was consumed in gaining control of the situation and forming waves, additional LVTs were procured for the transport of 1 1/2 waves of the Third Battalion (500 men) against Ennumennet Island.[20] The waves finally crossed the line of departure about 2:32 P.M., led by LCI gunboats and armored amtracs of Company D, 1st Armored Amtrac Battalion. During the delay, bombardment by both air and naval gunfire was prolonged and coordinated to coincide with the progress of the LVTs. At 2:46 P.M. the LCI's released their deadly cargo of rockets against both islands and the LVT(A)1s pushed through, firing their cannons on the move. Three minutes later the fire support ships, <u>Haraden</u> and <u>Porterfield</u>, augmented by the <u>Phelps</u>, lifted fire to allow final strafing by aircraft as the LVTs neared the beach. Three hundred yards offshore, the armored amphibians parted, and the troop carrying tractors passed through to the beach, landing between 3:12 P.M. and 3:15 P.M. Both islands were secured rapidly by the two attacking battalions (1000 men) with 24 Japanese defenders killed on Ennubirr Island and ten defenders killed on Ennumennet.[21]

Company A, 11th Amtrac Battalion immediately commenced landing the 75 mm pack howitzers of the 14th Marines and first elements finally reached Ennubirr at about 6:00 P.M.[22] This phase of the operation was difficult because the long trip through the Ennuebing pass and across the lagoon severely depleted the gasoline remaining in the tractors, thus restricting the amount of ammunition the tractors could haul to the various artillery sites and causing a net ammunition shortage. Arrangements had been made to station refuel ("bowser") boats near the landing beaches of Ennubirr and Ennumennet islands, but none materialized so tractors of this unit were forced to spend the night on the islands for lack of fuel.

At this point an error in coordination occurred when plans were changed to include an assault against Ennugarret Island, immediately north of Ennumennet. This island is closest to Namur and would be a valuable artillery and direct fire weapons site for later support of the main landings. Plans changed shortly before D-Day called for a landing at 4:00 P.M. but the late seizure of Ennumennet made this time impossible. A hurried conference was held between the 25th Marines regimental commander, Colonel Samuel Cummings, and Lieutenant Colonel Justice Chambers, the battalion commander of 2nd Battalion, 25th Marines, which had just taken Ennumennet. Colonel Chambers' amtracs were ordered elsewhere after taking Ennumennet except the two which carried his headquarters section because the 10th Amtrac Battalion, which was controlling amtrac allocation, did not receive the late change in plans.[23] The tractors had been reassigned to search for fuel since the Navy bowser boats which were to be stationed near the beaches of Ennumennet Island for refuel could not be located. Daylight was waning, but fortunately two more LVTs were procured while operating on an artillery mission. Colonel Chambers jammed 120 officers and men into and on top of the four amtracs and formed a tiny first wave to attack Ennugarret Island. He waited until 6:00 P.M., the most favorable tide, and launched them after a preliminary bombardment of mortars and 75 mm guns firing from half-track cars positioned on Ennumennet Island. Additional personnel were brought by these same four amtracs in a shuttle.[24] The first wave usage represents one of the heaviest personnel overloads (normal load is 20-25 Marines per amtrac) ever attempted for an assault landing. Fortunately, resistance was light, and the island was secured rapidly.

Figure 23. The Landing Craft, Vehicle, Personnel (LCVP). This craft, derived from boats designed for trappers and oil drillers of the lower Mississippi by Andrew Higgins, was the standard landing craft of all theaters of World War II and remains little changed to this day.

Ennugarret Island was secured about 7:15 P.M. and completed the tasks of the 4th Marine Division on D-Day, 31 January. At the end of the day, however, the dispersed operations of the 10th Amtrac Battalion and Company A of the 11th Amtracs had scattered the LVTs over a wide area. This was anticipated to some extent and plans called for reorganization of Company B at Ennuebing Island and Company C on Mellu during the late evening.[25] Company A, 11th Amtracs, partly because of lack of fuel and partly due to orders from the Navy Beachmaster (the Navy component of Marine Corps' Shore Party) also spent most of the night on Ennuebing Island.[26] Orders for the next day required the 10th Amtrac Battalion to lift the 24th Marine Regiment against Namur Island. To accomplish this, original plans called for the LVTs to reboard their "mother" LSTs for refueling, greasing, and crew rest. Plans called for the LSTs to mark themselves with distinguishing light patterns so that tractors returning to them during hours of darkness could find their way. This was not done for unexplained reasons. It appears, however, that the inexperienced crews of the LSTs feared Japanese fire if they displayed lights and failed to appreciate the total loss of direction that can overcome individuals during night operations. The result of this failure was to cause numerous tractors to lose their way in vain attempts to locate their LSTs while darkness closed on Kwajalein Atoll. As they wandered about, some sought shelter on nearby islands including Ennumennet Island and ten were lost by sinking when they ran out of gas at sea.[27] [The LVT(2) was equipped with a bilge pump dependent on the main engine for power and when the vehicles ran out of gas, the bilge pumps ceased to function and the tractors filled with water from the many holes caused by scraping over coral during the day's landings.] The number lost is approximate because seven tractors were listed as "probably sunk" at the end of the operation although their fate was not specifically known.[28] Directly related to this disastrous evolution was the reluctance of LST captains to take LVTs aboard which did not belong to them because gasoline was limited and skippers feared they would exhaust their supplies before their assigned LVTs appeared. The relationship between the LVT crews and the ship's crews of the various LSTs also was not the best. Inexperience on both sides caused a build-up of tensions due to the Navy crews lacking indoctrination in the basic reason for their existence to transport troops, and the Marines failing in some of their essential housekeeping chores.[29] Thus when Marines were in difficulty during the night of 31 January-1 February, there was less than full motivation on the part of the Navy to assist them.

As dawn approached on 1 February, the situation facing the 10th Amtrac Battalion was poor with respect to its mission for the day - lifting the 24th Marines against Namur Island with an assigned H-Hour of 10:00 A.M. Only a portion of its tractors had returned to their parent LSTs for refueling and maintenance with the remainder low on fuel and scattered between Mellu, Ennuebing, and Ennumennet islands. Communications remained poor because radios once soaked dried slowly, if at all. LSTs were ordered to discharge LVTs inside the lagoon to lessen the distance the tractors would have to travel to the line of departure, and troops were to be brought to the LSTs for transfer to the amphibians rather than the difficult transfer between the small LCVPs and the tractors. The movement of the LSTs into the lagoon created the first increment of delay since many had wandered as far as forty miles away from the atoll during the night's operations and took too much time to return to meet H-Hour.[30]

Further delay was required in order to procure sufficient tractors to carry the 24th Marines. Major Victor J. Croizat, Battalion Commander of the 10th Amtrac Battalion, notified Admiral Conolly during the early morning hours of the shortage of tractors for the morning landing. A replacement plan was devised which ordered the tractors of Company A, 11th Amtracs, assigned in support of the division's artillery, to report to the line of departure to assist in the transport of troops. This plan was not quickly successful and at 6:30 A.M. Colonel Franklin A. Hart, Regimental Commander of the 24th Marines, reported to General Schmidt that he was forty-eight tractors short of the 110 assigned for the landing on Namur.[31] The search for tractors intensified during the next two hours, but few additional tractors were found. Tractors of Company A, 11th Amtracs, were low on gas and required time to refuel before they could be loaded with troops. With these accumulating problems, the time of attack was delayed at 8:53 A.M. to a new H-Hour of 11:00 A.M.[32] Bombardment was prolonged to cover the considerable delay.

As the time approached to start the thirty-three minute run from the line of departure to the beach for an 11:00 A.M. landing, Colonel Hart was convinced his regiment was not yet ready. He requested another postponement and received word that W-Hour (H-Hour at Namur) would be delayed "until the combat team could make an orderly attack."[33] This message gave Colonel Hart the impression that timing was still flexible enough to allow him to fully organize and he set about getting his waves in final order. The new landing hour of 11:00 A.M. came and went without Colonel Hart feeling ready. However, Admiral Conolly was being pressured to launch the attack by several factors. Hydrographic conditions were favorable for an attack around the 11:00 A.M. hour, there was concern

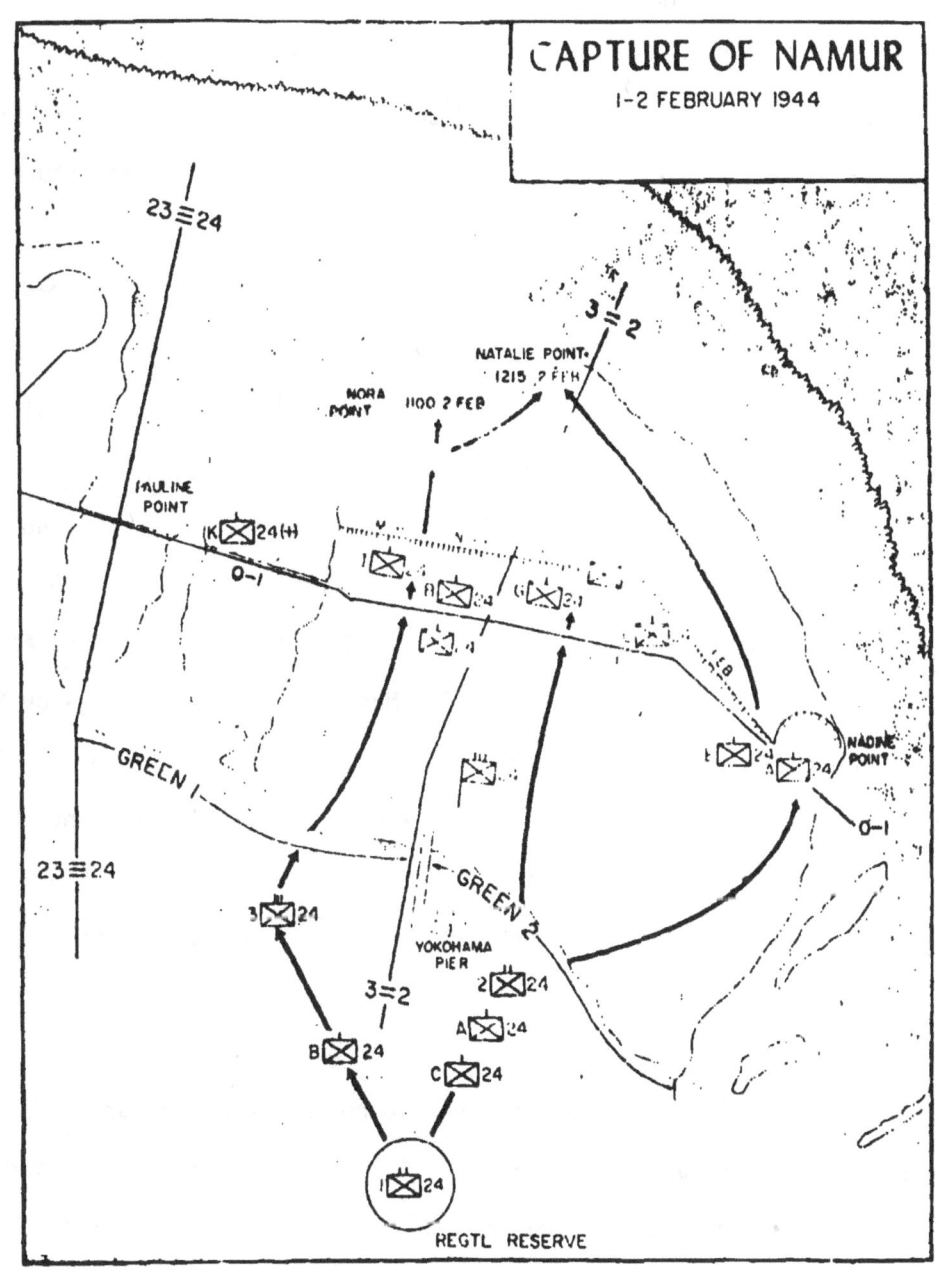

Map 9. Capture of Namur.

that the landing should not be delayed so that the neutralizing effects of the intensive preliminary bombardment would be dissapated, and tractors idling at the line of departure were consuming scarce gasoline. At 11:12 A.M. Admiral Conolly ordered the Phelps to drop the signal flag on her yardarm and thus the signal for crossing the line of departure was given. It caught Colonel Hart by surprise and his regiment was still not ready to make an organized assault. The landing on Namur Island resembled more of a ferry operation than a powerful assault but Admiral Conolly had correctly counted on the devastating effects of the aerial and naval bombardment to carry the landing.

Meanwhile, the situation that faced the 4th Amtrac Battalion and the landings on Roi was a contrast to the hectic morning of the 10th Battalion on Namur. The 4th had been withheld from D-Day landings to insure an adequate supply of tractors for the 23rd Marines for the landings on Roi, and although all tractors were on hand, the 4th Amtrac Battalion still experienced some of the same problems firing the initial unloading of their tractors from LSTs that had previously plagued the 10th Battalion on D-Day. Tractors loaded on the weather (upper) deck of the LSTs had to be driven up a steep ramp on the elevator in order to clear for lowering to the tank (lower) deck. At one point, to obtain clearance, crews on one LST were forced to use welding gear to cut off the tips of finders of the vehicles prior to lowering them.[34] Although this process delayed the 4th, the assault of the 23rd Marines was organized in time to meet the 11:00 A.M. H-Hour. The landing force was ready for landing long before the 24th Marines and impatiently waited as the H-Hour passed without any signal from the Phelps which was controlling landings on both Roi and Namur. Control was weakened within the 4th Battalion due to wet, inoperative radios, but the improved performance of Navy guide boats over the previous day overcame this weakness and when the signal came from the Phelps, the crossing of the line of departure proceeded in good order.

The attack on Roi was powerfully reinforced. In addition to the 4th Amtrac Battalion, the 23rd Marines were preceded by five rocket-firing LCI gunboats, thirty LVT(A)1s of Companies A and C, 1st Armored Amphibian Battalion, and twelve LVTs of the 4th Amtrac Battalion equipped with rockets.[35] The LCIs released their rockets 1,000 yards off the beach and cleared to either side to provide further support with their 40 mm cannon and machine guns. The LVT(A)1s of the 1st Armored Amphibian Battalion passed through and commenced firing their 37 mm cannon and machine guns. The rocket-firing LVT(2)s fired their rockets successfully, but they fell short, landing around the LVT(A)1s proceeding ahead of them. Incredibly there was no damage and the armored amtracs continued towards shore. The armored amtracs were particularly heavily concentrated in front of the right half of the beach with eighteen of the thirty vehicles attached to the 2nd Battalion, 23rd Marines, landing in that zone.[36] The armored amphibian wave had a tendency to narrow and widen its width in an accordian fashion, particularly after they got near the beach and the drivers closed their protective hatches. The reduced visibility through periscopes caused some tractors to collide, but they managed to maintain fair alignment as they hit the beach.[37] At Roi, the armored amtracs did not stand off the beach but preceded the troops inland. The attack hit with a great deal of momentum and the advance across Roi was so fast that it became disorganized. Tanks that had raced ahead had to be called back in order to get a coordinated attack to sweep the island.[38] During the

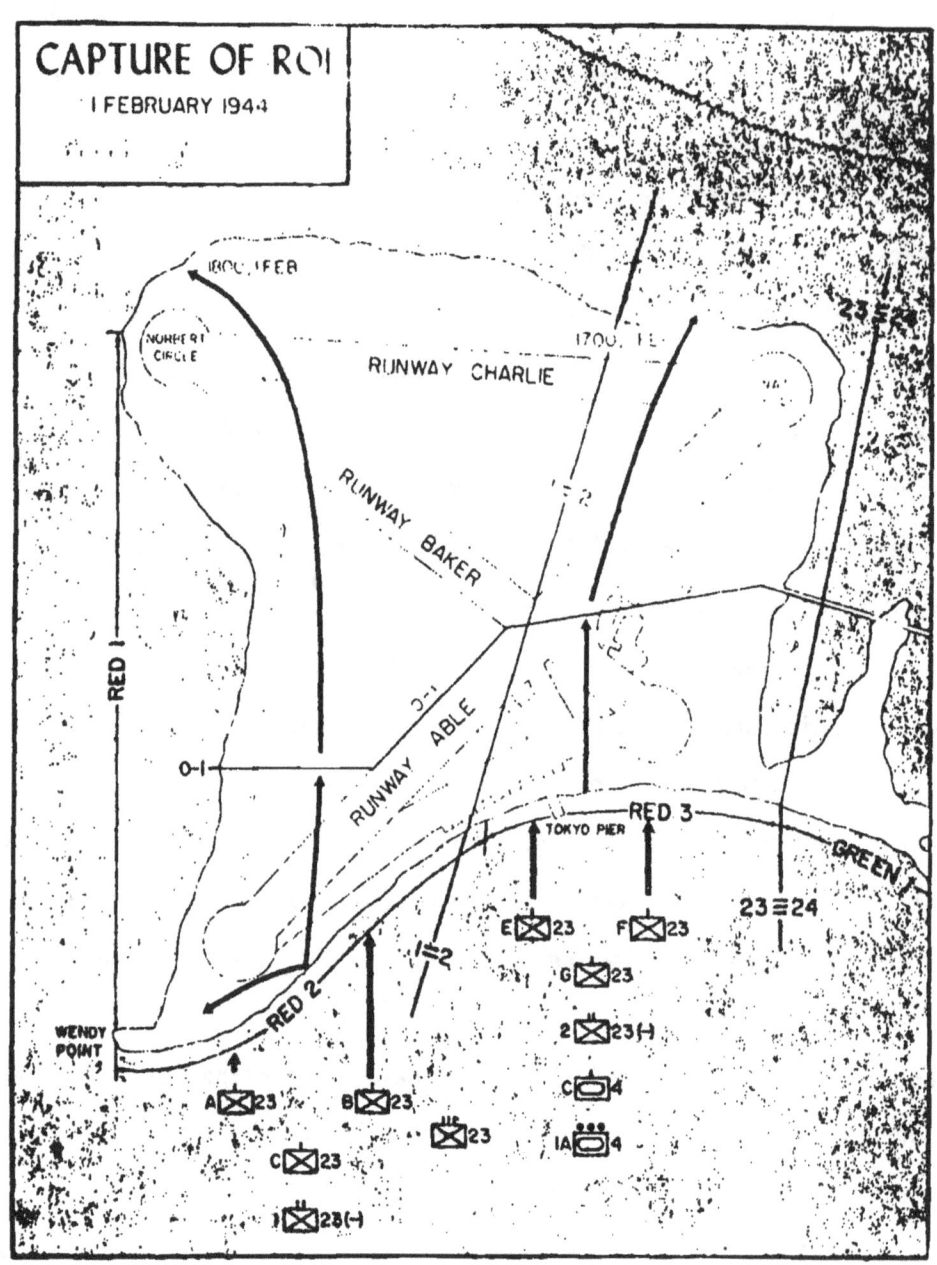

Map 10. Capture of Roi.

forward motion of the attack, the armored amphibians protected the right flank of the attack moving along the beaches with some armored amtracs in the water and some out, shooting at dugouts and sending the Japanese scurrying. The island was secured by the end of the day.

Back at Namur, the disorganized start of the ship to shore movement of the 24th Marines carried to the beach. The armored amphibians of Companies B and D, 1st Armored Amtrac Battalion, approached the beach under orders from the regimental commander to precede the troops to positions one-hundred yards inland, but they did not execute the order. About two-hundred yards from shore, they stopped and attempted to support the landing in place and allowed the troop carrying tractors to pass. The halt of the LVT(A)1s caused confusion, but the LVT(2)s managed to pass through, even though the armored amtracs continued to fire both their 37 mm cannons and machine guns after the LVT(2)s were in front of them.[39] This was a dangerous practice created by inexperience coupled with a greater amount of rubble on the Namur beaches and the presence of an anti-tank ditch just inland of the beaches which stopped a number of LVTs.[40] The 24th Marines met greater resistance as they attacked, due to the greater number of buildings and storage bunkers providing cover to the enemy and thick underbrush which gave the defenders further concealment. The 24th Marines' attack did not have the momentum of the attack on Roi due to the rough beach and the disorganized condition of their landing waves and the net result was congestion on the beaches involving troops, LVTs, and later light tanks that tried to come ashore to reinforce. The heavier construction of the few pillboxes and fortifications that survived naval gunfire was unaffected by the 37 mm cannon fire of the armored amtracs or the light tanks, which mounted the same 37 mm guns, and so the Regimental Commander relied on the 75 mm guns of his supporting armor half-tracks.[41] Despite the handicaps at the beachhead, the attack moved inland close to the scheduled pace, but suffered a major disruption at 1:05 P.M. when Marines attacking a storage bunker ignited a large cache of Japanese torpedo warheads. The ensuing explosion covered the entire island in a thick pall of smoke that convinced some Marines of a gas attack; many panicked looking for discarded gas masks.[42] Two more blasts followed detonated by Japanese to capitalize on the confusion. The three blasts, which caused chunks of concrete to become deadly missiles and tree trunks to fly through the air like toothpicks, accounted for about half of the 24th Marines' total casualties during the attack on Namur. The first blast was the biggest and accounted for twenty killed and one hundred wounded, most from Company F, 24th Marines, the attackers of the bunker.[43] As the problems of the attackers on Namur became known, support began to arrive. The company of medium tanks operating on Roi was switched to Namur over the connecting causeway and participated in the later advances as the spearheads. Light tanks and armored amtracs were also used, but their light guns were not decisive against many of the fortifications on the island and their chief service appears to have been firing cannister rounds to shred foliage or against personnel caught in the open.[44] Hard fighting continued throughout the afternoon and into the morning of 2 February. The island was finally secured at 2:18 P.M., 2 February 1944.[45]

Use of the LVT(2)s after the attacks on Roi and Namur was light. Logistical considerations for an attack on a small island are minimal and so was the use of the tractors of the 4th and 10th Battalions. The battalion command post of the 10th Amtrac Battalion was established on

Ennubirr Island on 1 February, and most of the 10th Battalion's tractors reorganized on that island after landing the waves at Namur. Maintenance and salvage operations were conducted for the remainder period in northern Kwajalein Atoll, although some tractors were used to clear tiny islands to the south of the target area between 2 through 5 February. No further difficulties were encountered.

While the Marines were assaulting the northern portion of the Kwajalein Atoll, the United States Army's 7th Infantry Division was attacking the southern end using the same overall approach of first securing the outlying islands for security and artillery positions, followed by a main attack on 1 February against the big island of Kwajalein. The Army Division had less than half the number of LVTs the Marines had. The 708th Provisional Amphibian Tractor Battalion was divided into four groups, Able, Baker, Charlie, and Dog, each with thirty-four tractors. Groups Able and Dog had participated in the D-Day landings against the outlying island and groups Baker and Charlie were fresh.[46] This parallels the Marines' use of the 10th Amtrac Battalion on D-Day and holding the 4th Amtrac Battalion fresh for the main landings the following day. The tractors used by the Army were forty-six LVT(2)s and fifty-six LVT(A)2s which the Army had requested as a modification of the unarmored LVT(2).[47] The armored version of the LVT(2) used by the Army suffered from reduced cargo carrying capacity because of the permanent attachment of its armor plate, but it was a tougher machine against enemy fire, and resistance was expected to be heavy. In addition to the LVT(A)2s of the 708th Provisional Amphibian Tractor Battalion, Company A of the 708th Amphibian Tank Battalion would precede the main landings with their seventeen LVT(A)1s. The Army supplemented the cargo capacity of its amphibians with the addition of one-hundred newly developed amphibious trucks, the two-and-one-half ton DUKW. This was to be one of the Army's greatest contributions to amphibious equipment and it became a workhorse during the remainder of the war. Sixty of these vehicles were assigned to transport artillery and forty were preloaded with emergency supplies to be used as floating dumps, available for instant dispatch to the beach as the situation required.[48] The vehicle was designed around the standard two-and-one-half truck chassis as a cargo carrier and therefore was not armored.

The 7th Infantry Division had been stationed in Hawaii near the planning center at Admiral Nimitz's Pearl Harbor headquarters and was therefore able to incorporate fully the latest schedules and tactical measures into its final rehearsals. The advantage of this was clear on 1 February as the 7th Division executed a smooth landing against the main island of Kwajalein. The only problem appeared to be the tendency of the LVT(A)2 to veer to the left, which caused drivers to overcompensate to the right, bunching waves in the right portion of their boat lanes. Rather than precede the leading waves, as at Roi-Namur, the Army stationed their armored amphibians on each flank of the leading wave, with the LVT(A)1s angled towards the beach at about forty-five degrees. From overhead, this formation, including the troop-carrying LVTs, looked something like a large "V".[49] This formation allowed the leading troop LVTs to use their machine gun power along with the firepower of the armored amtracs and cleared the armored amtracs from the path of the troop LVTs as they hit the beach. Thus, the confusion that occurred at Namur was avoided. Such an arrangement required a wider frontage for the first wave because the armored amtracs extended off each side of the first wave. It was successful at Kwajalein due to the relatively generous amounts of usable beach for the assault, equipped as it was with amtracs.

Preliminary bombardment by ships and air had been thorough, and little immediate resistance was encountered by the troops of the 7th Division as they landed on schedule at 9:30 A.M. An observer commented that the island "looked as if it had been picked up to 20,000 feet and then dropped."[50] The armor available was later increased with M-10 tank destroyers, which were a tank-like vehicles with an open turret mounting a powerful three-inch gun. With this amount of armor, with large guns already available, the armored amtrac was not to play a role in the fighting on Kwajalein. LVT(A)2s and the DUKWs acted in logistical support of the operation as the infantrymen fought the length of the island. It took the 7th Division four days to secure the island in fighting characterized by excellent Army tank-infantry coordination. The Japanese tended to infiltrate Army positions successfully at night, causing confusion and firing in all directions, but these incidents occurred in small numbers and did not significantly hinder the progress of the battalions. The buildings and fortifications on Kwajalein resembled those found on Roi-Namur although many of the heavy concrete structures were clearly designed for protective storage rather than for combat use.[51]

With the seizure of Kwajalein, the first phase of the conquest of the Marshalls was complete. It had been far quicker and cheaper than anyone had dared dream based on the intelligence gathered and the grim memories of Tarawa. The 4th Marine Division lost 313 killed and 502 wounded while the 7th Division lost 173 killed and 793 wounded.[52] The Kwajalein Atoll had been seized with greater speed than anticipated and General Holland Smith and Admirals Spruance and Turner all felt that a speed-up in the timetable for the complete conquest of the Marshalls - the attack on Eniwetok - was in order.

Admiral Nimitz had planned the capture of the Eniwetok Atoll during the early preparation for the seizure of the Marshalls. During January 1944, the 2nd Marine Division and the 27th Infantry Division, United States Army, were designated the landing forces for the atoll which lay in the western reaches of the Marshall group, 326 nautical miles from Roi-Namur. The lagoon measures twenty-one miles in length and seventeen miles in width with ample space for a major fleet anchorage. The three islands within the atoll were Engebi, Parry, and Eniwetok, all principal bases. None of the islands were large, varying only from one to two miles in length with widths from one mile to six-hundred yards. Engebi Island contained the atoll's only airfield, completed in July 1943, which occupied almost all of the island's area. Intelligence gathered prior to the departure of the task force from Hawaii for the Marshalls was limited to a few overhead photos. Material captured during the attacks on Kwajalein Atoll included a detailed hydrographic chart of the Eniwetok Atoll which greatly assisted in attack planning. Photo coverage was gradually expanded during January 1944, and the enemy force in Eniwetok was estimated from this source to be from 2,900 to 4,000 men. This force was constituted mainly from the 1st Amphibious Brigade which arrived in the area on 4 January 1944, to garrison the atoll and erect fortifications. The brigade was 3,940 men strong and General Yoshima Nashida, its commander, distributed his strength among the three principal islands on the atoll, Parry, Eniwetok, and Engebi, with brigade headquarters on Parry Island. The force sent to Engebi numbered 736 from the brigade, some aviation, civilian, and labor personnel, and totaled about 1,200 men.

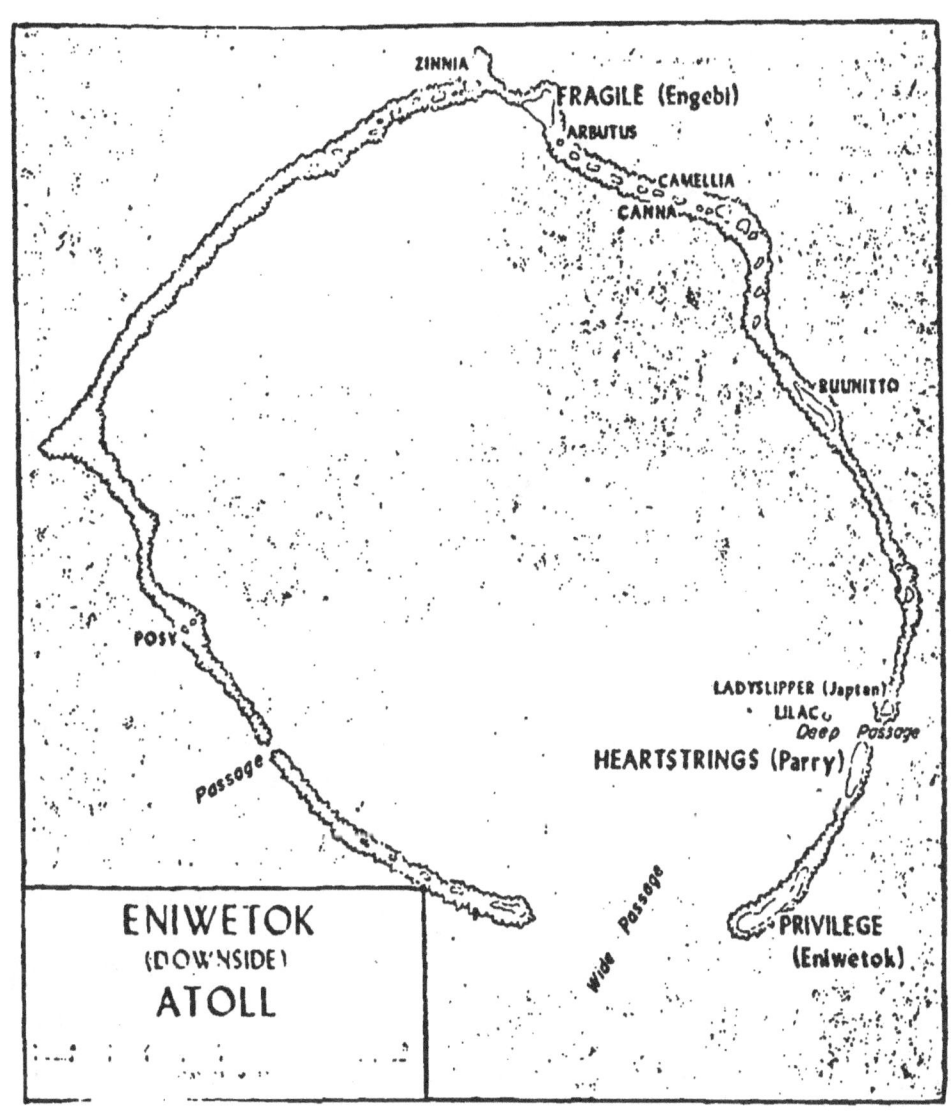

Map 11. Eniwetok Atoll.

General Nishida maintained 1,115 brigade men to defend Parry and his headquarters, and Eniwetok had about 908 brigade soldiers. Defenses were trenches, dugouts, log barricades at the beaches, and "spider traps" consisting of fighting holes interconnected with oil-drum tunnels dug into the earth. Each hole was covered with a sand cover, palm frond, or ordinary piece of metal. It allowed a sniper to pop up, fire, and disappear from sight, and if necessary to abandon his hole via the tunnels.[53] The Japanese approach, as it had been at other atolls, was to attempt to destroy the landing force at the beach by fire and counterattack.

The reserves designated for the Kwajalein landings were immediately available against the Japanese forces at Eniwetok Atoll. They consisted of the 22nd Marine Regiment and the 106th Regimental Combat Team from the 27th Infantry Division. With the Japanese split among three islands, the available forces numbering 10,000 assault troops were sufficient to achieve superiority at each island. Because forces were immediately available in the Marshalls area, the timetable for attack against Eniwetok was radically accelerated. Previous dates considered for the attack had been in the March-May 1944 period. The new date set for the landings was 15 February, but this was ultimately shifted to 17 February to allow additional time for carrier strikes against the Japanese bastion in the area, Truk Naval Base, 669 miles southwest of Eniwetok. Truk was a major staging area, repair facility, and naval and air base, which would require neutralization to conduct unmolested landings at Eniwetok.

With Kwajalein secured only on 5 February, little time remained for planning. The Eniwetok plans resembled those executed against Kwajalein. Three outlying islands would be seized on D-Day, 17 February, for use as artillery positions to support the landings the next day by the 22nd

Marines on Engebi. After seizure of Engebi, when it became clear that the reserves designated for use in that landing would not be needed, landings would be conducted by the 106th Regimental Combat Team against Eniwetok and two hours later against Parry Island. Aerial photos assured intelligence analysts that most of the atoll's defenders were concentrated on Engebi with smaller detachments on Parry and Eniwetok.[54] From this conclusion came the decision to use the more highly trained 22nd Marines against Engebi and the less experienced Army unit, supported by one battalion of the 22nd Marines, against Parry and Eniwetok.

Although preliminary naval gunfire support and air strikes were not as heavy as those against the Kwajalein Atoll, they wreaked havoc among the defenders. One prisoner of war estimated that fully half the defenders of Eniwetok were killed by the naval gunfire and air strikes that hit the atoll during 17 and 18 February, from cruisers, destroyers, and aircraft.[55] There was a heavy air strike against Truk simultaneously with the landings and the airfield at Engebi had been heavily damaged by carrier raids on 30 January and again on 10-12 February. The few defenses which the Japanese had been able to construct during the six weeks prior to the American landings suffered heavily from the efficient and effective preliminary fires. The sole American weakness was the failure to use heavier bombs against Eniwetok, which had the highest elevation - up to twenty feet above sea level, and thus yielded the Japanese more earth in which to bury their spider traps and resist air attack.[56] Nevertheless, the atoll's defenders were near starvation when the United States Navy finally and boldly steamed into the lagoon of Eniwetok Atoll through the narrow deep passage in the southern end of the atoll.[57]

The landings were to be supported by the 708th Provisional Amphibian

Tractor Battalion, minus one group remaining at Kwajalein Atoll. This support totaled forty-six LVT(2)s and fifty-six LVT(A)2s, plus seventeen LVT(A)1s of Company A, 708th Amphibian Tank Battalion.[58] The latter was the team that had performed so well during the Kwajalein Island landings of the 7th Infantry Division. About ten tractors were used during the preliminary landings on D-Day, 17 February, thus leaving the bulk of the battalion rested and fully ready for the landings against Engebi and Eniwetok on 18 February.

The LVTs for the Eniwetok landings were carried to the atoll in LSTs, but in contrast to the Navy-Marine cooperation problems at Roi-Namur, Navy-Army cooperation between the LSTs and the 708th Amphibian Tractor Battalion was excellent. Histories do not offer explanations for this, but it appears probable that the traumatic experiences of the LVT crews during the assault on Roi-Namur developed some lessons on cooperation which the LST crews at Eniwetok understood and took action to implement. The LSTs stationed themselves within one-thousand yards of the line of departure and thus reduced the run required by the LVTs.[59] Because the operation was staged from within the lagoon, eliminating the rough passage at sea experienced by LVTs at Roi-Namur, radios stayed drier and schedules were met.

The Engebi H-Hour was set at 8:45 A.M. Preliminary landings the day before had been successful and artillery would join the naval gunfire bombarding the island as the LVTs approached the beaches. Cruisers were to cease fire when the LVTs were within one-thousand yards of the beaches, but destroyers were instructed to keep firing with their five-inch guns until the LVTs were three-hundred yards from the beach.[60] The Engebi ship-to-shore movement was power laden. Six LCI gunboats preceded the

LVTs and armored amtracs to fire their rockets and automatic fire. Next came the leading five waves of LVTs carrying troops. Each wave consisted of eight to ten tractors for each of the two battalions, the 1st and 2nd battalions of the 22nd Marines, making the landing against Engebi.[61] Five LVT(A)1s were echeloned on the outside flanks of the leading troop LVT wave, and the remaining seven were a "V" shape between the two battalion formations of LVTs, with the open end of the "V" pointing towards the beach.[62] This formation thus produced an integrated troop carrying and LVT(A)1 formation, similar to that used against Kwajalein Island by the Army.

The troop transfer proceeded smoothly using the same methods employed at Kwajalein Atoll. The Amtrac Battalion Commander was directed to take position in the control vessel at the line of depature and after the LVTs landed, they were to report to him for further orders. LVTs were preloaded with water and ammunition to permit a fast build-up of supplies at the beach. The LVTs crossed the line of departure at 8:15 A.M. LCI gunboats released their rockets and veered away, but the rockets fell short. At 8:43 A.M., two minutes ahead of schedule, the LVTs hit the beach against light resistance. Although scheduled to proceed inland for about one hundred yards for fast penetration and to provide fire support with their machine guns, LVTs were forced to stop on the beaches by the rubble of coconut tree logs and other material churned up by the preliminary bombardment. This initially created some congestion but did not seriously impede the landing. Some LVTs of the left zone landed two-hundred yards too far to the left, but junior officers and non-commissioned officers quickly reorganized and pressed inland. On the right, one platoon was late in landing due to mechanical break-down. This platoon belonged to

Company A, 1st Battalion, 22nd Marines, which held the right flank sector in the attack across Engebi. Company C of the 1st Battalion was to attack Skunk Point, to the right rear of A Company, to secure that point as A Company swept inland. The late platoon hurried into position, but too late to prevent Japanese flushed by Company C's attack from penetrating into a widening gap between A and C Companies as A Company's attack progressed inland. The terrain was tangled undergrowth and it was necessary to halt the advance of A Company and call on tanks, which had just landed, to rectify the situation.[63]

The fighting on Engebi resembled the contrasts that occurred between Roi and Namur. On the left, the 2nd Battalion moved rapidly through the open terrain of the airfield on Engebi, and Newt Point at the far end of the island in the 2nd Battalion's zone was seized at 1:10 P.M.[64] It was not all quick work because the Japanese had entrenched medium tanks with 47 mm guns in this area and they were overcome only with combined artillery and 75 mm tank fire. On the right, fighting moved more slowly as Japanese took refuge in the dense undergrowth and staged a last-ditch fanatical defense. The few pillboxes encountered on Engebi were in this area as well as many spider traps. The Marines quickly discovered that by throwing smoke grenades into the passages of the spider web, they could readily locate the network's terminal fighting holes and seal them with explosives. In this way, the Marines punched forward supported by tanks and half-tracks carrying 75 mm guns. LVTs, both armored and cargo, were not used due to the extreme ruggedness of the terrain and the need for the heavier gun power of the medium tank, M4, known as the General Sherman. Because of the devastating effect of the preliminary bombardment, the island was secured far faster than might have been the case with less preparation. Despite the fanatical defense of Japanese in the 1st Battalion's zone, the island was declared secure at 2:50 P.M. by the Landing Force Commander, Brigadier General Watson.[65]

Although mopping-up was to continue on Engebi for another day and a half, it was time to commence the next phase of the Eniwetok Atoll operation, the attack of Eniwetok Island itself. The 3rd Battalion, 22nd Marines and the 2nd Separate Tank Company with its M4s, was ordered reembarked for this landing. The 3rd Battalion was the floating reserve for the landing which was made by the 1st and 3rd Battalions of the 106th Regimental Combat Team (RCT), and the Marine tanks were attached to the 106th for support.

H-Hour was set at 9:00 A.M. on 19 February for Eniwetok Island. Because it was believed that this island was more lightly defended than Engebi, naval gunfire and air strikes had been more harassing than deliberately destructive in nature. Only 204.6 tons of projectiles were thrown against Eniwetok Island with none larger than eight-inch, in contrast to the 1,179.7 tons fired against Engebi.[66] H-Hour was delayed first to 9:15 A.M. and then to 9:22 A.M. due to fears that the armor, reembarked from the landings at Engebi, would not arrive on time. The armor was on time and assault troops were ordered across the line of departure at 9:09 A.M., with troops hitting the beach at 9:16 A.M.[67]

Trouble began at once. The LVT(A)1s were under orders to proceed one-hundred yards inland, but were stopped by a log barricade at the beach. The area was heavily fortified with spider traps and the Army attack stalled. The Japanese counterattacked around noon with three-hundred to four-hundred men but the attack was beaten down with some Army casualties. Despite this success, the Army attack continued forward only by inches mainly because many defensive installations survived the preliminary naval gunfire and in fact most of the spider traps were untouched due to their greater depth. Against this tough nut, the 106th, an inexperienced outfit, made very slow progress. A Marine Battalion in floating reserve was landed at 1:30 P.M. to impart momentum to the attack and was thrown into the line heading south against the rear of the island main defenses, fighting alongside the 1st Battalion, 106th Regimental Combat Team (RCT). The Marine battalion did accelerate the attack but gaps opened between it and the lagging Army unit, into which troublesome Japanese infiltrators moved causing some confusion until in each case they were eliminated. Fighting frequently occurred in dense underbrush which limited observation and log emplacements were sometimes not discovered until the attackers were less than thirty-five yards away. Due to the close proximity, naval gunfire or other heavy caliber support could not be used and individual action was required by groups of infantrymen to silence these defenses.[68] Problems were also encountered in allocation of the tank support and the Regimental Commander, Colonel Ayers, did not appear willing to release tanks from either the Marine medium tank company or the Army light tank company to the Marine battalion despite repeated requests. They remained in support of Army units who were also having difficulty with the enemy situation. It required another day, until 2:45 P.M. on 20 February, to secure the southern end of the island; the northern end was not secured until 2:30 P.M. on 21 February.[69]

As on Engebi, armored amtracs did not take part in the combat on the island because the defenses were too heavy for the vehicles' light 37 mm gun. Cargo carrying LVTs reverted to logistical roles after the landing.

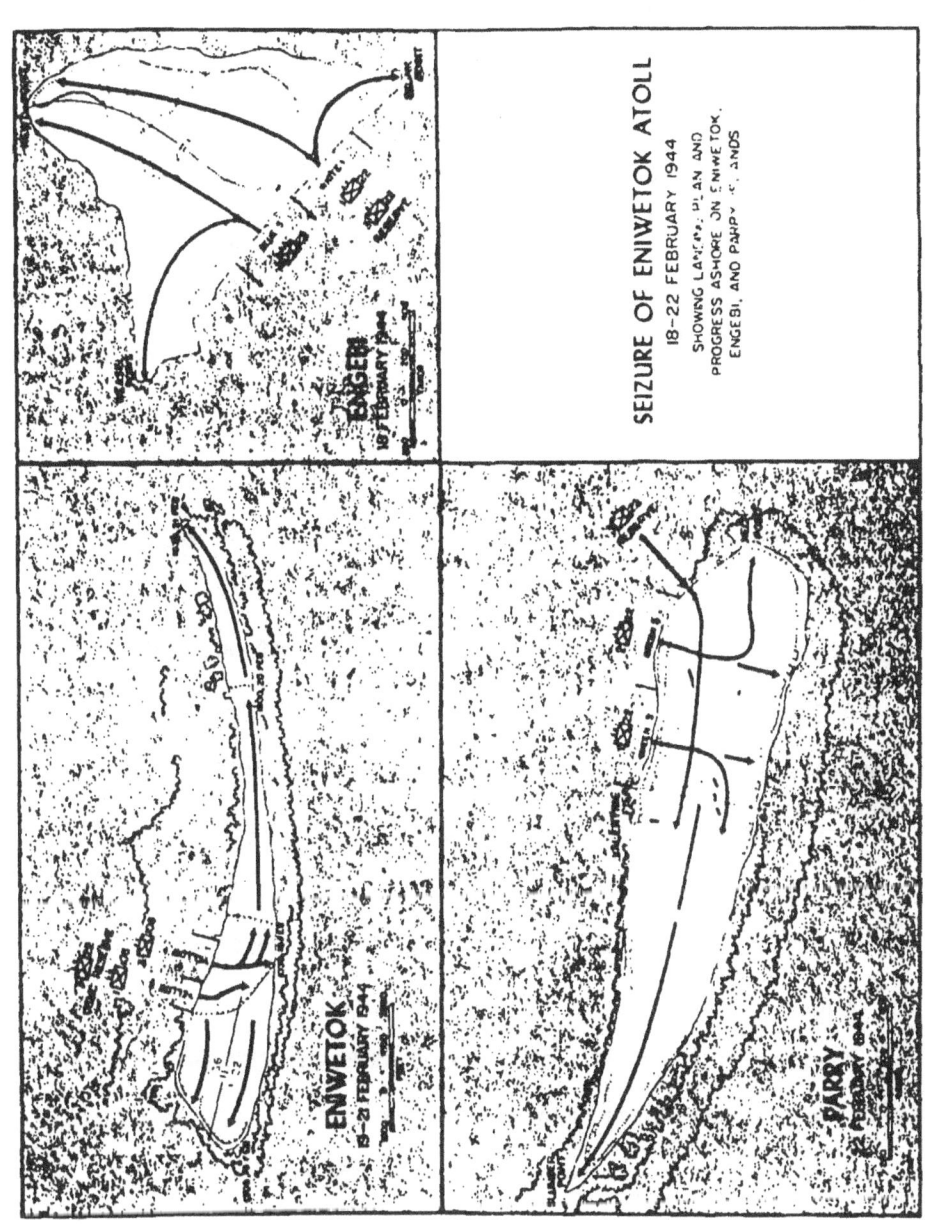

Map 12. Seizure of Eniwetok Atoll.

The unexpected toughness of the Eniwetok fight forced changes in plans for the attack on Parry, the last objective. This had been scheduled for the 106th, but it was clear that to keep a rapid timetable, it would be necessary to give this mission to the 22nd Marines, the victors of Engebi. H-Hour was scheduled for 9:00 A.M. on 21 February, and both the 1st and 2nd Battalions of the regiment were available in time for that original H-Hour. Timetables were delayed, however, when General Watson decided to postpone the landing until the 3rd Battalion, fighting on Eniwetok, would be available as a floating reserve. The new time was 9:00 A.M. on 22 February. With the unexpected resistence rising, preliminary bombardment of Parry was increased and the island rocked under an intense load of shells including 143 6-inch, 751 14-inch, 896 8-inch, and 9,950 5-inch shells into an area of only 200 acres.[70] Another significant change was the decision by General Watson to compress the frontages originally planned for the landing beaches because he felt they were too large and in doing so, he also shifted their location three-hundred yards northward. However, this information was not completely distributed, and caused problems during the ship-to-shore phase of the landing.[71]

Utilization of the LVTs remained the same as previous landings executed by the 708th Amphibian Tractor Battalion. The first waves crossed the line of departure at 8:45 A.M. preceded by LCI gunboats, as usual. Naval gunfire continued during the early part of the approach and three LCI gunboats on the right flank were struck by 5-inch shells from ships firing on radar because of the smoke. They lost thirteen men killed, forty-six wounded, but stayed on station and fired their rockets before leaving the area.[72] As the LVTs approached the shore, they were guided by Navy guideboats towards the originally planned beaches, three-hundred yards too far south. This drift affected the LCIs and appears to be the cause of the friendly fire hitting the right flank gunboats. Bouys to within 500 yards of the beach, along the division between the two landing teams, were to guide the LVTs, but the wind was carrying the smoke from the naval gunfire out over the incoming waves and drivers could not see any of the bouys or landmarks.[73] The Marines of the first wave landed 300 yards too far south, but succeeding waves, lost in the smoke, landed at varying positions along the beach. This confusion was corrected, as it had been in the past, by the aggressive leadership of junior officers and non-commissioned officers. Resistance on the beach was heavy but companies rapidly pushed through, assisted by the medium tanks of the 2nd Separate Tank Company. Three Japanese tanks were part of the defense of Parry and were not entrenched as stationary pillboxes as on Engebi. For unknown reasons, the Japanese chose to wait until Marine armor had landed before conducting a tank attack with their three tanks. (Japanese tanks throughout the war remained flimsy with inferior gun power by American standards.) The attack was disastrous for the Japanese, losing all three tanks and crews, with no damage to the General Shermans of the 2nd Separate Tank Company.[74] Tank-infantry coordination was excellent during the Parry fighting, assisted by the light tank company of the 106th RCT, and this support led to the rapid elimination of the defenders of Parry even though many spider traps and trenches had survived the shelling. Although a narrow strip of land at the southern end remained contested at nightfall, the Regimental Commander, Colonel Walker, declared the island secure at 7:30 P.M. on 22 February.[75] With this declaration, the final objective of the Eniwetok operation, code named CATCHPOLE, was completed.

As in the Kwajalein Atoll, for six weeks after Eniwetok there were follow-up landings on tiny islets ringing the atoll. The procedure usually involved a low-level aerial photo run by a PBY flying boat, which delivered photos to the landing force consisting of an LST carrying the assault troops and six to nine LVTs. Two LCI gunboats, a destroyer escort for gunfire support, and a mine sweeper to clear the approaches to the islets and atolls being visited made up the remainder of the miniature task force. Resistance varied from none to intense fire fights where a maximum of eighteen Japanese were killed on one island. Units of the 22nd Marines performed many of these landings, but a force of 199 Marines from the 1st Defense Battalion also conducted some operations during this phase. The last landings were made on 21 April 1944. Only four atolls were by-passed which contained airfields and sizeable enemy forces: Maloelap, Wotje, Mille, and Jaluit atolls. These targets were kept neutralized by the 4th Marine Aircraft Wing which began entering the Marshalls bases at Roi and Engebi during February 1944.

The Marshalls campaign represents a rugged test of the family of LVTs available at that time because it exploited the full range of LVT capabilities and was the first extensive use of the armored amphibian LVT(A)1 which mounted the 37 mm gun as its main armament - the same gun as the light tank, M5, extensively used by both Army and Marine units. As far back as Tarawa, however, the 37 mm gun had demonstrated its inability to destroy many of the substantial Japanese fortifications commonly encountered in the Pacific. In contrast, the 75 mm gun of the M4 Medium Tank, the General Sherman, was highly effective and frequently responsible for destroying pillboxes impeding infantry progress. It was clear that the armored LVT needed a heavier gun to become a more valuable support weapon to the Marine infantry fighting their way inland. Another point requiring review was the type of gun needed because the capabilities of the gun would shape the ultimate tactical utilization of the vehicle. The 37 mm gun was a flat trajectory tank gun which tended to force the LVT(A)1 to attempt to assume the role of the tank, an attempt generally unsuccessful since the overall power of the gun was insufficient and the vehicle was frequently blocked from proceeding inland by beach debris. It appeared that the tank made the best tank and the gun chosen for the armored LVT should be complimentary to the tank gun rather than try to duplicate its characteristics.

The LVT(2) and (A)2 were heavily used during the Marshalls and in many ways stood the test, but problems became obvious. The loss of many LVT(2)s of the 10th Amtrac Battalion at Roi-Namur due to sinking focused attention on the need for an additional bilge pump for the incoming water from coral and bullet holes when the vehicle's engine stopped. Water inside the vehicle also caused considerable trouble with communications so a better installation of the radios was required to water proof them. In response to the frequent loss of communications plaguing LVT operations, Marine tractor crewmen were now required to learn semaphore signalling which was frequently used to control the LVT in the water later in the war.[76] The desirability of adding a ramp to the design of the LVT had long been recognized. It was necessary to lift cargo over the side of the LVT(1) and (2); the incorporation of a ramp would greatly speed the loading and unloading of cargo as well as make room for the possible loading and transport of vehicles within the LVT. Maintenance continued to be a prime consideration in the availability of the LVT. The track grousers (cleats) required continual tightening and wore down rapidly when in contact with the coral or rock. A worn grouser reduced the speed of the LVT in the water which in turn had a direct bearing on its ability to execute assault and logistics runs. The grouser also had a direct bearing on the response and control of the vehicle in the water - never an outstanding feature of the LVT. As one former crewman recalled, control in water was like "being in a bathtub with an oar."[77]

Despite the technical problems, the tactics evolved for the use of the LVT in the assault role resembled those standardized for the remainder of the war. The placement of the LVT(A)1 in the lead wave or ahead of the lead wave of troop tractors gave the landing fire power and momentum right up to the sand. The Army practice of placing the LVT(A)1s to each side of the leading wave simplified the control problem encountered at Namur when the LVT(A)1s were placed directly ahead of the troop carrying LVTs and endangered friendly troops by firing over their heads with their tank guns as the troop LVTs passed ahead to make the landing. The use of rocket firing troop LVTs was only a marginal success, but experimentation continued with this type of fire support with later models. Roi-Namur emphasized the need for detailed briefing of the LVT crews on all aspects of the landings so that beaches would not be missed and the correct troops were carried ashore. Another refinement needed was a smoother transfer of troops to the LVTs because the complex business of offloading troops from their transports and boating them over to LSTs for loading into LVTs consumed so much time that an 4:30 A.M. reveille was required for a landing at 9:00 A.M. The rest and feeding of the troops immediately before they landed was important and two to three hours of riding around in LCVPs and LVTs before actually landing was destructive for moral and troop efficiency.

The Marshalls was atoll warfare. Although it was characterized by an overwhelming naval gunfire preparation that General Holland M. Smith, the overall landing force commander, described as "historic", it nevertheless required the services of the LVT to overcome the ever-present coral reefs that surrounded every island in the area. The whole Marshalls campaign was accomplished with a light cost in lives due in no small part to the continued use of the LVT. General Holland Smith summarized his feelings on the use of LVTs by stating, "Our amphibian tractor proved effective but . . . our control and employment of amtracs was capable of improvement."[78] Everyone from engineers at Food Machinery Corporation to Marines in the field were working on just such improvements so that Operation GRANITE, the capture of the Marianas, would be swift. The first objective was a large island called Saipan.

NOTES

[1] Robert D. Heinl and John A. Crown, The Marshalls: Increasing the Tempo (Washington D.C.: Historical Branch, G-3 Division, Headquarters, United States Marine Corps, 1954), p. 13.

[2] Henry I. Shaw, Bernard C. Nalty, and Edwin T. Turnbladh, Central Pacific Drive, Vol. III of The History of United States Marine Corps Operations in World War II (5 vols.; Washington D.C.: Historical Branch, G-3 Division, Headquarters, United States Marine Corps, 1966), p. 135.

[3] Ibid., p. 136.

[4] Ibid., pp. 140-141.

[5] Ibid.

[6] Heinl and Crown, The Marshalls, p. 44.

[7] Jeter A. Isely and Philip A. Crowl, The United States Marines and Amphibious War (Princeton: Princeton University Press, 1951), p. 262.

[8] 10th Amtrac Battalion, Report on Operations of the 10th Amtrac Battalion During Operation Flintlock (In the Field: 10th Amtrac Battalion, 1944), p. 2.

[9] Shaw, Nalty, and Turnbladh, Central Pacific Drive, p. 128.

[10] Ibid., p. 137.

[11] Ibid., p. 152.

[12] 10th Amtrac Battalion, Report on Operations, Enclosure (a), p. 2.

[13] Ibid., Enclosure (a), p. 8.

[14] Heinl and Crown, The Marshalls, p. 44.

[15] 10th Amtrac Battalion, Report on Operations, Enclosure (a), p. 6.

[16] Ibid.

[17] Ibid.

[18] Heinl and Crown, The Marshalls, p. 46.

[19] Ibid., p. 48.

[20] Ibid., p. 49.

[21] Ibid., p. 50.

[22] 10th Amtrac Battalion, Report on Operations, Enclosure (c), p. 3.

[23] Ibid., Enclosure (a), p. 1.

[24] Heinl and Crown, The Marshalls, pp. 51-52.

[25] 10th Amtrac Battalion, Report on Operations, Enclosure (a), p. 7.

[26] Ibid., Enclosure (c), pp. 3-5.

[27] Ibid., Enclosure (d), p. 2.

[28] Ibid.

[29] Isely and Crowl, U.S. Marines and Amphibious War, p. 273.

[30] Heinl and Crown, The Marshalls, p. 67.

[31] Shaw, Nalty, and Trunbladh, Central Pacific Drive, p. 157.

[32] Ibid.

[33] Ibid., p. 158.

[34] Ibid., p. 157.

[35] Heinl and Crown, The Marshalls, pp. 68-69.

[36] Shaw, Nalty, and Turnbladh, Central Pacific Drive, p. 161.

[37] Heinl and Crown, The Marshalls, p. 69.

[38] Ibid., p. 75.

[39] 10th Amtrac Battalion, Report on Operations, Enclosure (a), p. 12.

[40] Ibid., Enclosure (a), p. 9.

[41] Isely and Crowl, U.S. Marines and Amphibious War, p. 283.

[42] Heinl and Crown, The Marshalls, p. 89.

[43] Ibid.

[44] Shaw, Nalty, and Turnbladh, Central Pacific Drive, p. 172.

[45] Heinl and Crown, The Marshalls, p. 98.

[46] Ibid., pp. 100-101.

[47] Shaw, Nalty, and Turnbladh, Central Pacific Drive, p. 190.

⁴⁸Ibid., p. 134.

⁴⁹Ibid., p. 175.

⁵⁰Isely and Crowl, <u>U.S. Marines and Amphibious War</u>, p. 277.

⁵¹Heinl and Crown, <u>The Marshalls</u>, p. 103.

⁵²Shaw, Nalty, and Turnbladh, <u>Central Pacific Drive</u>, p. 180.

⁵³Heinl and Crown, <u>The Marshalls</u>, pp. 118-120.

⁵⁴Ibid., p. 124.

⁵⁵Isely and Crowl, <u>U.S. Marines and Amphibious War</u>, p. 124.

⁵⁶Ibid., p. 299.

⁵⁷Shaw, Nalty, and Turnbladh, <u>Central Pacific Drive</u>, p. 194.

⁵⁸Ibid., p. 190.

⁵⁹Isely and Crowl, <u>U.S. Marines and Amphibious War</u>, pp. 296-297.

⁶⁰Shaw, Nalty, and Turnbladh, <u>Central Pacific Drive</u>, p. 189.

⁶¹Ibid., p. 190.

⁶²Heinl and Crown, <u>The Marshalls</u>, p. 131.

⁶³Shaw, Nalty, and Turnbladh, <u>Central Pacific Drive</u>, pp. 200-201.

⁶⁴Heinl and Crown, <u>The Marshalls</u>, p. 134.

⁶⁵Shaw, Nalty, and Turnbladh, <u>Central Pacific Drive</u>, p. 203.

⁶⁶Heinl and Crown, <u>The Marshalls</u>, pp. 136-137.

⁶⁷Shaw, Nalty, and Turnbladh, <u>Central Pacific Drive</u>, p. 206.

⁶⁸Heinl and Crown, <u>The Marshalls</u>, p. 139.

⁶⁹Ibid., p. 142.

⁷⁰Shaw, Nalty, and Turnbladh, <u>Central Pacific Drive</u>, p. 211.

⁷¹Ibid., p. 210.

⁷²Heinl and Crown, <u>The Marshalls</u>, p. 146.

⁷³Ibid.

⁷⁴Shaw, Nalty, and Turnbladh, <u>Central Pacific Drive</u>, p. 213.

[75] Heinl and Crown, The Marshalls, p. 149.

[76] Interview with MGYSGT Thomas J. Grover, USMC, 15 June 1975.

[77] Ibid.

[78] Holland M. Smith, Coral and Brass (New York: Charles Scribner's Sons, 1949), pp. 148-149.

PART VI

SAIPAN: EMPLOYMENT IN MASS

The Combined Chiefs of Staff shaped the final strategy for winning the Pacific War against Japan during the Casablanca Conference of January 1943. They decided that the decisive route of advance toward Japan would be the Central Pacific through the Marshalls, Truk, and then to the Marianas Islands. MacArthur's advance through the Southwest Pacific via the Solomons, New Britain, New Guinea, and the Philippines would provide flank security for the main Central Pacific operations. The next objectives after the capture of the Marshalls in February 1944, were among the toughest - Truk and the Marianas.

Truk had long been regarded as the anchor of Japanese strength in the Central Pacific area and was listed as a prime objective along the route of advance. It contained air fields, naval repair and staging facilities, and a sizeable garrison of ground troops, and with such strength any attempt to bypass it would create a threat in the rear of American units moving forward to other objectives. The Marianas also contained sizeable forces and would offer the United States a new set of important advanced bases for the final operations against Japan. The position of the Marianas, 1,200 miles south of Japan, became a key factor in early 1944 when the United States produced the B-29 bomber which, with a combat range of 3,250 miles, could span the distances to Japan. Bases developed for the B-29 in China began operations on 5 June 1944, but they were

considered insecure because there were doubts the Chinese could hold them against Japanese attacks.[1] The Marianas offered the United States the first secure base for commencement of strategic bombing of the Japanese homeland with a heavy land-based bomber.

The strikes against Truk conducted by Naval carrier aircraft on 17 and 18 February, simultaneous with the Eniwetok landings, disclosed how weak Truk Atoll actually was. There were 365 planes caught on the ground by the 17 February raid and of the approximately one-hundred undamaged aircraft, none rose the next day to oppose the second raid of Navy fighter-bombers, apparently due to lack of pilots.[2] By the end of the second day of air attacks, two cruisers, four destroyers, nine auxiliary craft, and twenty-four cargo and transport vessels had been sunk.[3] The Navy had hoped for a decisive fight during the operations against Truk, but although none developed, the raids demonstrated just what a hollow shell the former bastion had become. The Japanese had withdrawn.

Original planning by Admiral Nimitz had included an attack on Truk and the date for operations against the Marianas was then set for 15 November 1944.[4] The Joint Chiefs of Staff, however, were looking for ways to accelerate the pace of the Pacific War and the rapid capture of the Marshalls coupled with the weakness of Truk created the opportunity they sought. On 12 March 1944, they issued a directive setting 15 June as the target date for the seizure of the Marianas Islands to secure secondary naval facilities and a potential B-29 air base.[5]

The Marianas Islands are fifteen islands stretching 425 miles in a north-south direction, in the West Pacific Ocean. They were former German possessions which the Japanese received as part of the League of Nations Mandate in 1921, with the exception of the American possession of

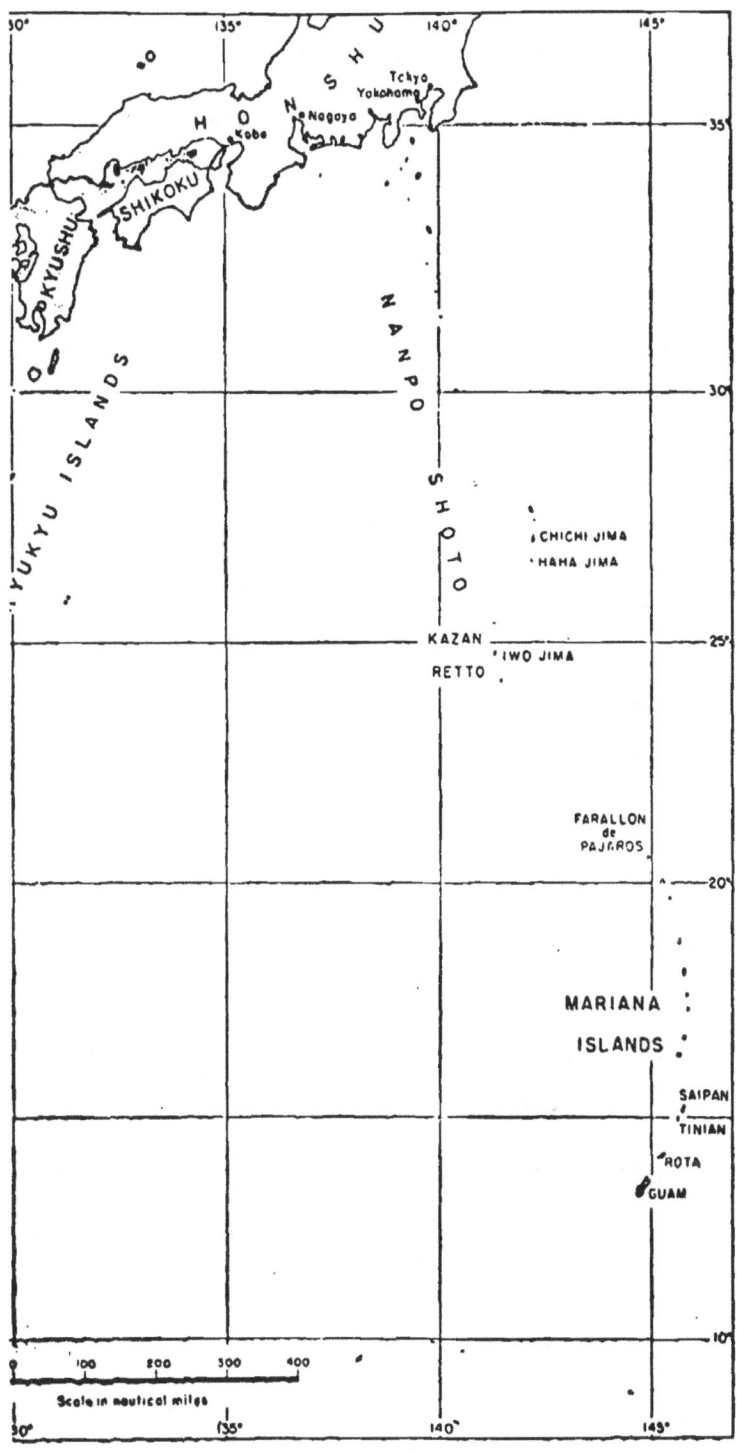

Map 13. The Marianas.

Guam, won by the United States in the Spanish-American War. Only those islands in the southern portion had military significance including Saipan, Tinian, Rota, and Guam. During the first days of World War II, Guam had been seized by the Japanese despite the valiant stand of the few American military personnel on the island. Because the Japanese kept their activities cloaked in secrecy during the pre-war years, little was known of the islands until they became amphibious objectives during World War II.

The first target was the island of Saipan, the administrative headquarters for Japanese forces in the Marianas and location of several large airfields. It had ample room for construction of maintenance facilities and placement of artillery to fortify the later assault on Tinian, three miles to the south. The selection of Saipan as the first objective in the Marianas was therefore a logical one that lowered the risks in the attack against Tinian. It should be noted that the 2nd and 4th Marine Divisions were scheduled to attack Saipan as well as conduct the shore-to-shore operation against Tinian; three days after the landings on Saipan, the 3rd Marine Division and the 1st Provisional Marine Brigade would attack Guam. The reserve for the overall attack of the Marianas was the Army's 27th Infantry Division.

Saipan is an irregularly-shaped island with a length along the north-south axis of approximately 14.2 miles by 6.5 miles wide or a land area of about seventy-two square miles, far larger than the tiny atolls that Central Pacific forces had been attacking in the Gilberts and Marshalls. In contrast to the maximum elevation on Eniwetok of twenty feet above sea level, the highest point on Saipan is 1,554 feet on Mount Tapotchau, located near the center of the island. The northern and eastern sections are rolling hills and plateaus which drop sharply into the sea in well-defined cliffs. The only exception to this is Magicienne Bay on the east coast with a usable beach and a coral reef, the only one on the east coast. The southern part of the island features a low-lying plain on which the Japanese built Aslito Airfield with a 3,600 foot main runway. The west coast has a coral reef along almost its entire length which narrows to between five-hundred and 1,300 yards in width.[6]

The beaches on the southern part of the west coast of Saipan offered the best entrances into the inland portions of the southern plains. This area was chosen as the landing beaches for the 2nd and 4th Marine Divisions on 15 June 1944. The presence of the coral reef dictated the use of LVTs in this landing and with two combat divisions landing abreast, each with 17,465 personnel, they were to be employed on a scale not seen up to this point in the war. Six battalions or six-hundred troop LVTs would be used and two battalions (or about 136 armored amphibians) would precede them to the beach. This massive application of the LVT on Saipan featured the use of the latest modifications off the production lines, and these changes represented significant improvements in LVT design.

The new cargo model was the LVT(4). The design was developed by the Food Machinery Corporation which utilized many of the basic components of the LVT(2) but included the much-needed ramp in the rear. The numbering system in this case appears out of sequence because of the concurrent attempt of Borg-Warner to develop a ramped LVT. Borg-Warner, it will be remembered, developed the Model A as the first armored amphibian but its design was rejected in favor of the Food Machinery models which became the LVT(A)1 and LVT(2). After its initial failure, Borg-Warner continued development and next produced a prototype ramped LVT, the Model B, which was to be called the LVT(3). Production difficulties delayed its completion and so the Food Machinery designed LVT(4) was the first ramped LVT to see action.[7]

The design changes in the LVT(4) were built around the requirement to incorporate a ramp feature into the cargo LVT, a feature recommended almost from the first operations involving LVTs in the Solomons. With both the LVT(1) and (2), it was necessary to hoist all cargo, personnel, and weapons over the side of the vehicle to load into the cargo compartment. This cargo compartment was in the middle of the LVT with the driver's station forward to provide visibility, and the engine was in the rear. Food Machinery Corporation maintained the driver's position forward, but also moved the engine forward to a position just behind the driver which allowed the rear area to become the cargo compartment with the back side hinged and lowered. The hinged portion became the loading ramp into the vehicle and eliminated the need to hoist the load over the side. Cargo could now be rolled, pushed, and generally man-handled far faster than ever possible using the old over-the-side method with earlier LVTs. Despite the extensive re-design to obtain this ramp, much of the vehicle used time-proven components including substantially the same track, engine, and transmission as the LVT(2). In order to give the rear loading ramp strength, substantial reinforcement was necessary. This, combined with the manually operated winch necessary to lower and raise the ramp, added about 2,600 pounds of weight to the vehicle and reduced land speed from thirty-one mph for the LVT(2) to twenty mph for the LVT(4); the water speed remained nearly the same for both vehicles, about six mph. Despite its added weight, the recommended maximum cargo for the LVT(4) was 2,500 pounds more than that for the LVT(2) due mainly to the

Figure 25. The LVT(4) and LVT(2) in a floating comparison. Note that the LVT(4) floats about one foot higher.

Figure 26. A rear view of the first ramped LVT showing the massive ramp which formed a separate watertight compartment. This vehicle is at the LVT Museum, Camp Pendleton, California.

increased size of the cargo compartment, no longer cluttered and obstructed by the drive line. Both the LVT(2) and LVT(4) had the same ninety-four inch wide cargo space, but the LVT(4)'s space was longer at 150 inches versus 129 inches for the LVT(2). Production started on the LVT(4) during December 1943, too late for the Marshalls, but in time for Saipan. The following is a summary data table for comparison of the LVT(2) and the LVT(4):

	LVT(2)	LVT(4)
Length	26' 1"	26' 1"
Width	10' 10"	10' 8"
Height	8' 1"	8' 1"
Crew	3 to 6	2 to 7
Weight: empty	24,400 lbs.	27,400 lbs.
Weight: loaded	30,900 lbs.	36,400 lbs.
Ground Clearance	18"	18"
Engine: make	Continental	Continental
Engine: type/model	Radial-Gasoline W670-9A	Radial-Gasoline W670-9A
Engine: horsepower	250	250
Fuel Capacity	110 gallons	140 gallons
Radius: land	200 miles	150 miles
Radius: water	60 miles	75 miles

Sources: War Department Technical Manual 9-775, February 1944, and Robert J. Icks, "Landing Vehicles Tracked", in Armored Fighting Vehicles in Profile, ed. by Duncan Crow (New York: Doubleday & Company, Inc., 1972), p. 162.

The ramp feature allowed for the first time, loading a military jeep into an LVT or, with the muzzle elevated, a 105 mm howitzer. This ability to carry small vehicles and artillery pieces up to 105 mm greatly expanded the variety of applications for the LVT as the battle for Saipan approached.

The new armored amphibian was designated the LVT(A)4. The origin of

Figure 27. Side view of the LVT(4) with a 105mm howitzer loaded. The LVT(4) was the first LVT capable of carrying this artillery piece.

Figure 28. Inside view of the 105mm howitzer load. The tube is near full elevation.

the skip in numbering from the LVT(A)2 to the LVT(A)4 is obscure, but plans appear to have been made to build an armored version of the LVT(4), to receive the designation LVT(A)3, which would be armored with a heavy gun, but without a turret. Although these plans were never completed, Food Machinery's new armored amphibian received the designation LVT(A)4.[8] This vehicle retained definite similarity to the basic configuration of the LVT(A)1 but used a different turret and gun. The basic change in this case was more than just a heavier gun, in fact it replaced the LVT(A)1 tank gun with an artillery howitzer. Since the capabilities of the gun determine the tactical usage of such a fighting vehicle, the new LVT(A)4 moved away from the attempt to make the armored amphibian a tank and towards the role of an artillery weapon and an assault gun. A detailed comparison of gun performance will be useful:

	LVT(A)1	LVT(A)4
Caliber	37 mm	75 mm
Muzzle Velocity	2,900 feet per second (Armor piercing ammunition)	1,250 feet per second (High explosive ammunition)
Max. Range	12,850 yards	9,610 yards

Source: E. F. Hoffschmidt and W. H. Tantum IV, United States Military Vehicles, World War 2 (Old Greenwich: W. E. Inc., 1970), pp. 56, 89.

The prime mission of the 37 mm gun in the United States arsenal of weapons was to defeat enemy armor. This called for a high-speed, armor-piercing round of ammunition with a flat trajectory. While valuable in some limited applications against light fortifications, the 37 mm rounds did not have either the penetration power or explosive charge required to damage heavy Japanese fortifications. The heavier explosive charge packed in the 75 mm howitzer of the LVT(A)4 capitalized on the demonstrated

Figure 29. Side view of the LVT(A)4. A machine gun mount is on top of the turret.

Figure 30. Overhead view shows the open-top construction of the turret.

effectiveness of 75 mm guns used on Tarawa, Roi-Namur, and Eniwetok. However, as seen from the table above, the howitzer uses high explosive ammunition which gains its effect through blast rather than penetration, as in the case of the armor-piercing round of the 37 mm tank gun. Because howitzer rounds are larger, slower, and travel in an arching manner or high trajectory, targets shielded from the direct fire of the 37 mm tank gun may be reached by the 75 mm howitzer since its rounds fall more from above than those of the flat-shooting tank gun. The 75 mm howitzer mounted in the LVT(A)4 represented a definite break with previous gun and mission thinking with respect to armored LVTs.

Another significant difference was that the new armored amphibian's turret did not provide for gyro-stabilization of the main gun. Gyro-stabilization is a system that maintains the gun in a constant elevation set by the gunner, despite the rolling, pitching, and lurching of the vehicle. The LVT(A)1 had this system in its turret for the 37 mm main gun. Without gyro-stabilization, accurate shooting on the move is impossible. The best technique for firing the main gun of the LVT(A)4 was a form of snap-shooting or firing as the target appeared to be nearing the cross hairs of the sight and not waiting for an ideal or perfect sight picture prior to firing.[9] The reason the LVT(A)4 lacked gyro-stabilization stems from the military approach to use standardized and time-proven components of tank and armored vehicles to achieve quick and workable solutions to a problem. Thus, when the turret of the M3 light tank was used on earlier LVTs, gyro-stabilization was included because it came as standard equipment with the turret and gun. In contrast, in searching for a larger 75 mm gun for an improved armored LVT, the turret of the M8 self-propelled howitzer was considered to be the satisfactory answer, but this turret did not come with gyro-stabilization because the mission of the M8 was to fire from a stationary position as artillery.

Saipan's planning called for troop LVTs and LVT(A)4s of the 4th Marine Division to penetrate inland to capture high ground dominating the beach. It was hoped to capitalize on the armored mobility and fire power of the LVT and the armored amphibian combination to cover ground rapidly at the outset. The high ground was designated the O-1 Line and required a movement of 1,500 to 2,000 yards inland.[10] This plan had the definite side benefit of clearing the narrow beaches which averaged only twenty to thirty yards wide and allowing the large number of troops in succeeding waves room to land. Initially, the plan to penetrate inland was to apply to both the 2nd and the 4th divisions but General Watson, Commanding General of the 2nd Marine Division, took strong exception to using this method in his zone of action because heavy woods lay just behind the narrow beaches and he feared loss of control of the troops over an extended period of time while they continued inland in LVTs. Also, he felt the grouping of men into the vehicles would expose them unnecessarily to fire as they moved inland.[11] In his zone, General Watson secured permission from General Smith to have movement no more than 200 yards inland to a tractor control line marked by a railroad line. The troops were to disembark at this point while the armored amphibians [LVT(A)1s and a few LVT(A)4s of the Army's 708th Amphibian Tank Battalion] delivered overhead support fire from the vicinity of the beach. Troop-carrying LVTs were also to deliver overhead support fire from their machine guns until the next wave reached the control line. They were then to return to the LVT pool for further use as directed by the control vessel at the line of departure.[12]

The plans thus formed did not differ substantially from earlier use of the cargo LVT or armored amphibian except that a deep penetration was to be attempted to high ground by General Schmidt's 4th Marine Division. Subsequent use of the LVT(A)4 was to be reinforcement of the artillery or to support infantry by direct fire. In contrast to earlier landings, two full tank battalions, the 2nd and 4th, supporting their parent divisions, would land and assume the missions appropriate for tanks, thus preempting this role for armored amphibians. Saipan's plans therefore moved the armored amphibian more towards artillery fire support and direct fire support as an assault gun - that is, from behind a screen of infantry - rather than attempting to lead infantry as was frequently done by tanks.

The plans laid for the LVT, particularly in the 4th Marine Division zone, were not based on the comprehensive knowledge of the terrain needed for operations across such an extensive land mass. Intelligence gathering for the Saipan landing suffered from problems stemming from too few aircraft for too many concurrent missions in the various theaters of war in the Pacific. Aerial photo coverage fell far short of ideal considering the size of the objective and the complexity of the terrain. Intelligence officers had little knowledge of the island until carrier planes attacked Saipan on 22-23 February 1944. Aerial photos were taken of certain portions of the islands during these raids, but these photos were made by attack planes whose targets did not always coincide with areas required for proper landing force intelligence. Also, enemy anti-aircraft fire made it unhealthy for attacking aircraft to linger over areas that needed photo coverage. General Smith's Intelligence Officer wanted coverage ninety, sixty, thirty, and fifteen days prior to 15 June but the demands on carrier aircraft caused Admiral Spruance to deny further photo runs from carrier aircraft.[13] Between 17 April and 6 June, seven additional photo runs were finally made by high level Navy bombers, but these photos were not available to the landing force when it left Hawaii. They were delivered to the force when it staged at Eniwetok Atoll for some transfer of troops among the shipping, but the slower elements in the LSTs had already set sail by the time the photos arrived and only the division headquarters had access to this latest update. Map makers, working with the photos taken during the 22-23 February carrier raid as well as other scanty information, developed maps where slopes were assumed to be uniform unless shadows indicated a sharp rise or depression. Clouds, trees, and the angle at which the photo was taken sometimes helped to hide the true nature of the terrain and the maps were in error. Many cliffs, for example, were mapped as gentle slopes. While the 2nd Marine Division was aware of the difficulties for LVTs due to the presence of a heavy forest in their zone, the 4th Marine Division's plans, based on the erroneous terrain maps, would be frustrated by the rugged terrain that would prove more than a match even for LVT mobility. Intelligence further failed to establish an accurate count of the Japanese forces on the island. The final estimate was 15,000 to 17,600 Japanese consisting of 9,100 to 11,000 combat troops, 900 to 1,200 aviation personnel, 1,600 to 1,900 Japanese laborers, and 400 to 500 Koreans. The actual count was about 30,000 soldiers and sailors plus hundreds of civilians.[14]

As the task forces churned towards Saipan, preliminary bombardment commenced with carrier aircraft attacks on 11 June, which surprised the Japanese and destroyed 150 Japanese aircraft on the ground and in the air, and heavier aircraft bombing runs on 12 June.[15] On 13 June a group of fast battleships arrived to begin shelling the beaches and other island

targets. These were newer battleships, built since 1939, and the
Missouri and the New Jersey were among this class of powerfully armed
ships. Despite their modern equipment, their bombardment was not as
effective as it could have been. It was not certain if the waters off
the west coast of Saipan had been mined by the Japanese, and, because the
fast battleships had arrived before the slower minesweepers, the area
close to shore had not been officially "swept" or cleared. As a result,
the battleships were required to stand off at ranges over 10,000 yards to
fire rather than the 2,000 yards normally employed to achieve pinpoint
destruction. The spotters and crews of the fast battleships were not as
well trained as the old battleships which up to this point had been the
mainstay of the naval bombardment; many targets remained intact. In
addition, the fire tended to be area fire rather than the methodical
point-by-point destruction required to clear the way for a landing. The
fire of these ships, however, was not intended to replace but rather to
supplement the close-in work by the veteran gunfire crews of the older
battleships scheduled to arrive the next day.[16] On 14 June, the old
battleships arrived and began their short-range destruction of targets
around the beaches, however, Japanese use of camouflage was excellent with
many mobile guns enabling them to move out to shoot, then duck under
skillfully constructed natural covers in caves or hillsides. Other
factors mitigated the effect of the bombardment. Naval ships were
required to conserve ammunition for the bombardment of Guam, scheduled
three days later, and on D-Day no naval gunfire was to fall more than
1,000 yards inland, leaving only aircraft to attack inland targets. The
latter order was issued to conserve precious time required to coordinate
fires but in fact resulted in many targets escaping fire from the weapon

best suited to destroy them.[17] Overall, there was also the basic problem of insufficient time. The destruction by the experienced naval gunfire ships was scheduled for one day only, hardly adequate to do the job. There would be many more Japanese on the beaches than expected.

The gunfire plan for the approach of the LVTs to the beach was a product of amphibious experience and represented tightly coordinated fire support. The line of departure for Saipan was 4,000 yards offshore. When the LVTs reached a point, 1,000 yards from the beach, the main batteries of the old battleships were to cease fire on the beaches and shift inland. Aircraft would start their final neutralization runs when the LVTs were 800 yards from shore, flying over the path of the naval shells. Five-inch guns were to continue to fire until the LVTs were only 300 yards from shore. Aircraft were to continue to attack the beach right up to the point of landing.[18]

The task forces approached the island and went into positions seaward of the line of departure on the morning of D-Day, 15 June 1944. There was considerably less shuffling of troops to load LVTs than previously in the Marshalls because during the staging at Eniwetok, six days earlier, assault troops had been transferred to the LSTs carrying the LVTs that were to land them. After six days in a cramped LST, the marines were mean enough to attack anybody.[19] Other lessons learned in earlier engagements were now applied. LVTs at Saipan were supplied with bundles of wooden plugs to pound into holes punched in the hulls by gunfire or coral to seal them until they could be welded.[20] Cargo LVTs in the lead waves were given two sand bags, partially filled with sand, which were placed on the rear of the cargo compartment, with instructions to the crew to throw the bags over any grenades landing inside the vehicle. The

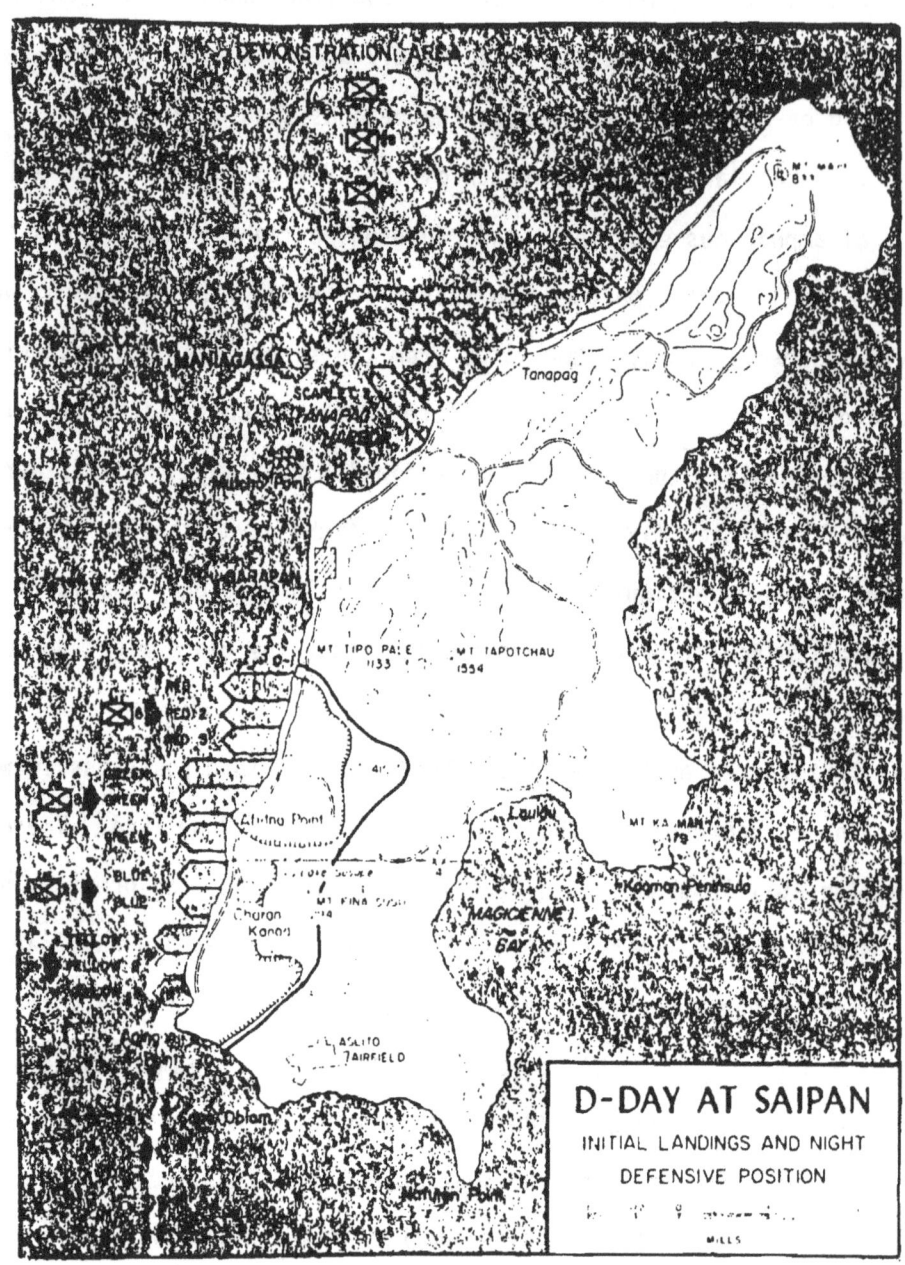

Map 14. D-Day at Saipan.

operation orders gave further grim instructions, "If you can't get a sand bag, place your helmet over it. If at all possible throw it out. You may lose your hand, but that's better than your life."[21] The crew chief's position was behind the driver to enable him to observe the front and sides and assist the driver in steering by the "hand tap" method. The operations orders cautioned, "Remember, this boy has little or no vision. The crew chief is his eyes."[22] All cargo LVTs were loaded with certain assault supplies to assist in immediate supply of the infantry and to keep their own machine guns firing. This included four expeditionary cans of water for the infantry, four cases of belted machine gun ammunition, two cases of rifle ammunition, two cases of carbine ammunition, two cases of grenades, and about four rounds of either 81 mm or 60 mm mortar ammunition.[23]

The plans for the formation of armored amphibians and cargo LVTs resembled the tactics of the Marshalls on a massive scale. The outer flanks of troop-carrying LVTs were protected by six armored amphibians and the gaps between the battalion-sized landing teams were filled with a wedge-shaped formation of six more armored amphibians. This allowed firing by both the first wave of cargo LVTs and the armored amphibians simultaneously. Following waves were only to fire if they were attacked by aircraft. Three LCI gunboats were to precede each battalion landing team. LVT(2)s comprised the first three waves with the last wave consisting of LVT(4)s because these vehicles were better suited to carrying the heavier loads of headquarters elements, including wheeled vehicles.[24]

The forty-seven LSTs carrying the armored amphibians and LVTs reached their assigned positions 1,000 yards seaward of the line of departure at about 7:00 A.M., on the morning of 15 June and began unloading at 7:00 A.M. Some LSTs were late in starting because the armored amphibians, positioned ahead of the LVTs on the main or tank deck, were difficult to debark.[25] This and other minor problems caused the task force commander, Admiral Kelly Turner, to postpone H-Hour ten minutes from 8:30 to 8:40 A.M. Navy guide boats led the LVTs to their lines of departure where most of the waves were formed around 7:30 A.M., but some as late as 8:00 because one LST could not get its bow doors open.[26] The signal to cross the line of departure was given at 8:05 A.M. and the leading waves composed of ninety-six LVTs, sixty-eight armored amphibians, and twenty-four LCI gunboats churned towards the line of old battleships pounding the beaches at ranges of 2,000 yards.[27] The interval between the LVTs varied but averaged forty yards, although that of the lead wave was a little less due to its additional armored amphibians. The time interval between the waves varied slightly but ran generally at three minutes between the first and second waves, five minutes between the second and third waves, and eight minutes between the third and fourth waves. The compressed timing of the early waves was to land men and guns rapidly to secure a foothold. The early part of the 4,000 yard run from the line of departure to the beach was uneventful, only scattered Japanese fire falling near the line of departure. As the tractors closed on the barrier reef (about 1,000 to 1,500 yards offshore) however, Japanese fire became more intense and increased closer to the beach. There was high surf at the reef's edge, estimated by one battalion commander to be from twelve to fifteen feet, and one to two tractors per battalion were lost by overturning in the rough water. Mortar and anti-boat fire increased as the LVTs moved from the reef towards the shore, although the first two waves suffered only light losses from this fire. The third and fourth waves came under more accurate fire and losses increased to about one to two LVTs per battalion. Despite the efforts of the Japanese, the first waves hit the beach between 8:38 A.M., and the following three waves of LVTs came in five to nine munute intervals. The relatively light losses were due in part to the spot armoring of the cargo LVTs with 1/4 and 3/8-inch armor on the hull, and 1/2-inch armor on the cab and bow. Although some did penetrate, many rounds as well as much schrapnel were turned.[28] Control craft guiding the LVTs were unable to cross the reef and the LVTs were on their own from the reef to the beach. The deadly fire of the Japanese and a strong northerly current made it difficult for the LVT drivers to maintain direction and many battalions were landed 400 to 600 yards too far left in their zones. This caused troop concentrations that were vulnerable targets for enemy fire and losses were particularly high in the 2nd Marine Division's zone of action.

As the tractors hit the beach, the cost of the poor intelligence and aerial photography became more apparent. Terrain assumed to consist of uniform slopes now was seen to be sheer cliffs. Dense woods blocked the tractors in the 2nd Marine Division and they were unable even to reach the tractor control line, 200 yards inland; most could not go more than thirty yards from the beach.[29] The rugged terrain blocked the planned armored thrust to the dominant ridge in the 4th Marine Division's zone and most troops were forced to debark at the beach under fire. It was the plan of the Japanese commander, General Hideyoshi Obata, to attempt to defeat the Americans at the beach, and the rugged terrain, concealing Japanese positions which escaped the preliminary bombardment, and the overall failure of American intelligence to gauge properly the nature of the terrain or the number of the enemy, combined to make the fight for Saipan's beaches one of the toughest in the history of the Marine Corps. Japanese mortar and artillery fire, guided by observers on the dominant ridgeline which was to have been seized by the abortive armored thrust of the 4th Marine Division, caused severe casualties, particularly among later waves of troops when the Japanese fire on the beach became extremely accurate. By 1:00 P.M., one regiment in the 2nd Division lost an estimated thirty-five per cent wonded or killed.[30] Artillery and mortar fire took a heavy toll among the armored amphibians which remained on the beach after landing to furnish fire support for the assault troops. Figures on the losses of armored amphibians are confused, but the earliest official history of the campaign lists three armored amphibians disabled prior to reaching the shore and twenty-eight damaged on the beach or attempting to move inland.[31] LVTs returning to the line of departure were also fired on by artillery and anti-boat guns, which inflicted some losses until discouraged by the crews zig-zagging in the water. In a number of cases, when the tractor began to zig-zag, the fire ceased.[32] The LVTs gave as good as they had received, and one cargo battalion expended 50,000 rounds of caliber .50 machine gun ammunition and 175,000 rounds of caliber .30 during the run to the beach.[33]

Immediately after the landing, cargo LVTs returned to their control vessels for further orders, a trip made difficult by the high surf at the reef which caused a few tractors to overturn. (Their crews were rescued.) Badly needed reserves were transferred from LCVPs to LVTs at a transfer line seaward of the reef, and landed at about 10:30 A.M. As the day progressed, more LVTs were utilized in the logistical duties vital to support a major landing of two Marine divisions. Generally, this meant some LVTs were retained by the shore party organizations of the two divisions for runs inland to dumps while others made runs between the ships and the beach carrying supplies. Outgoing LVTs were used to evacuate the casualties to hospital ships.

The armored amphibians continued to furnish assault gun fire support to the infantry. In the 4th Marine Division zone, some isolated groups were able to penetrate to the ridgeline. Eight LVTs supported by three armored amphibians, probably LVT(A)1s, sprinted through the Japanese defenses on the only available road beyond the town of Charan Kanaoa on the beach, and prepared a perimeter defense on a hill astride the ridgeline, a position isolated and exposed to direct small arms fire and mortar fire. The LVT(A)1s, fearing possible destruction from concentrated fire, remained at the base of the hill and did not provide fire support at that point. The outpost was recalled after dark to friendly lines. A similar breakthrough occurred further south in the 4th Marine Division zone involving five armored amphibians and three cargo LVTs. This breakthrough was also unsupported by the remainder of the battalion and had to be recalled or risk possible destruction by surrounding Japanese.[34]

At the end of the first day, it was necessary for the cargo LVTs to return to their LSTs for the night because there was no room on the beachhead for them or their maintenance shops due to the shallow penetrations of the landing forces. Darkness fell as they struggled through the high surf at the reef and some LVTs, finding it difficult to locate their "mother" ship, as they had in the Marshalls, tied up to any available ship for the night, unable to refuel or conduct maintenance.[35] Although this meant the LVTs were scattered during the night, improved command and control organization was able to muster them without difficulty the following morning. This improved control included the use of a control vessel remaining exclusively on station at the line of departure, unlike the Marshalls where the control vessel at one point left station and temporarily became a fire support ship. In addition, the 5th Amtrac Battalion used an LVT officer stationed on the control vessel who was in constant communication with the LVT battalion command post ashore. Landing force logistical requirements for which LVTs would be needed were given to the LVT battalion command post and these were relayed to the LVT officer on the control vessel who in turn had radio and visual communications by semaphore with the LVTs afloat in the LVT pool area.[36] The 2nd Amtrac Battalion used a liaison officer stationed with the shore party and as missions were ordered requiring the use of LVTs in their zone, the liaison officer would radio the mission to the floating battalion command post which then used either radio message or semaphore to designate a tractor to execute the mission.[37]

On the second day of operations, the logistical mission included landing reserves and elements of the shore party, and hauling ammunition, water, medical supplies, and other supplies as part of the unloading of amphibious shipping. Some LVTs were attached to the attacking battalions to haul supplies directly to their dumps inland, a requirement that was continued for twenty days in the 2nd Marine Division zone.[38] Also during the second day, a small boat channel was discovered which was free of coral shallows and allowed some landing craft to proceed to the beach in the 4th Marine Division zone. This eased the strain on the LVTs but the limited capacity of the channel was inadequate during the critical early days to eliminate the necessity of reef-crossing with LVTs.[39] In order to avoid the difficulties in finding LSTs in the dark, LVT operations on the second day were secured at about 6:30 P.M. to allow enough daylight to locate mother ships. This procedure was successful and LVTs were able to refuel and conduct maintenance during the second night at Saipan.

General unloading continued on the third day, and the various cargo battalions were able to transfer their operations ashore because the landing force, after a stiff fight, carved out a beachhead 2,000 to 3,000 yards deep and finally controlled the ridgeline that was to have been seized on the first day. During this time the LVTs became the mainstay for movement of supplies because few wheeled vehicles had landed, a situation continued for far longer than had been planned because the Japanese main battle fleet had sortied to defend Saipan and American Naval Task Forces were redeployed between 17 through 22 June (during which time the Navy severely pounded the Japanese in the Battle of the Philippine Sea). Because the transports and LSTs were now vulnerable to Japanese air attack by being bunched so close to shore, they had to move out to sea and so their unloading operations stopped. LVTs continued as the prime cargo movers of supplies inland from the beaches for the landing force, a continuous operation which wore down the number of vehicles remaining operational each day. This strain was increased by the landing of the Amphibious Corps Reserve, the 27th Infantry Division, during the night of 17 June, a decision made by General Holland Smith because he foresaw the vicious fight necessary to secure the rest of the island, and realized that the reserve would otherwise have to stay at sea with the redeployed Navy forces and would therefore be lost to the landing force on Saipan.

With the landing of the 27th Infantry Division, the campaign for Saipan became a three-division thrust, initially fanning out east and south, and then realigning for the push to take the northern half of the island. Although wheeled vehicles were landed after the return of the Navy from the Battle of the Philippine Sea, some LVTs continued logistical runs throughout the campaign. The majority of cargo LVTs were able to perform maintenance and repair functions as the need for their services diminished. On several occasions, LVT battalions were ordered to supply men, machine guns, and sometimes vehicles to augment beach defenses along the west coast. Also, one battalion furnished LVT crews to act as listening posts inland of some of the 2nd Marine Division's supply dumps. A variety of tasks were also completed to lend further support to the drive north to capture the remainder of Saipan. Samples of the range of missions listed by the 2nd Amtrac Battalion were:

    a. Working with demolitions teams to assist in blowing a small boat channel through the reef.

    b. Salvaging many landing craft stuck on the beach and reef by driving up to the craft and pushing it backwards off its stranded perch.

    c. Supplying LVTs for use as fire-fighting vehicles at beach dumps.

    d. Experimenting with and constructing portable bridgehead ramps.

    e. Evacuating casualties to hospital ships.[40]

The LVT played a pivotal factor in the highly satisfactory unloading of Navy ships between D-Day and 25 June. During this time the majority of shipping was unloaded, and at low tides only the LVT and DUKW were usable because of the very shallow waters over the reef. The few boat channels in the reefs rapidly became congested and the narrow beach frontage was piled high with supplies, an inviting target for the Japanese. Only the LVT and DUKW were able to bring their cargoes out of the water and haul them inland to dumps, a vital factor which reduced beach congestion which might otherwise have become a monumental obstacle in the attempt to support three divisions attacking abreast.[41]

The armored amphibians, despite their heavy early casualties, rendered valuable support as assault guns. The tanks of the 2nd and 4th Marine Divisions landed during D-Day but suffered costly losses by dropping into potholes on the way to shore and drowning in the deep water. In one company, only four of the company's fourteen medium tanks made it to shore in working order.[42] Other companies were more fortunate, but all suffered from the journey across the reef. Until the lost tanks could be salvaged, additional pressure was placed on the armored amphibian to provide needed close-in fire support, a service they continued to provide. Remarked one battalion commander, ". . . I shall always remember the excellent support given to my battalion by the Army LVT(A)'s."[43] This was in reference to the excellent service rendered by the Army's 708th Amphibian Tank Battalion, armed predominantly with the old LVT(A)1s. The added power of the 75 mm gun on the LVT(A)4 was well used because the forticications encountered at Saipan were frequently substantial with the toughest installations concentrated near the beaches. As the medium tanks of the two Marine tank battalions were salvaged and returned to service, use of the armored LVTs diminished, although they remained in action during the push north whenever the Marines or Army were fighting along the coast. For this task the armored amtracs were used on the beach to provide fire support into the shore line cliffs which frequently harbored Japanese hidden in caves. The northward push to complete the conquest of Saipan was rugged fighting, characterized by close-in encounters as Marine and Army infantry dug the Japanese out of their caves. This cave fighting was the singular characteristic of the fighting on Saipan.

When American forces continued to pressure the Japanese and forced them into a compressed pocket in the northern end of the island, the Japanese decided to stage what was to be the largest banzai (suicide) attack of the entire war. During the night of 6-7 July, from 1,500 to 3,000 Japanese soldiers poured through a 300 yard gap in the line of the 27th Infantry Division and surged about 1,500 yards into the rear of American lines. They overran the batteries of the 10th Marine Artillery Regiment that was firing in support of the 27th Division from positions about 600 yards in the rear and continued until stopped by their own losses and the actions of the 27th Infantry Division Commander, General Griner, who committed his reserves.[44]

The tragic consequences of Japanese propaganda on local civilians became clear as the Americans closed on the northernmost tip of the island, Marpi Point. Japanese military had convinced civilians they would be tortured and killed by the Americans, and thousands leaped to their deaths from high cliffs over the sea. Mothers threw their babies ahead of them or jumped with them in their arms.[45] It was a spectacle few who were there care to remember but one they can never forget.

The island was declared secure on 9 July 1944. Additional mopping-up was conducted to include the attack of Maniagassa Island, a small island situated outside the main usable harbor on Saipan and thus a threat to American shipping. Although the island was tiny, 250 yards wide by 300 yards long, preparations were as complete as those for a large landing. Naval gunfire support was furnished by the 40 mm machine guns of one LCI gunboat. Fifteen minutes prior to the 11:00 A.M. H-Hour, the 10th Marine Artillery Regiment showered 920 105 mm and 720 75 mm shells on the island.

The 3rd Battalion, Sixth Marines attacked the island using 25 LVTs of the 5th Amtrac Battalion, preceded by five LVT(A)4s of the 2nd Armored Amphibian Battalion. It was over within an hour with twenty-nine Japanese defenders captured or killed and one Marine wounded.[46]

A review of the campaign leads to certain conclusions about LVT development to this point. The new LVT(4) passed its first combat test with flying colors, yet not all Marines thought highly of it. Remarked one Marine concerning the LVT(4), "You had the engine in your hip pocket."[47] This referred to the forward position of the engine which made the driver's position in the cab hot and noisy. The winch for raising and lowering the ramp was placed high on the wall inside the cargo compartment, requiring a crewman to expose himself to fire to operate it; it was also considered too weak by many and repeated failures were recorded.[48] Also, despite the plain lessons of the Marshalls, the LVT(4) at Saipan did not have hand-operated bilge pumps in addition to the power driven models. This failure did not create problems at Saipan because operations during the first two days were not as confused as those at the Marshalls and operations from the third day on were conducted from land bases. The sustained operations during the early days of the operation highlighted the need for greater maintenance capability within the LVT battalion. Recommendations were made to provide more mechanics and welders as well as for the design of a specialized retriever LVT that could tow other LVTs and could be equipped with a boom to lift engines and LVTs for repair.[49] Communications aboard the cargo LVTs continued to suffer from lack of waterproofing. A pioneer effort was made during the Saipan operation to equip LVTs with multiple receiver-transmitter radio sets for use of command vehicles. While the operation was in its landing and early beachhead phase, such a vehicle could provide the battalion commander with a mobile command post and sufficient communications nets to handle his needs until his full command post came ashore. This concept was to gain a firm hold in future operations, but during the landing at Saipan, these vehicles still suffered from inoperative, flooded radios.[50]

The armored amphibian received its share of punishment during the Saipan operation. Both the LVT(A)1 and (A)4 were used to support the landing and then to continue to give fire support at the beach or to move inland to spearhead a drive for quick seizure of commanding terrain. The intensive artillery fire delivered by the Japanese wreaked havoc with the armored amphibians in all zones of action once they lumbered out of the water and became vulnerable on land. While in the water, the armored LVT presented a low profile and those parts above water, principally the turret, were the more heavily armored parts of the vehicle. Once on land, the high silhouette of the vehicle and its lightly armored hull made it vulnerable to powerful anti-tank guns and direct hits from artillery. Twenty-eight of the sixty-eight armored amphibians in the lead wave were destroyed or damaged by Japanese artillery although some were later repaired. This type of attrition is eloquent testimony to the limits of use of the armored LVT against heavy resistance at the beachhead. It stands in stark contrast to the heavily armored tank which can take a great deal more punishment from artillery hits and survive direct hits up to 105 mm. The inability of the armored LVT to act as a tank did not destroy its usefulness at Saipan because it did give valuable fire support to Marines pinned down on the beach. The point raised by Saipan was that, once forces project inland, the usefulness of the armored amphibian begins to decrease dramatically as it confronts the full range of anti-tank threats inherent in land combat. The medium tank must come ashore early to spearhead any inland drives against fairly large land masses such as those encountered at Saipan.

The damages incurred by the armored amphibians at Saipan stirred a controversy over the open-turret design of the LVT(A)4. The LVT(A)1 had a fully enclosed turret of a light tank while the (A)4 had the open turret of a gun carriage used on self-propelled artillery. Many thought that the armored LVTs might have survived longer with a closed turret. The argument was not settled during World War II because all armored LVTs, the (A)4, and the later (A)5 retained the open turret design. General Louis B. Metzger, commander of early armored amphibian battalions in World War II, wrote in 1948:

> Armored amphibians should never be employed as land tanks, but only as assault guns. The difference being that LVT(A)s should always operate behind a screen of infantry and support such infantry by direct fire. If this concept is adhered to, the requirements for turret covers are reduced considerably.[51]

As a final highlight to this point, a review of casualties suffered by the various armored amphibian battalions and the tank battalions should prove instructive. All figures are total casualties including killed, wounded, and missing:

2nd Armored Amphibian Battalion	12 officers	136 enlisted
708th Amphibian Tank Battalion	0	184
2nd Tank Battalion	0	18
4th Tank Battalion	6	53
762nd Tank Battalion	6	75

Source: Casualty tables, Appendix III, Hoffman's *Saipan*.

The casualty figures show the superior ability of the medium tank to take battle punishment.

The hard fight for the beaches of Saipan took a heavy toll on LVT crews but did not diminish the overall service these vehicles were able to render in the conquest of Saipan. The cargo LVT continued not only to act as the assault landing craft for the infantry but also as a vital logistics asset that helped to make the difference between chaos and progress in logistical support operations. Its versatility now extended to carrying artillery and the beginning was made in the use of the command LVT for communications for the commander in a mobile combat situation. Improvements were needed on the LVT(4), but its basic redesign to incorporate the ramp greatly added to its overall versatility and value to the landing force.

The armored amphibian's role was placed in true perspective by the Saipan campaign. It became clear that it was not a tank and although it could render direct fire support to the infantry, once the tanks came ashore, the LVT(A)4 was adaptable to providing indirect fire support similar to artillery. This adaptability, however, was not extensively utilized and histories simply note that the vehicle was used to reinforce fires or tanks, artillery, and mortars. From this it is difficult to determine if the fire delivered was direct fire similar to that of the tanks, or overhead fire of mortars and artillery. The full range of capabilities of the 75 mm howitzer does not appear to have been used on Saipan. The LVT(A)1 remained in use and due to the high velocity tank gun it mounted, it was usable only in the direct fire role. The land mobility of the armored amphibian, however, frequently did not compare with that of the tank and its failure to lead the way inland in the 4th Marine Division zone of action is partially due to this problem. The greater power and track width of the medium tank made it the vehicle to overcome the terrain inland from the beaches of Saipan.

Within the Marianas, the fight for Saipan was the toughest test of the new LVTs. The subsequent operation to take Tinian was characterized by General Holland M. Smith as the perfect amphibious operation.[52] The LVTs performed their functions with a high degree of effectiveness and their ability to continue inland from the beach was critical to the success of the Tinian landings because the tiny beach of only 200 yards in width held no room for dumps, maintenance stops, command posts or any of the normal beach activities. Given favorable terrain, the LVTs ability to project toward the center of the island with its load allowed the landing force simply to displace normal beach functions inland. This approach permitted Holland Smith to land his Marines at the rear of the Japanese who held heavily fortified lines in the south of the island near Tinian Town. The outcome of the battle against the island's 9,000 defenders was never in doubt. The LVTs amphibious capability allowed the Marines to execute a classic surprise landing.

Sterner tests lay ahead for the LVT and the Marines under General Holland M. Smith. The new B-29 was taking heavy losses over Japan and there were no fighters with sufficient range to escort the big bombers from Saipan or Tinian. An intermediate stop was needed that could provide a landing site for damaged B-29s and a launch point for fighter escort over Japan. The island chosen was Iwo Jima.

N O T E S

¹John W. R. Taylor, Combat Aircraft of the World (New York: G. P. Putnam's Sons, 1969), p. 455.

²Robert D. Heinl and John A. Crown, The Marshalls: Increasing the Tempo (Washington D.C.: Historical Branch, G-3 Division, Headquarters, United States Marine Corps, 1954), p. 127.

³Heinl and Crown, The Marshalls, p. 27.

⁴Carl W. Hoffman, Saipan: The Beginning of the End (Washington, D.C.: Historical Division, Headquarters, United States Marine Corps, 1950), p. 18.

⁵Ibid., p. 20.

⁶Ibid., map 2.

⁷Marine Corps Schools, Amphibious Operations, The LVT and LVT(A) (Quantico: Marine Corps Schools, 1948), p. 11.

⁸Food Machinery Corporation, Water Buffalo (Mimeographed Historical/Technical pamphlet, no location: 1944), p. 4.

⁹Lt. J. I. Williamson's letter to the Special Marine Corps Amphibian Tractor Board, 5 May 1948.

¹⁰Hoffman, Saipan, p. 51.

¹¹Ibid., p. 52.

¹²2nd Amtrac Battalion, Operation Order No. 1, Forager (In the field: 2nd Amtrac Battalion, 1944), p. 2.

¹³Henry I. Shaw, Bernard C. Nalty, and Edwin T. Turnbladh, Central Pacific Drive, Vol. III of The History of the United States Marine Corps Operations in World War II (5 vols.; Washington D.C.: Historical Branch, G-3 Division, Headquarters, United States Marine Corps, 1966), p. 245.

¹⁴Ibid., p. 246.

¹⁵Hoffman, Saipan, p. 35.

¹⁶Ibid., p. 37.

¹⁷Ibid., p. 41.

¹⁸Shaw, Nalty, and Turnbladh, Central Pacific Drive, p. 250.

[19] Hoffman, Saipan, p. 34.

[20] 2nd Amtrac Battalion, Operations Order No. 1, Forager, Annex A, Special Landing Instruction for LVT Personnel, p. 7.

[21] Ibid.

[22] Ibid., p. 9.

[23] 2nd Amtrac Battalion, Operations Order No. 1, Forager, Appendix 1 to Annex A, Special Instructions for LVT Personnel, p. 1.

[24] 2nd Amtrac Battalion, Special Action Report (In the field: 2nd Amtrac Battalion, 1944), p. 1.

[25] Ibid.

[26] 715th Amphibian Tractor Battalion, Special Action Report (In the field: 715th Amphibian Tractor Battalion, 1944), p. 1.

[27] Shaw, Nalty, and Turnbladh, Central Pacific Drive, p. 264.

[28] 2nd Amtrac Battalion, Special Action Report, p. 6.

[29] Ibid., p. 2.

[30] Shaw, Nalty, and Turnbladh, Central Pacific Drive, p. 269.

[31] Hoffman, Saipan, p. 50.

[32] 715th Amphibian Tractor Battalion, Special Action Report, p. 3.

[33] Ibid.

[34] Shaw, Nalty, and Turnbladh, Central Pacific Drive, p. 273.

[35] 2nd Amtrac Battalion, Special Action Report, p. 3.

[36] 5th Amtrac Battalion, Special Action Report, (In the field: 5th Amtrac Battalion, 1944), p. 1.

[37] 2nd Amtrac Battalion, Special Action Report, p. 3.

[38] Ibid.

[39] 715th Amphibian Tractor Battalion, Special Action Report, p. 2.

[40] 2nd Amtrac Battalion, Special Action Report, pp. 3-4.

[41] Hoffman, Saipan, p. 164.

[42] Ibid., p. 60.

[43]Ibid., p. 56.

[44]Ibid., pp. 227-228.

[45]Ibid., p. 245.

[46]Ibid., p. 246.

[47]Interview with Master Sergeant C. J. Peterson, USMC, 13 June 1975.

[48]2nd Amtrac Battalion, Special Action Report, Enclosure B, p. 1.

[49]Ibid., p. 2.

[50]2nd Amtrac Battalion, Special Action Report, p. 6.

[51]Lt. Col. Louis B. Metzger letter to Special Marine Corps Amphibian Tractor Board, 17 May 1948.

[52]Holland M. Smith, Coral and Brass (New York: Charles Scribner's Sons, 1949), p. 201.

PART VII

TRACTION IN THE BLACK SAND

Iwo Jima translated means Sulphur Island, an appropriate name because of sulphur deposits just below the surface all over the island. During much of its history it was a desolate, sparsely populated spot of land whose inhabitants scratched a bare living from sugar and sulphur refining and farming in the sub-tropical climate. It is geologically a new island, thrust up from the ocean floor as the visible tip of a volcano now inactive. The island's volcanic origin also gave its beaches black sand, sand that was to be burned into the memory of thousands of Marines who were to attack Iwo Jima during February 1945.

Iwo Jima is part of the Bonin Islands which in turn are part of a larger grouping of islands known to the Japanese as the Nanpo Shoto. This chain stretches from Tokyo Bay south for a distance of 750 miles, coming to within 300 miles of the Marianas Islands. Few of these islands were militarily important when World War II opened, but Chichi Jima and Iwo Jima became of the utmost importance as planners looked beyond the Marianas. Chichi Jima was the primary harbor in the Bonins but was too rugged for extensive airfields. By contrast, Iwo Jima had no significant harbor but possessed a plateau suitable for extensive airfield construction. In 1943, one airfield had been completed by the Japanese and twenty aircraft were stationed there.[1] Two additional airfields were also constructed, but by July 1944, most of the island's air complement had been destroyed by American Attacks.[2]

The strategic significance of Iwo Jima crystallized with the progress of the war. On 12 August 1944, the Joint War Planning Committee of the Joint Chiefs of Staff issued a plan for the seizure of the Bonins which listed the operation as desirable to provide fighter cover for bomber operations against Japan, to deny the strategic outposts to the enemy, to provide air defenses for positions in the Marianas, and to provide air fields for staging bombers against Japan.[3] During this period and after, final reviews were taking place on possible attacks on Formosa or the China Coast, as the terminal operations of the Central Pacific Drive. It was determined by Admiral Nimitz that both operations were of questionable value since forces of the size required were not available, and the seizure of Iwo Jima and Okinawa - for which suitable forces were available - would accomplish substantially the same objectives. Admirals Nimitz and King conferred over this situation and King, as a member of the Joint Chiefs of Staff, proposed to that body the seizure of Okinawa and Iwo Jima. On 3 October 1944, the JCS accepted Admiral King's proposal and issued the directive which guided the Pacific War to its conclusion. It provided for the capture of Luzon in the Philippines by 20 December 1944, the acquisition of Iwo Jima by 20 January 1945, and the seizure of Okinawa by 1 March 1945.[4] General Holland M. Smith, Commanding General of the newly-created Fleet Marine Force Pacific command, received word from Admiral Nimitz on 9 October 1944 that Iwo Jima would definitely be the objective for the next Central Pacific attack.[5]

The overall commander for Iwo Jima was Admiral Raymond A. Spruance and General Smith himself was designated Commander of Expeditionary Troops. The Marine forces immediately available for the operation were the 3rd,

4th, and 5th Marine Divisions, which were assigned to the Fifth (V) Amphibious Corps, commanded by General Harry Schmidt, Smith's immediate subordinate in the chain of command and commander of the landing forces. With the designation of the forces available, the LVT picture was also set. The 2nd Armored Amtrac Battalion, with sixty-eight LVT(A)4s would provide the armored amtrac support. Four battalions of cargo amtracs, the 3rd, 5th, 10th and 11th, would provide the troop-carrying amtracs for the landing and subsequent logistics support. These battalions were equipped with the LVT(2) and the LVT(4) plus the latest modicications. A new cargo amphibian was in production, but it was not available for Iwo Jima. The new LVT(3) would be used for the first time on Okinawa.

At the time of designation, the experienced 3rd Marine Division was on Guam reorganizing after its capture of that island. The 4th Marine Division, veteran of Roi-Namur, Saipan, and Tinian, had just returned to its camp site on the island of Maui. Although the new 5th Division would see combat for the first time, it was composed of veterans who had served with other divisions and who spread the hard lessons of combat among the new recruits. The 5th Division embarked for Hawaii during August 1944 and made its camp there on the big island. Because all major planning staffs in the chain of command were in the area of the Hawaiian Islands, except the 3rd Marine Division in Guam, planning was greatly facilitated as was completion of the details of what was to be the Corps' toughest fight.

While American planning was underway, the Japanese were harboring no illusions about the fate of Iwo Jima. They were well-aware that the island was only three hours flying time from Tokyo and was suitable for development as a major air base. The island also held special significance for the Japanese people who claimed Iwo Jima by right of colonization as early as 1593 when it was first discovered by the Japanese explorer Sadayori Ogasawara.[6] The Marines were literally attacking Japanese soil in the inner defense ring of the Empire.

The work to fortify Iwo Jima began in earnest during the invasion of the Marshalls. The Japanese high command could see that the Carolines-Marianas defense line was in danger and the inner defense ring had to be strengthened to gain time to prepare the homeland for the expected invasion. By April 1944, the strength of Iwo Jima had climbed to 5,000 Army troops with thirteen artillery pieces, 200 light and heavy machine guns, fourteen 120 mm coast defense guns, twelve heavy anti-aircraft guns, and thirty 25 mm dual mount anti-aircraft guns.[7] In May the Emperor appointed a new commander of the island defense forces, General Tadamichi Kuribayashi, a tough martinet who had served in Manchuria and who commanded the Imperial Guards prior to his appointment. Kuribayashi had a keen appreciation of American Military potential opposing him because as a captain he had served as an attache in the United States for two years in the late 1920s. During this period he had written in a letter to his wife:

> The United States is the last country in the world that Japan should fight. Its industrial potentiality is huge and fabulous, and the people are energetic and versatile. One must never underestimate the American's fighting ability.[8]

When Tojo gave Kuribayashi command, he emphasized that the eyes of the entire nation were focused on Iwo Jima.[9]

The new commander arrived on the island during June 1944, in time to witness heavy air attacks that reduced his aircraft complement to near zero. Kuribayashi's ideas on the defense of the island were derived from observation of the futility of past Japanese attempts to defend the beachhead and to attempt banzai counterattacks that wasted lives. His approach was to construct defenses not at the water's edge where they would be destroyed by naval gunfire, but in depth throughout the island. The beaches were to be defended by sighting weapons to fire along the long axis of the beach and emplacing only some infantry and automatic weapons at scattered strongpoints along the shore. Further, Kuribayashi issued directives against the fanatical suicide counterattacks because even though it was to be a defense to the death, he would conduct it to exact the maximum loss of American life, and that meant staying in position rather than charging the Americans. His measures were controversial, but he had his way.

To conduct a prolonged defense of the island, construction of the heaviest fortifications were required to withstand bombs and naval gunfire. Kuribayashi had witnessed American air attacks and was determined to burrow underground for protection and build the toughest pillboxes possible above ground for his guns. Concrete of superior quality was possible when the volcanic ash of the island was mixed with cement and walls were as much as four-feet thick of reinforced concrete. Sand was piled in front of some positions for as much as fifty feet for additional protection. The pillboxes were relatively blind with narrow fields of fire and small openings for additional protection of the inhabitants, but the large number of positions overcame this limitation.[10] The main communications center for this vast fortification called Iwo Jima was a mammoth room seventy-five feet underground that measured 150 feet long by seventy feet wide with a roof ten feet thick and walls five feet thick, and twenty radios with operators on every two to three radios.[11] If the Americans wanted to kill the Japanese, it was Kuribayashi's intention that American bombs and naval gunfire would not be the instruments of death.

The American Marine with his rifle would personally have to come and get them.

American intelligence concerning this activity was initially derived primarily from aerial photographs and captured Japanese maps from the Saipan campaign. However, unlike the aerial photo scarcity encountered before Saipan, Navy photographic squadrons proceeded to amass aerial photos with no fewer than 371 sorties over the island to take pictures. This excellent coverage resulted in the creation of a photo map of great detail on 6 December 1944, and even this was updated with later photographic coverage. Close-in photographic coverage of the beach areas was provided by submarines and beach studies were conducted which indicated that the traction in the loose sand would be difficult even for men. Only tracked vehicles were expected to move effectively. American intelligence noted that defenses were sited to repel the invasion once it had landed and discerned one of the two main lines of defense which stretched the entire width of the island. American experts could tell it was going to be a tough fight, but they made two significant errors. The first was the underrating of Japanese strength on the island by estimating 13,000 to 14,000 personnel while the real figure lay between 21,000 and 23,000. This underestimation was due to the excellent camouflage employed by the Japanese which masked their true defensive strength to aerial photographs. The second error was that intelligence analysts felt the Japanese would repeat their past tactics of attempting to throw the invasion back into the sea at the water's edge by concentrated fire of all available weapons and banzai counterattacks.[12] This view was supported by the past defensive lines, clues that the toughest battle would be inland and after the landing rather than at the beach. It would be a rude shock when the

Japanese later coolly remained silent during the early phases of the landings and then opened fire with devastating effect after the landing had moved inland some distance.

Against this formidable island the Marines planned to employ 70,647 assault troops, augmented by Army garrison troops and naval personnel assigned to shore duty in construction and beach logistics, bringing the expeditionary force up to 111,308 men.[13] The ship-to-shore landing movement for this massive effort was to be spearheaded by LVTs. The first five waves of the landing would use 400 LVTs carrying eight battalions of the 4th and 5th Marine Divisions onto the southeastern beaches of Iwo Jima. The cargo tractors would be preceded by a wave of sixty-eight LVT(A)4s of the 2nd Armored Amtrac Battalion who in turn would be preceded by LCI gunboats firing rockets and 40 mm machine guns. The Iwo Jima plans gave primary emphasis to heavy gun power in the first wave by placing the LVT(A)4s in line formation so each vehicle could have maximum freedom of fire with its 75 mm howitzer and machine guns. The LVT(A)4s were to land and proceed inland for a short distance to assist the assault troops. Troop tractors were to land and discharge their troops at the beach and return to sea for logistics duties. The line of departure for this landing was 4,000 yards offshore and a thirty-minute run was expected. Interval between waves of LVTs was to be 250-300 yards.[14] The net width of the landing beaches for the two assault divisions was 3,500 yards, which put an armored amtrac every fifty yards as the first wave approached the beach. It was a planned power punch.

The scheme of maneuver once ashore was simple. The 4th and 5th Marine Divisions would land abreast with the 3rd Marine Division in Reserve, the 5th on the left. The extreme left-hand regiment of the 5th was the 28th

Marine Regiment led by Colonel Harry "The Horse" Liversedge, who was famous for his outstanding combat leadership in the Munda campaign in the Solomons. This regiment was to attack straight across the narrow neck of land and then turn southwest to take Mount Suribachi. It was this regiment that was later to have the honor of staging the most famous combat picture of World War II, the flag raising on Mount Suribachi. Other regiments of the division were to attack forward, then turn right and attack northeast up the long axis of the island. The 3rd Marine Division was to land over the same beaches about three days after D-Day (D+3) and move into the center between the 4th and 5th Marine Division. Both the 4th and 5th Tank Battalions would land on call over their parent division's beaches for support in the early phases of the landing because it was anticipated that the tanks' firepower would be needed to get the troops off the beach quickly.

A significant point should be noted here with respect to the use of LVTs at Iwo Jima. The island rose steeply out of the sea and the beaches were open to the full force of the sea, complete with pounding surf; there was no offshore reef. Therefore, one of the primary motives for using the LVT in the assault mode was not present at Iwo Jima. At Tarawa, the Marshalls, and Saipan, the fringing reef around the islands necessitated the LVT to land the attacking waves of troops, but at Iwo Jima there were other requirements. Even though intelligence experts underestimated the size of the enemy garrison and were not able to foresee the change of Japanese tactics, they did predict a tough fight, and judging from past Japanese practice, they expected it at the beach. Analysts considered the armored protection of the LVT and the firepower of the armored amtrac to be absolutely necessary to get the troops ashore against the anticipated

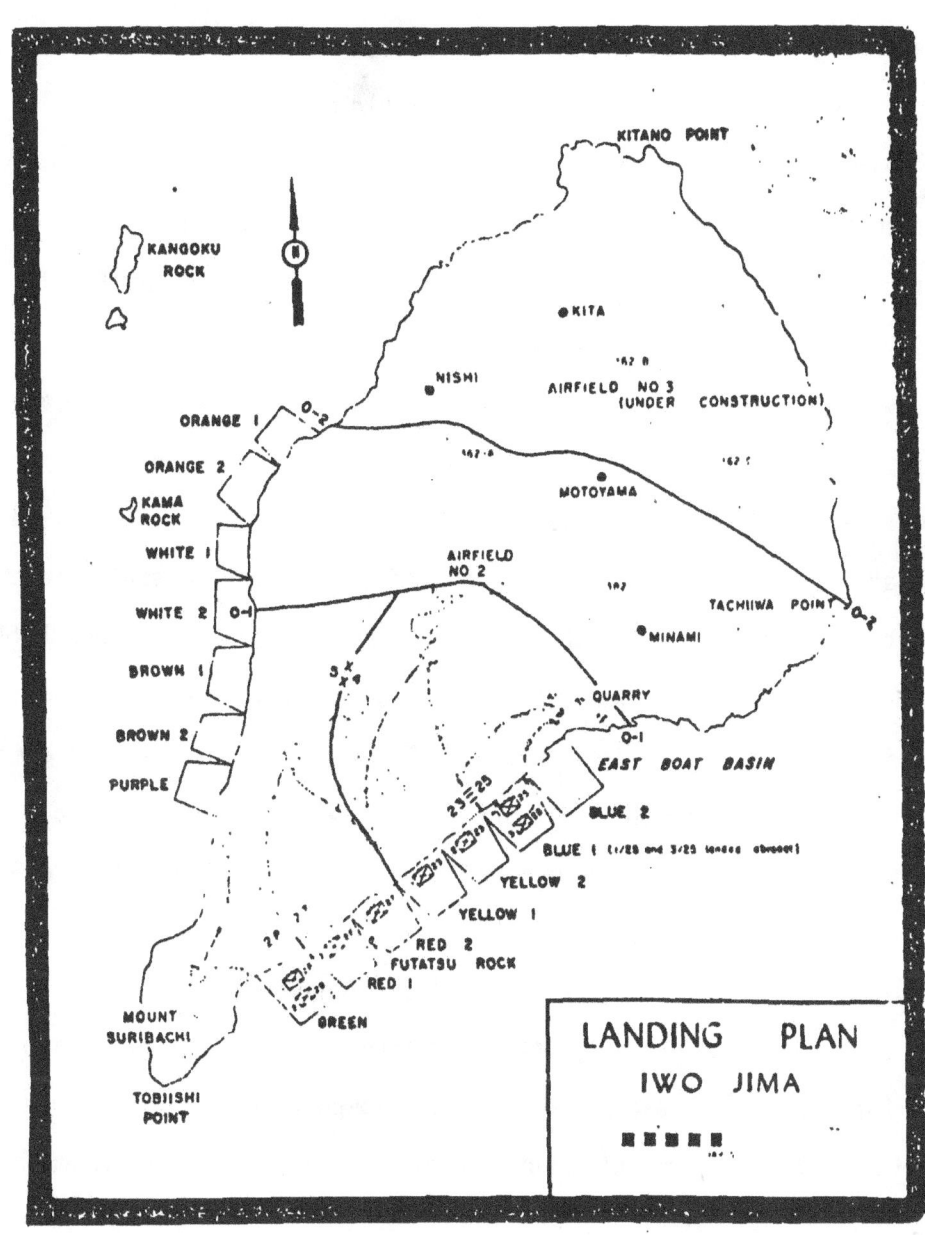

Map 15. Landing Plan, Iwo Jima.

resistance. Further, beach studies conducted by daring Underwater Demolitions Teams of the Navy (UDTs) under the very noses of the defenders, revealed that the sand on the beaches would be loose and hard going for wheeled vehicles but tractors would manage more easily.[15] This consideration favored the use of LVTs not only to land the troops, but also to establish the early logistics effort until surfaced roads could be laid in the loose sand. The decision to use LVTs at Iwo Jima was to prove right on both counts.

However, before any troops could be landed in the LVTs and before troops could be expected to stay on the beaches, it was clear that Iwo Jima had to be thoroughly softened by bombardment. Iwo Jima received the most intensive and prolonged preparation given any objective in the Pacific in World War II.[16] The initial phase began on 8 December 1944, with B-24 bombers and Marine B-25 bombers striking the Bonin Islands for seventy-four consecutive days from high level with bombs with Iwo Jima receiving special attention. It should be noted that on 18 November D-Day was postponed from the original 20 January 1945 date set by JCS to 3 February 1945, and on 6 December 1944 it was moved to 19 February. Both adjustments were made due to the lack of naval forces, which were still engaged in unexpectedly tough fighting in the Philippine Islands under MacArthur.[17] These postponements allowed greater time for preparation by the bombers which were attempting to neutralize the airfield, destroy fixed gun positions, and unmask additional targets. These raids used large numbers of 100-pound bombs and fragmentation bombs and were not intended to destroy the heavier bunkers and pillboxes. They did, however, destroy anti-aircraft positions, disrupt communications, and finally neutralize the airfield.[18] The Japanese found it necessary to detail 2,000 men, with as many as fifty men to a bomb crater, to keep the airfield active and on 2 January 1945, used 624 men, eleven trucks, three rollers, and two bulldozers for twelve hours to put airfield number 1 back into working order.[19] This effort was not enough and operations appear to have ceased on 3 January 1945. A captured list of aircraft using airfield number 1 shows two aircraft landing there on 3 January; there is no record of their ever having departed.[20] Despite their success against the airfield, the bombers did not achieve substantial destruction of heavier gun positions and pillboxes. On 9 February 1945, additional photo coverage of Iwo Jima showed the number of heavy installations of all types had actually increased![21] The lightweight bombs and the inability of the high-level bomber to achieve pin-point accuracy against small, hardened pillboxes, resulted in negligible impacts that threw the burden of destruction on naval gunfire and eventually on the ultimate weapon, the Marine rifleman.

Naval gunfire for Iwo Jima was an area of controversy. General Holland M. Smith, the Expeditionary Troops Commander, fought for additional naval gunfire preparation above and beyond that recommended by the Navy. Smith had seen the results of inadequate preparation at Tarawa and Saipan and did not want a repetition on a target as tough as Iwo Jima. As he later explained:

> My own study of early air photographs indicated that a situation of an incredible nature existed on the island. It was plain that Iwo Jima had fortifications the like and extent of which we had never encountered. Mindful of Tarawa, where most of the fortifications were above ground and were still standing when the Marine landed, my opinion was that far more naval gunfire was needed on an island five times the size of Tarawa, with many more times the number of defenses, most of them deep underground.

> I could not forget the sight of Marines floating in the lagoon or lying on the beaches at Tarawa, men who died assaulting defenses which should have been taken out by naval gunfire. At Iwo Jima, the problem was far more difficult. If naval guns could not knock out visible defenses, how could they smash invisible defenses except by sheer superabundance of fire?[22]

The first request forwarded by General Schmidt, Commander of the Landing Force, and strongly backed by General Smith, was for a preparation of ten days' duration by a cruiser division and three battleships.[23] The Navy, however, had planned a supporting attack, the first by carrier aircraft, against the Japanese aircraft industry on the mainland, a target so far untouched. Admiral Spruance's concern was that a prolonged bombardment at Iwo Jima offered the Japanese an opportunity to attack the amphibious task force from the mainland (only three hours away) using the feared Kamikaze tactics that did such great damage in the Philippines. The American carrier strike against the Japanese mainland also required the services of two new, powerfully armed, fast battleships, the North Carolina and the Washington, which were diverted from duty at Iwo Jima to escort the carrier force because both ships had the latest in anti-aircraft installations, a high-priority requirement in view of the suspected Kamikaze threat.[24] The net result was the Navy's firm decision to bombard Iwo Jima for no more than three days, even after General Schmidt proposed a four-day preparation in a subsequent discussion. It should be noted here that the Navy was further faced with conflicting strategic requirements because the same ships firing on Iwo Jima would also be delivering fires on Okinawa a short time later. This forced the ships to conserve ammunition because a prolonged bombardment would have exhausted their magazines with insufficient time to resupply and still meet the timetable for Okinawa which involved seven days of firing before D-Day on 1 April 1945.

Naval gunfire support at Iwo Jima prior to D-Day was executed by a force of four battleships, four heavy cruisers, one light cruiser, and sixteen destroyers, an insufficient force in view of the 724 priority A and B targets identified for destruction. Priority A targets threatened ships, aircraft, and UDT operations while priority B concerned threats to the landing force in its movement to shore. The bombardment commenced at 8:00 A.M. but unfavorable low clouds and poor visibility limited the effectiveness of the first day's firing. The second day was marked by Japanese unwillingness to withhold their fire completely as directed by their commander, General Kuribayashi, and a heavy exchange took place during covering operations in support of a UDT beach reconnaissance. The battleship <u>Nevada</u>, closing to point-blank range at 3,000 yards, had four men wounded from Japanese fire while the cruiser <u>Pensacola</u>, closing to 1,500 yards, took successive hits from a 150 mm gun which destroyed her command center, catapult airplane, and holed her hull. She withdrew with seventeen killed and 120 wounded, but the gallant ship stayed on station at a greater range and continued to fire in support of the UDT effort, ceasing fire only when surgical operations were underway or for blood transfusions. Further heavy casualties were taken by crews of twelve LCI gunboats assisting the UDT swimmers by supplying fire support from 1,000 yards out. During a forty-five minute exchange with heavy caliber Japanese guns, all twelve were damaged, one capsized and sank, and a total of seven crewmen were killed and 153 wounded. While these battles raged, the UDT swimmers managed to accomplish their mission with the loss of only one man. The UDT discovered no underwater minefields or underwater obstructions.[25]

The opposition experienced by the bombardment force on the second day did not inspire optimism; indeed, gloom prevailed. For the third and last day of preparation, Admiral Blandy, commander of the task force provided the naval gunfire support, approved a Marine recommendation that all available firepower be concentrated on the beaches. The ships closed to 2,500 yards, but unfavorable weather again interfered and results were less than desired. The overall assessment of the effort is inescapable. As ominously understated by Isely and Crowl, the preparation was "inadequate".[26]

Weather on the morning of D-Day was clear and calm, with unlimited visibility. Although some consideration was given to continuing naval bombardment for a fourth day, Admiral Blandy, concerned that weather would deteriorate and jeopardize the ship-to-shore movement, stayed firm on a three-day preparation bombardment. At 6:40 A.M. on 19 February, the pre-H-Hour bombardment began. H-Hour was set for 9:00 A.M. The battleships North Carolina and Washington, having returned from the raid on Japan, joined the bombardment, raising the total battleship count to six firing in support of the landing. In addition to the big ships, forty-two LCI gunboats fitted with 4.5-inch and 5-inch rockets, and 4.2-inch mortars began firing at 7:30 A.M. Almost 10,000 rockets were launched during the pre-H-Hour bombardment.[27] The signal to commence landing was given at 7:25 A.M. and in twenty minutes 400 tractors carrying the eight assault battalions were in the water and moving to rendezvous areas to form into waves as the pounding of the beaches continued. At 8:05 A.M., naval gunfire ceased and 120 fighters and bombers from the carriers, including twenty-four F4U Corsairs, a powerful fighter-bomber of Marine Fighter Squadron 124, swarmed to the attack with rockets, napalm, and machine guns. Pilots were given clear orders for this run from the

Deputy Air Commander Landing Force, Colonel Vernon E. Megee, USMC, who told them to "go in and scrape your bellies on the beach."[28] They did.

While the air attack proceeded, gun fire ships closed range for their final assault and at 8:25 A.M., bombardment was resumed, concentrating on the beaches and adjacent areas. The amtracs reported all in readiness to cross the line of departure at 8:15 A.M., and at 8:30 A.M. the pennant dipped on the Control Vessel, sending sixty-eight armored amtracs across the line of departure on time with waves of cargo amtracs following at 250 to 300 yard intervals. As the amtracs approached the beach, naval gunfire never ceased, but instead used a rolling barrage technique which shifted fire inland in 200 yard increments ahead of the troops. The overall effect of this tremendous pummeling was to stun the Japanese into temporary silence and inactivity. It is estimated that only five amtracs were put out of action by enemy fire during the initial movement to shore.[29] Naval bombardment was supplemented by further runs of Marine Fighter Squadron 124, which used forty-eight F4U Corsairs and F6F Hellcats to strafe the beach ahead of the troops. Pilots were ordered to pull out at 600 feet because of the presence of naval gunfire below that altitude.[30]

Problems began almost immediately with the loose sand on the steep beaches. As the first armored amtracs contacted the sand between 8:59 and 9:00 A.M., many could not get traction up the steep gradient of the beach. This was particularly true in the 5th Marine Division zone on the left where the armored amtracs, after failing to climb the incline, backed into the water and continued to supply overhead fire as the troops pushed inland. Armored amtracs in the 4th Marine Division were more successful, although everywhere the sand was loose, deep, and difficult. Cargo amtracs, not required to penetrate far inland, stopped near the water's edge to

Figure 31. The first waves of LVT(4)s head for beaches at Iwo Jima. Note the Naval Gunfire Ships, including a battleship, well inside the line of departure.

Figure 32. LVT(4)s churning for the shoreline. This is one of the later waves of LVTs.

discharge troops. Even troops found the sand sucking in over their boot tops and many, loaded with packs weighing up to 100 pounds, found just moving forward difficult.

After about fifteen minutes, penetrations of up to 300 yards inland were made, but by then the Japanese began to recover from the tremendous naval fire they had received and concentrated mortars and artillery on the LVT and other vehicles attempting to move around on the beach. To add to this increasing litter of damaged vehicles at the water's edge, many LCVPs, which carried later waves of troops, were stuck with their ramps buried in the loose sand, unable to retract with the rough surf, and broached sideways to the shore. There they remained until salvage could later extricate them, and so they added to a litter that was among the worst seen in amphibious operations. Tanks of Company A, 5th Tank Battalion landed at 9:25 A.M., but had great difficulty getting ashore, and four tanks broke their tracks and one had its engine drowned before they found an exit off the beach.[31]

Inland, progress was slow and little room yet existed in the early hours to establish supply dumps on the beach. Marston Matting, hinged steel plates connected together and used for the first time to establish quick roads over the sand, had not yet been laid to permit wheeled vehicles to operate. In this situation, the LVT became the primary means of getting the supplies to the troops. On the initial run into the beach, each cargo LVT carried 700 pounds of high priority cargo to be dumped on the beach and used immediately by the combat troops. It was anticipated that from one-half to two-thirds of these supplies, consisting mostly of water, ammunition, rations, signal equipment, and medical supplies, would be lost to enemy fire or washed out to sea, but recovery exceeded all

Figure 33. Two LVTs in action during the early phases of the landing. The leading vehicle has just received a direct hit from Japanese artillery.

Figure 34. This is an early example of the terrible beach litter that clogged efforts to land supplies.

expectations because sixty to seventy percent was retrieved and stacked by troops and advanced elements of the shore party landing in the sixth wave.[32] Later runs by the LVTs went directly from supply ships and floating dumps offshore to front line troops, a situation which continued through 22 February in the 5th Marine Division zone, and through 25 February in the 4th Division's area. Up until these dates, ninety percent of the cargo for these two divisions was carried directly from the sea to the troops in cargo LVTs.[33] Even after these days, LVTs were extensively used to move supplies because of poor roads and very rough terrain.

This intensive application of the LVT produced rapid mechanical deterioration and after four day's hard service, the number of cargo LVTs shrank from 400 to 267, a definite handicap in the early days of the operation and in part due to the recurrence of an old issue.[34] As in the Marshalls, problems were once again experienced with the LST crews that carried the LVTs to the objective area. LSTs were reluctant to draw near the line of departure on D-Day, thus lengthening the run for the LVTs, and later, they refused to service any LVT except those they had carried. Most of the experienced LST crews of previous campaigns had been sent to the Philippines and Iwo Jima had green crews whose indoctrination was not complete. An innovation provided by LST mother ships was bunks, hot baths, and food for weary LVT crews forced to work continuously all day and sometimes at night during the early days of the landing.[35]

Refueling of the LVTs also became a problem. Bowser boats were too few in number and too hard to find. Medium landing craft, as well as the lighter Bowser boats, were bobbing about too much in the heavy seas to effect safe refueling. The only method that seemed to work was the slow one of ferrying gasoline drums from attack transports to the LSTs which in turn conducted refueling operations.[36]

The strain of this logistics work was lightened to some extent by three companies of DUKWs competently handled by their Army crews. Also, a new, small amphibian vehicle was working hard on the scene. This was the M29C Weasel, a small, fully tracked cargo carrier with a very light ground pressure of 1.9 pounds per inch (psi), making it very mobile in the loose sand. It carried its payload of 1,200 pounds smartly about the island considering its tiny sixty-five horsepower engine, could travel thirty-six mph on land but only four mph in water, and was not considered suitable for the open water travels of the larger LVT.[37]

The fighting slowly moved inland against the toughest forticications the Marines had ever faced. Kuribayashi had constructed two main lines of resistance across the island with a secondary line in the far northern part of the island. Due to the inadequate preliminary bombardment, a large number of the fortifications remained to be taken by artillery, tanks, flamethrowers, and, as always in war, finally the rifleman.

The 3rd Marine Division was brought ashore on 24 February 1945, and with it came its 3rd Tank Battalion. A total of three tank battalions or 150 tanks were on the island to provide critically needed gun power for destroying pillboxes. Against these heavy fortifications, the less powerful howitzer of the LVT(A)4 was not effective; the higher velocity 75 mm gun of the M4A2 Sherman tank provided almost twice the hitting power of the short-barreled 75 mm howitzer in the LVT(A)4. The LVT(A)4 supplied direct fire during the critical early hours of the landing but was rapidly replaced by the early-arriving tanks.

As the drive proceeded slowly along the northern axis of the island,

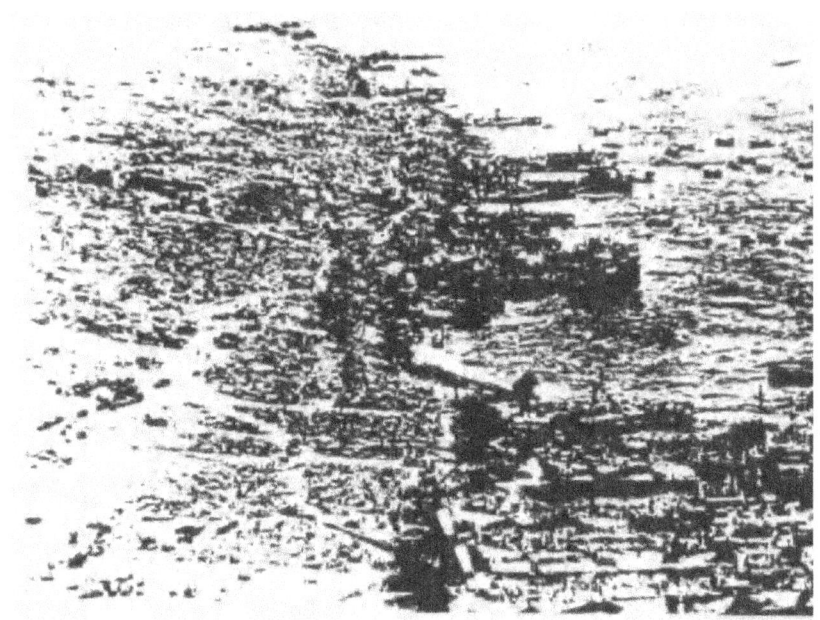

Figure 35. The beachhead in the later stages of development after the troops had pushed inland. This is a view from Suribachi showing the workhorse LST unloading supplies.

Figure 36. This view shows the hectic logistic activity within the beachhead. Note the vast array of shipping out to sea.

LVT(A)4s floating in the ocean attempted to shell Japanese caves lining the cliffs that faced on the sea. Each time this was tried, however, the armored amtracs tended to spray their fire over a wide area and were forced to cease fire because their wild shooting endangered friendly troops. This is directly attributable to the lack of gyro-stabilization in the turret of the LVT(A)4 and snap shooting when troops are close is not an acceptable practice. Their fire remained accurate on land and they were used in the direct fire mode where tanks could not be obtained.

As the campaign neared its final phase, the fighting never ceased. It remained a pillbox-by-pillbox destruction contest with no quarter given or asked by the Japanese defenders. Casualties were exacted from the Marines to the last and General Kuribayashi himself perished somewhere in the northern part of the island by unknown means. Some experts say he participated in one of the few banzai attacks that were staged but others feel that he may have committed suicide along with many other Japanese soldiers who preferred death to surrender. The General had done his job well. As of 26 March 1945, when the island was secured, only 216 Japanese had been captured and the rest of the 21,000 to 23,000 defenders had died; Marine casualties totaled 5,885 killed or died of wounds, and 17,272 wounded. Experts inspecting the fortifications at Iwo Jima reported they had never seen a position so thoroughly defended. Isely and Crowl stated in their excellent analysis of the campaign, "Comparisons are difficult, but it is probable that no other given area in the history of modern war has been so skillfully fortified by nature and by man."[38]

In surprising contrast to the ferocity of the fight on Iwo Jima, casualties were light among the LVT personnel. The following table gives figures for the four cargo LVT battalions (each numbering about 500 personnel):

	Wounded/Died of Wounds	Wounded
3rd Amtrac Battalion	8	17
5th Amtrac Battalion	10	35
10th Amtrac Battalion	8	27
11th Amtrac Battalion	2	34

Source: Whitman S. Bartley, Iwo Jima: Amphibious Epic (Washington, D.C.: Historical Branch, G-3 Division, Headquarters, United States Marine Corps, 1954), p. 221.

Separate figures are not available for the 2nd Armored Amtrac Battalion, but casualty counts appear to be low for this unit also. The explanation for the low casualty figures is in part due to the heavy logistical use of the cargo LVT behind the lines which kept it out of front line action after the early days, and the heavy pre-H-Hour bombardment which stunned the Japanese into silence and allowed the LVTs to land the early waves relatively unmolested. Also, tanks landing early replaced the armored amtracs and lowered their overall exposure to the heaviest fighting.

The vehicles used at Iwo Jima differed little from those used at Saipan. The principal vehicle modification was the addition of machine gun shields to protect the operators of the vehicle's two machine guns mounted forward. This was a recommendation forwarded by amtrac personnel as a result of the Saipan landing and incorporated at the factory.

The true significance of Iwo Jima in the history of the development of the LVT was its use on an island that did not have a coral reef. The LVT was now more than just a means of landing over a coral reef and represented the desire of the commanders to supply the troops with armor protection and mobility during the critical early phases of the landings. The mobility of the LVT in difficult terrain conditions was never more clearly demonstrated than at Iwo Jima when they managed to move over the black sand with the vitally needed supplies during the first four days of fighting. Isely and Crowl supply a succinct evaluation,

> . . . Without the cargo amphibian tractors, however, and especially the later model equipped with a ramp, it is impossible to see how any advance could have been sustained, for these almost alone supplied the fighting troops during the first several days of the assault.[39]

This evaluation is for more than just a dull routine of shuttling supplies to the troops and evacuating casualties to the ships. The hectic role of the amtrac is described graphically by a Marine Captain who was at Iwo Jima:

> Whatever happened the amtracs kept coming - they kept coming in all night. They were the only link between the 40,000 men ashore and the ships. They had to keep coming. One tractor, on its way to the front with ammunition, was diverted into action by a Marine patrol held up by some Japs protecting an artillery position. When the Japs attacked with hand grenades the amtrac crew fought them off with their machine gun, but not until a grenade had landed in the tractor and wounded one of the Marines. The crew killed eight of the enemy and occupied the position, turned it over to the infantry, and went on its way.[40]

Iwo Jima was declared secured on 26 March 1945, but even before this airfield construction had started behind the lines. The first B-29 in distress landed at Iwo Jima on 4 March on the then-usable airfield number 1. By 26 March, thirty-five other Superfortresses in trouble had landed, and by the end of the war 2,251 B-29s made emergency landings with 24,761 crewmen aboard, of which a large number would have lost their lives if Iwo had not been available.[41] Iwo Jima became a major staging base in the B-29 air war over Japan and the launch base for P-51 Mustang fighter cover for the bombers. Beyond this, it stands as a monument to the highest type of courage that won World War II. Fierce battles have been fought in Korea and Viet Nam, but the twenty-four Medals of Honor, many of them posthumous, fully justify the words of Admiral Nimitz in his Pacific Fleet Communique of 17 March 1945: "Among the Americans who served on Iwo Island, uncommon valor was a common virtue."[42]

As this epic became history and legend, the last battle in the Central Pacific campaign was nearing. It was to be the largest amphibious operation yet and would have to brave the "Divine Wind", the Kamikaze, before it would capture the island called Okinawa.

NOTES

[1] Whitman S. Bartley, *Iwo Jima: Amphibious Epic* (Washington, D.C.: Historical Branch, G-3 Division, Headquarters, United States Marine Corps, 1954), p. 6.

[2] George W. Garand and Truman R. Strobridge, *Western Pacific Operations*, Vol. IV of *The History of United States Marine Corps Operations in World War II* (5 Vols.: Washington D.C.: Historical Branch, G-3 Division, Headquarters, United States Marine Corps, 1971), p. 452.

[3] Bartley, *Iwo Jima*, p. 20.

[4] Ibid., p. 22.

[5] Ibid., p. 23.

[6] Ibid., p. 2.

[7] Garand and Strobridge, *Western Pacific Operations*, p. 449.

[8] Ibid., p. 451.

[9] Ibid., p. 450.

[10] Bartley, *Iwo Jima*, p. 13.

[11] Ibid., p. 14.

[12] Garand and Strobridge, *Western Pacific Operations*, pp. 473-475.

[13] Ibid., p. 475.

[14] Bartley, *Iwo Jima*, p. 52.

[15] Ibid., p. 28.

[16] Ibid., p. 39.

[17] Garand and Strobridge, *Western Pacific Operations*, p. 469.

[18] Ibid., pp. 485-486.

[19] Ibid., p. 459.

[20] Bartley, *Iwo Jima*, p. 15.

[21] Garand and Strobridge, *Western Pacific Operations*, p. 486.

[22] Holland M. Smith, *Coral and Brass* (New York: Charles Scribner's Sons, 1949), p. 243-244.

[23] Ibid., p. 244.

[24] Jeter A. Isely and Philip A. Crowl, *The United States Marines and Amphibious War* (Princeton: Princeton University Press, 1951), p.446.

[25] Garand and Strobridge, *Western Pacific Operations*, pp. 495-497.

[26] Isely and Crowl, *U.S. Marines and Amphibious War*, p. 446.

[27] Garand and Strobridge, *Western Pacific Operations*, p. 503.

[28] Robert Sherrod, *History of Marine Aviation in World War II* (Washington: Combat Forces Press, 1952), p. 347.

[29] Isely and Crowl, *U.S. Marines and Amphibious War*, p. 478.

[30] Sherrod, *Marine Aviation*, p. 347.

[31] Bartley, *Iwo Jima*, p. 57.

[32] Isely and Crowl, *U.S. Marines and Amphibious War*, p. 521.

[33] Ibid., p. 522.

[34] Ibid., p. 524.

[35] Ibid.

[36] Ibid.

[37] E. J. Hoffschmidt and W. H. Tantum, *United States Military Vehicles World War II* (Greenwich: WE Inc., 1970), p. 118.

[38] Isely and Crowl, *U.S. Marines and Amphibious War*, p. 486.

[39] Ibid., p. 521.

[40] Raymond Henri, "Logistics Afloat" in *The United States Marine Corps in World War II*, ed. S.E. Smith (New York: Random House, 1969), p. 769.

[41] Bartley, *Iwo Jima*, p. 210.

[42] Garand and Strobridge, *Western Pacific Operations*, p. 712.

PART VIII

BIGGEST FOR LAST

The decision that brought the Marines to the sands of Iwo Jima also took them to Okinawa. On 3 October 1944, the Joint Chiefs of Staff issued a directive giving the final objectives of the Pacific War. MacArthur was to invade the Philippines on 20 December 1944, Iwo Jima was set for 20 January 1945 (and later delayed as seen in Part VII), and Okinawa was targeted for 1 March 1945.[1] These final targets represented a shift from the former objectives of Formosa and the China coast to be used as staging areas for the eventual invasion of the Japanese home islands. Concern had grown that both Formosa and the China coast would require more troops than were available and after careful study it was concluded that Okinawa could be seized with far less force and offered a fully adequate staging area for mounting the invasion. The capture of Okinawa, after securing Iwo Jima to aid the air war, would provide the full range of required facilities for preliminary strategic bombing followed by a massive amphibious expedition against Japan itself.

Okinawa was strategically located only 350 nautical miles south of the southern Japanese home island of Kyushu and offered two major fleet anchorages, numerous locations for airfields, with three major existing airfields, and sufficient land area to train assault troops for the upcoming invasion. Okinawa is an irregularly shaped island, sixty miles long, with the jutting Motobu Peninsula at its widest point of eighteen

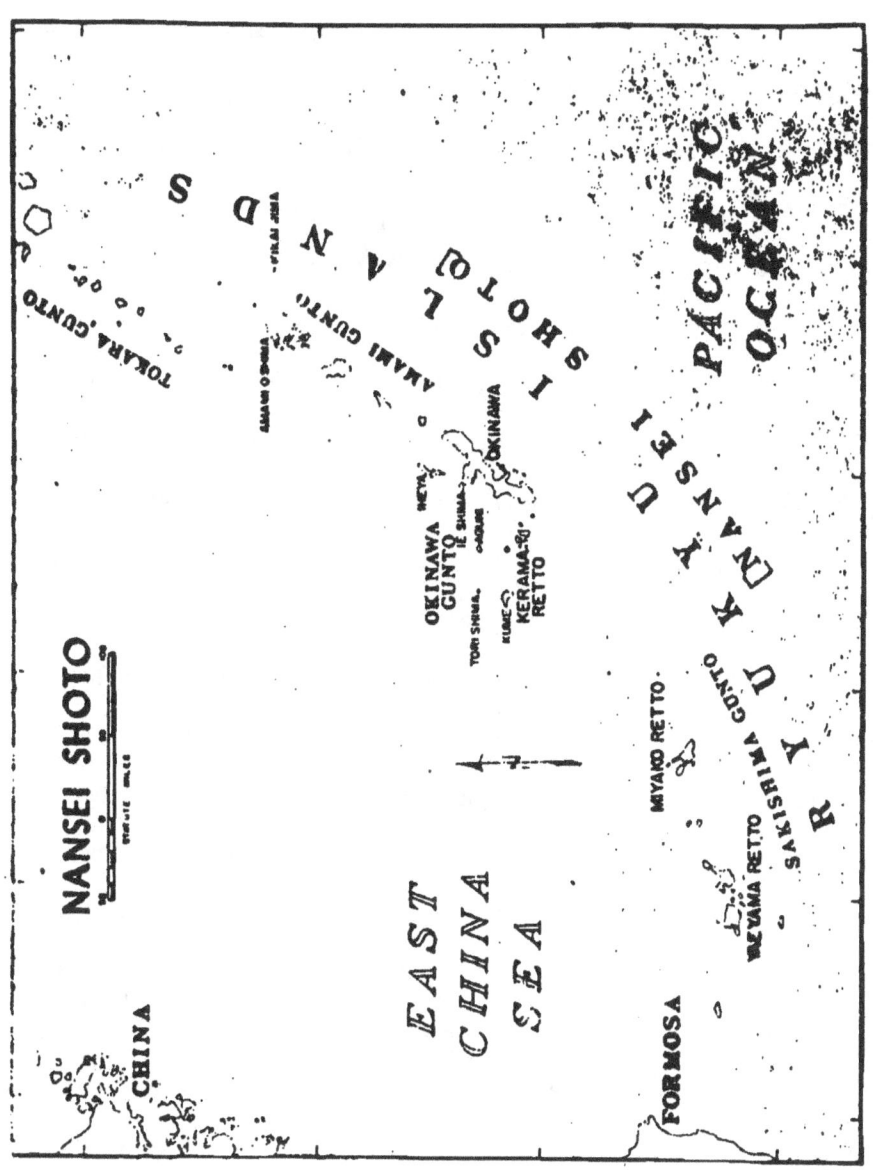

Map 16. Nansei Shoto.

miles, and the Ishikawa Isthmus its narrowest width of two miles. The northern two-thirds of the island is mountainous and covered with scrub pines with a rocky and percipitous shoreline; the southern one-third is rolling lowlands broken by deep ravines. Beaches in this area are reef-bound and often backed by sea cliffs. Usable beaches for a landing existed on the west coast near the town of Hagushi, on the east coast within the large fleet anchorage of Nakagusuku Wan, and south near the town of Minatogawa. In contrast to former island objectives of the Central Pacific drive, Okinawa had a significant civilian population of around 500,000, most of whom were farmers and some fishermen. About fifteen percent of the population lived in the major town of Naha in the south, which also contained port facilities.[2]

Okinawa remained in the background of the war until April 1944, when the Imperial General Headquarters, Japan's supreme agency for direction of the war, created the 32nd Army and assigned it the mission of improving the defenses of Okinawa and surrounding islands. By this time it was obvious that the outer defenses were crumbling and something had to be done to strengthen the inner lines. Prior to 1944, Okinawa boasted only a minor naval base and a few small army garrisons, but steps were taken immediately to increase the number of troops on the island and to use these troops to construct a defensive network to stop the Americans. As part of this construction, the Japanese implemented their new doctrine on island defense because it was clear to the Japanese on Okinawa, as it was to General Kuribayashi on Iwo Jima, that Americans could not be stopped on the beach. The combination of American naval gunfire, methodically destroying even heavy pillboxes, and pinpoint bombing from aircraft was too powerful to be overcome simply by beach defenses. The Japanese therefore adopted the same approach used on Iwo Jima of constructing one or more belts of defenses across the entire width of the island, well inland and away from the heavy preliminary bombardments on the beach. The objective of this defense was to exact the highest casualties from the enemy after they had landed in an attempt to bleed them to a standstill.

Major Japanese reinforcements arrived between June and August 1944 and included the veteran 9th Infantry Division with battle honors dating back to the Russo-Japanese War of 1904-05, the 24th Infantry Division (the largest tactical unit with over 14,000 Japanese and Okinawan conscripts), and the 62nd Infantry Division with fewer than 12,000 men, almost all infantry.[3] Beyond these three infantry divisions, there were many reinforcing units consisting of an armored regiment with 750 men organized into one light and one medium tank company, a tractor-drawn artillery battery, an infantry company, a maintenance company, an engineer platoon, and 9,000 naval personnel, few of whom were trained for infantry work. In addition, there were super-secret sea-raiding units not previously employed consisting of seven squadrons of one hundred hand-picked men and one hundred boats laden with explosives, charged to destroy amphibious shipping by suicide-ram tactics. Most of these units were stationed on Okinawa, but three were on Kerama Retto, an island group west of Okinawa.[4]

The strengthening of Okinawa's defenses focused on the south where two main lines of defense were constructed with the strongest anchored in the Shuri Region. Positions were constructed underground using the many natural caves in the area and each was mutually supporting. Also, many defenses were organized as reverse slope defenses, using the back side of a hill away from the enemy which permitted the defenders to shoot

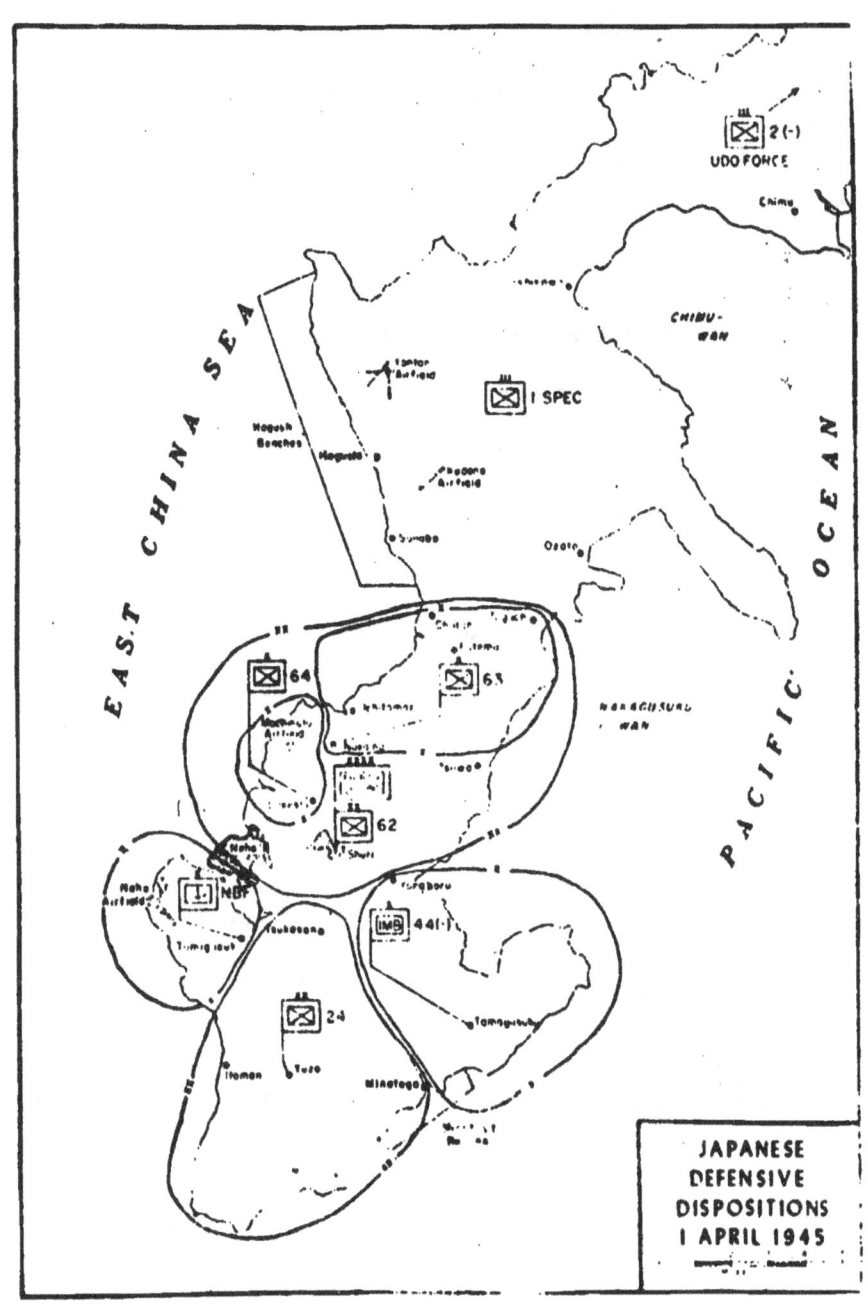

Map 17. Japanese Defensive Positions, 1 April 1945.

the exposed attackers off the skyline as they came over the top of the hill. The Japanese were applying all their hard-earned experience as they organized the island on a schedule to get them ready to meet the Americans when they came ashore. To keep the morale of the troops up, the commanders created a battle slogan:

> One Plan for One Warship
> One Boat for One Ship
> One Man for Ten of the Enemy or one Tank[5]

The landing force for this invasion was to be the largest in the history of the United States' Central Pacific Drive and consisted of two corps (one Army, one Marines) of infantry divisions, the III Amphibious Corps under Major General Roy S. Geiger, USMC, and the XXIV Corps, under Major General John R. Hodge, USA. The III Amphibious Corps included the 1st and 6th Marine Divisions, while the XXIV Corps had the 7th and 96th Infantry Divisions. In addition, the 77th Infantry Division was assigned to take Ie Shima and Kerama Retto, island groups west of Okinawa, the 2nd Marine Division was to stage a diversionary demonstration in the south, and the 27th Infantry Division was named the floating reserve. Within this massive force a large complement of LVTs from the 780th Amphibian Tank Battalion (USA), the 1st and 3rd Armored Amtrac Battalions, the 1st, 4th, 8th, and 9th Amtrac Battalions, and the 534th Amphibious Tractor Battalion (USA) would carry the troops ashore over the reef-blocked beaches of Hagushi and against the outlying islands off both east and west coasts.

American intelligence of the islands was meager at first but between 29 September 1944 and 28 March 1945, 224 photo reconnaissance missions were run over Okinawa which produced an accurate photo mosaic map of the area and rubber relief models to facilitate briefings. It was possible to see some of the enemy's strength in the south and intelligence analysts initially figured an enemy strength of 48,600. Thereafter, estimates varied widely as additional reports and information were received and reached a peak of 87,000 in January; by April the number had fallen to 75,000 men based on the news that a division had departed from Okinawa for the Philippines.[6] The actual total is not certain because the number of Okinawan home guard participants is not known; from available estimates, however, it appears there was a trained infantry of 67,000 men, an Okinawan home guard of about 23,500, and the Japanese Navy of 9,000 personnel.[7] This totals to 100,000 Japanese defenders versus an American assault landing force of 541,866 men.[8]

The plan for the main landings at Okinawa over the Hagushi beaches and the seizure of the outlying islands was a three-phase operation. Phase one would be seizure of the southern part of Okinawa because it was most suitable for airfields required to bomb Japan and for port facilities to stage naval expeditions. The second phase would capture the remainder of Okinawa and the large island of Ie Shima, on Okinawa's west coast, and the third phase would take additional bases in the archipelago. Eventually, the realities faced during the campaign reversed the first two phases and later logistical considerations and favorable progress eliminated the requirement for the third phase.[9]

The planning for the employment of LVTs followed the successful patterns of past landings. The first wave would be entirely LVT(A)4 armored amphibians, preceded by rocket and mortar-firing LCI gunboats, followed by five to seven waves of cargo amphibians of both the battle-tested LVT(4) and the new LVT produced by Borg-Warner, the LVT(3). To confuse enemy forces and immobilize them, the main landing at the Hagushi were to be loaded over its ramp. The Model B was only 24' long by 11' wide versus a 26' 1" length and 10' 8" width for the LVT(4).[11] Another feature was the addition of a four-speed and reverse automatic transmission which had successfully been powering the M5 tank and had proven its reliability and which relieved the driver from anticipating contact with the beach and shifting into a lower gear just before touching. This shifting had been the most difficult part of driving and was now eliminated. The suspension of the Model B used the time-proven torsilastic principle of previous amtracs and the same grouser proven optimum in early tests conducted by Food Machinery in 1943 and battle-proven since then. Borg-Warner was aware of the early lessons of combat vulnerability of the cargo LVT and had added 3/8 inch of armor to the cab and sides of the vehicle covering the engine and gasoline tank.[12]

The Continuing Board for the Development of Landing Vehicle, Tracked, the Navy's chief body for guiding the development of LVTs within the Bureau of Ships, had become interested in the Model B while it was being developed, and reviewed the vehicle's progress. It was clear that the increased cargo capacity of the Model B was justification for a contract and Borg-Warner at last received the green light to produce the LVT(3), the official designation given to the final version of the Model B. Although production of the LVT(3) commenced in April 1944, it was one year before it received its baptism of fire at Okinawa, a lag caused by the requirement to produce sufficient spare parts for the vehicle to replace battle damage and the need to train the crews and mechanics in the operation of the new components of the vehicle, particularly the transmission, prior to committing them to action.[13] The following is a further comparison between the LVT(3), the second ramped amphibian, and the first ramped vehicle, the LVT(4):

	LVT(3)	LVT(4)
Cargo Capacity (no armor)	12,000 lbs.	9,000 lbs.
Weight (empty)	26,600 lbs.	27,400 lbs.
Ground Clearance	19 inches	18 inches
Speed (land)	17 mph	20 mph
(water)	6 mph	7.5 mph
Cruising Radius (land)	150 miles	150 miles
(water)	75 miles	75 miles
Gasoline Load	130 gallons	140 gallons
Engine	Cadillac V-8 (two engines)	Continental radial W 670-9A
Horsepower	220 HP (each)	250 HP

Source: Robert J. Icks, "Landing Vehicles Tracked," in Armored Fighting Vehicles in Profile, ed. Duncan Crow (New York: Doubleday & Company, Inc., 1972), p. 162.

The LVT(3) was the culmination of the development of the cargo LVT during World War II because no further modifications were produced before the war ended. The LVT(3), with modifications including a covered cargo space, became the standard cargo LVT of the post-War Marine Corps. The key role played by the LVT in the Central Pacific drive was recounted in colorful language to new crewmen in an early LVT(3) training manual:

> Maybe you're new in this business, and maybe not - but either way you should have heard of the record the Bushmaster's mammy and pappy set at Bouganville, Tarawa, Kwajalein, Saipan and other places. They were the Alligator LVT(1) and the Water Buffalo LVT(2) - two damn fine tractors! Most of the guys who gave the Japs the old one-two punch at those islands will tell you it would have been murder to hit the beach in anything but an amphibian tractor. Anything else would have had its guts ripped open by the reefs surrounding the islands - and provided a sitting duck target for some slant-eyed son of heaven, ashore.[14]

As in previous operations, the LVTs were conveyed to their target, Okinawa, in LSTs, and because these ships did not contain adequate accommodations for large numbers of soldiers. The assault troops that were to ride the LVTs to the beach were transported most of the way to

Figure 41. Side view of the LVT(3).

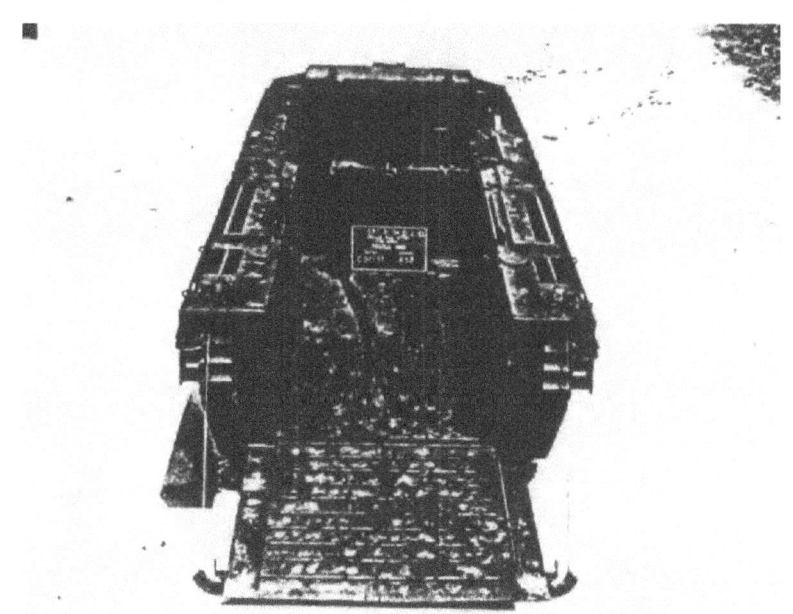

Figure 42. Rear view of the LVT(3) with ramp lowered.

Figure 43. The front view of the LVT(3). This shows the machine gun mount on the left and the attached armor plate.

Okinawa on the faster troop transport ships and then transferred to the LSTs at Ulithi Lagoon, a vast lagoon captured without resistance in September 1944, lying midway between the Marianas and the Palau Islands.

Carrier planes first struck Okinawa hard on 10 October 1944, with raids again on 3 and 4 January 1945. During this period, United States Navy submarines ranged the Pacific and fast carrier task forces were also striking Formosa and Tokyo to reduce the enemy's ability to reinforce the beleaguered garrison on Okinawa. By mid-February 1945, Okinawa was effectively isolated from support from the nearby homeland except for one potent force, the Kamikaze.

Because substantial American naval support was retained in the Philippines area when the fighting took an unexpectedly heavy turn, the date for Iwo Jima was set back twice. This in turn postponed the landing for Okinawa since the same naval gunfire forces at Iwo were also required at Okinawa. The final date for Okinawa was 1 April 1945.

The first American units to appear off Okinawa were the trusty minesweepers, clearing the way for the battleships to begin bombardment on 24 March 1945, as well as preparing the way for the seizure of the Kerama Retto on 26 March by the 77th Infantry Division. This latter operation proceeded on schedule using the LVT(4)s of the 534th Amphibian Tractor Battalion and LCI gunboats firing rockets and mortars ahead of them. Most of these landings were battalion-size or smaller and in two days the Kerama Retto was available for conversion to a valuable naval base and logistical staging area for the upcoming main landing at Okinawa.

On 26 March, during the landings at Kerama Retto, the Kamikaze struck the landing force for the first time. Between 26 and 31 March these planes rose from Okinawan airfields and damaged six ships including Admiral

Spruance's flagship, the <u>Indianapolis</u>; near misses accounted for damage to ten others.[15] This was the beginning of a deadly campaign that was to cause the United States Navy to suffer more men killed during the Okinawan campaign than either the Army or the Marines received fighting on the land.[16] It was the valiant work of the Navy, especially its picket ships (destroyers with early-warning missions), that allowed the Okinawa landing to proceed with clock-work precision. The total number of ships involved in the landings was a record 1,213 and these would have been lucrative targets for the Japanese had the Kamikaze been allowed to get through.[17] During the three-month campaign on Okinawa from 1 April to 1 July, anti-aircraft defenses coordinated by the Navy accounted for an astounding 7,830 Japanese aircraft destroyed.[18]

Naval gunfire commenced on 25 March and fired a total of 27,226 rounds, 5-inch caliber or larger, most of which was directed into the beaches and fell on virtually empty space. Due to the failure of American intelligence to discover fully the dispositions of the Japanese, it was felt that the Japanese would defend at the beaches as they had done in the past with the notable exception of Iwo Jima. In fact, there was little defense at the beach and little damage was done by the heavy naval gunfire preparation except to the airfield at Yontan. The main lines of defense to the south escaped a heavy pounding.

On 30 March, valuable support was given by Navy UDT swimmers who destroyed 2,900 underwater obstacles, most of them wooden posts six to eight inches in diameter, by hand-placed charges.[19] The UDT also supplied valuable intelligence, basically favorable, concerning the beach conditions at Hagushi.

There were calm seas and good weather for the landing on the morning of 1 April 1945. Air support orbited overhead as LSTs discharged their tractors at 7:00 A.M. H-Hour was set for 8:30 A.M. and prior to that hour the beaches were subjected to a fierce pummeling by ten battleships, nine cruisers, twenty-three destroyers, and 177 LCI gunboats. Unfortunately for the attackers, as already noted, this fire fell for the most part on empty space. Japanese response was only scattered, ineffective fire. The pennant dropped from the control ships at 8:00 A.M. and sent the first wave of LVT(A)4s across the line of departure, 4,000 yards offshore, behind mortar and rocket firing LCI gunboats. The run was estimated to take one-half hour. During this time the main battery fire of the battleships continued and 138 planes strafed the beaches. The landings proceeded on schedule and within twenty-five minutes the LVT waves were ashore with no losses to enemy fire. LVT(A)s moved to the flanks of their units to protect them during the landings. There were difficulties only in the sector of the 1st Marine Division where the rough reef caused some units to be late.[20] As the troops stormed out of their LVTs, they were greeted by an unusual silence. The Japanese were not there.

Later waves of troops were brought to the beach using the transfer line technique which established a rendezvous line seaward of the reef where troops were transferred from LCVPs to LVTs for the trip across the reef. Later, at high tide, direct beaching was possible for some of the landing craft, including those carrying tanks. The first tanks hit the beach within thirty minutes of the first wave using the new T-6 floatation gear; thirty minutes later, tanks were being directly beached by landing craft. The T-6 floatation gear, which worked very well in the calm waters off Okinawa, consisted of pontoons fastened to the M-4 tank by spot welds,

Figure 44. LVT(A)4s crossing the line of departure.

a makeshift steering device, and small, electrically detonated charges to detach the pontoons after the tank had landed. The tracks of the tanks provided the drive through the water.[21]

By 3:30 P.M. on D-Day the majority of assault forces were ashore. The advance inland was halted for the day between 4:00 and 5:00 P.M. to allow troops to dig positions and commence patrolling the front to find the enemy. The average penetration was a considerable 3,500 yards and both Yontan and Kadena airfields had been captured. L-Day on Okinawa (different letters used due to the many different landings executed at Okinawa - L-Day was used for the main landing) was an unqualified success.

After the first day, the fortunes of the two corps, the XXIV and the III Amphibious Corps, began to vary widely. The Army units of XXIV Corps were ordered to turn south and in so doing discovered the true strength of the Japanese defenses in the Shuri Castle area of southern Okinawa. Meanwhile, the Marines striking north were met by little or no resistance because the enemy had left only token forces to hold the area. The toughest fight for the Marines in the early days in the north was the fight for Motobu Peninsula where the rough mountainous country of that peninsula hid a Japanese force of over 1,000 men which required four days of close fighting to eliminate. Due to the rough terrain, neither tanks nor any type of LVT could be used to support the fighting.

The rapid progress of the Marines in the north led to the decision to capture Ie Shima, lying off northern Okinawa's west coast, ahead of schedule. It had been anticipated that the fight for Motobu Peninsula would require an amphibious landing, but naval forces that might have been required for that operation were now free to land the 77th Infantry Division against Ie Shima. The 77th had been at sea in transports waiting for the word to attack and had endured an attack of eight kamikazes which scored three hits and heavy loss of life to one of the regiments. As the day approached for the landing, observation planes and photos failed to disclose any sign of enemy activity. Despite this, the Commanding General, General Bruce, remained suspicious. Rather than land two companies on a daylight reconnaissance as had been suggested in view of the apparent enemy inactivity, he landed two battalions abreast on 16 April, despite kamikaze attacks largely defeated by the sturdy picket destroyers of the Navy. The General had been right in his suspicions about the island, for it masterfully camouflaged a force of 7,000 people, including 1,500 Okinawan civilians who fought fanatically for their island. The senior officer on the island, Major Masashi Igawa, must have been an outstanding leader for the civilian resistance was the fiercest experienced anywhere in the Okinawan campaign.

The landings on Ie Shima used Army LVT(4)s of the 534th Amphibian Tractor Battalion, with air and naval gunfire cover, but references give no mention to any use of LCI gunboats. The fight for Ie Shima was bitter and protracted due to the Japanese use of many caves and the necessity of taking high ground heavily defended and thickly strewn with mines and booby traps. The island was declared secure on 21 April, but mopping-up continued for four more days. Total Japanese losses were 4,706 killed versus the 77th's loss of 239 killed and 879 wounded.[22] These American casualties included the sad loss of one of the nation's most beloved war correspondents and friend of the GI, Ernie Pyle.

The 96th Infantry Division ran into the main defenses on Okinawa on 6 April and the pace in the south slowed to a crawl. Progress was curtailed by enemy artillery and mortar fire combined with counterattacks to seize lost or critical terrain. The 1st Marine Division was sent south to reinforce this attack and officially came into the line on 1 May. The whole Marine attack from this point would be re-oriented to the south.

LVT support during this phase was limited to logistical roles for the cargo LVTs and direct and indirect firing by armored LVTs. As in the past, the tanks of the Marine Division, with their more powerful 75 mm guns, were in front of the infantry blasting the caves and flamethrower tanks were invaluable for sealing caves as they had on Iwo Jima. Roads were few and the cargo LVT provided direct logistical support to Marine units as the drive southward progressed. An enemy counterlanding was attempted on the rear of the 1st Marine Division, but these attackers were destroyed by LVT(A)4 crews. Throughout this period operations of the cargo LVT were continuous and drained the availability of operational vehicles. The LVT(3), like its predecessors, required extensive maintenance which was not available because these vehicles were vitally needed to transport the massive requirements, particularly in ammunition, needed by the 1st Marine Division as it fought south.

The III Amphibious Corps entered the fight for the south on 6 May. To reinforce its attacks, LVT(A)4s were employed to fire artillery missions using high-angle fire under the control of artillery fire direction officers.[23] The LVT(A)s' role as artillery increased later in the campaign with six platoons (thirty vehicles) giving fire support on 19 May. When not engaged in fire support, the most common application of the LVT(A) on Okinawa was to guard the seaward flanks of the divisions as they drove south.

The progress of the attack was severely hampered by rains which fell in torrents for ten days starting 22 May and made movement of even a jeep or man difficult in knee-deep mud. Even the LVT was bogged down by this mud and the gap between logistical support and the requirements of battle widened to the point that air drops were required to supply the troops. LVTs were reassigned to supply the troops beach-to-beach using the sea as a supply route and were in continuous operation during the rainy ten days.

The 1st Marine Division had the mission of conducting a shore-to-shore amphibious landing against the Oroku Peninsula, which lies west of the principal city of Naha. This peninsula, after the fall of the main bastion of Shuri some days previously, was now defended only by the remnants of Japanese naval forces. D-Day was set for 4 June and for this operation a critical shortage of LVTs developed. Of the four battalions or 400 cargo LVT vehicles that had landed on Okinawa, only 72 were operational and these were in poor condition because of the continuous supply support required during the rains.[24] For this reason, the attack was reduced to regimental level with two battalions landing abreast. H-Hour was set for 6:00 A.M., but as the cargo LVTs formed on the line of departure at 5:30 A.M., five of those in the first wave had mechanical failure. Despite this loss of troop strength, the regimental commander ordered the assault forward and the remaining six vehicles of the first wave crossed the line of departure behind a line of LVT(A)4s. The landing was successful and this was due in no small measure to the pounding dealt by no less than fifteen artillery battalions which were supplying the preparation fires for the landing.[25]

LVTs were active to the last days of the campaign. LVT(A)s and LVTs were used to attack positions in the extreme south of Okinawa on 6 June. The island was declared secure on 21 June 1945 by General Geiger, who succeeded General Buckner who was killed by a mortar round on 8 June.

Figure 45. A platoon of LVT(A)4s waiting for orders during the fighting for the Oroku Peninsula on Okinawa.

The Okinawan campaign was the largest amphibious operation in the Pacific and represented the very latest thinking in LVT application. For the cargo amphibian, Okinawa represented the classic mix of assault delivery of troops against the enemy beachhead on D-Day followed by logistical support for the troops, often in situations where the LVT was the only vehicle that could get through. The latter occurred on Okinawa where sea resupply had to be used when the torrential rains made the island literally an ocean of mud. Figures are not available for a comparison of the stamina of the new LVT(3) versus its predecessor, the single-engined LVT(4), however, records show that the LVT(3) was very sensitive to the need for maintenance time in between operations or malfunctions would increase. Tracked vehicles as a family have this fault and even the long line of development leading to the LVT(3), using time-proven parts from the M5 light tank, did not greatly change its maintenance requirements.

The armored amphibian on Okinawa was used for the first time in large numbers to deliver artillery fire reinforcing conventional artillery, a use which has become a cornerstone of post-war doctrine and one which is totally compatible with the 75 mm howitzer design capabilities. The assault gun role of the LVT(A) was required in a landing until tanks came ashore to assume direct-fire infantry support. Occasional efforts have been made to design add-on equipment to float main battle tanks and the success of the T-6 floatation gear is notable. However, the Dual-Drive tanks of Normandy, which used a collapsible canvas screen errected to provide the necessary floatation, were generally lost at sea in the rougher waters of the English Channel. Until such time as a reliable floatation scheme can be designed for a main battle tank, and three decades later there has been no promise of such a successful apparatus, the role of the armored LVT is assured. The Marine Corps has continued to maintain the capability of reinforcing its landings with armored amphibians of the latest model rather than attempt to design floatation gear for its main battle tanks.

The disadvantages of the LVT(A)4 were well known and development was underway during World War II's last months to rectify the lack of a gyro-stabilization system in its turret. The LVT(A)5, essentially an LVT(A)4 with stabilization added, was scheduled for action in the Pacific, but the war ended before it could be employed.

World War II represented a period of intense development of the LVT for the speed with which new models arrived on the battlefield scene exceeded anything seen in post-war years. Necessity was, quite literally, the mother of invention. Yet, in retrospect, the LVT(1) possessed certain characteristics which were not matched by later LVTs, not the least of which was speed in the water. It must be recognized that the LVT represented a vital technical solution of a problem in warfare that had to be solved before victory could be achieved. It came to represent the desirable characteristics of armor protection, firepower, and mobility for the troops in the amphibious mode, and achieved the status of a required item for success with minimum loss of life. The confidence and state of mind of the LVT crews was clearly expressed in the closing pages of an early training manual on the LVT(3):

> Yeah, it's been a long way. What's more, there's still a long tough road ahead. Don't kid yourself that it's going to be a picnic. It's not. These little yellow B-------s we're trying to exterminate are screwy, fanatical fighters who get crazier the closer they get to home. They've got beliefs, too, even if they don't agree with ours. Before you can get them to change their minds, you'll probably have to ram an LVT down their oriental throats. And we hope you do it![26]

These might seem harsh, racist words today, but they represented the state of mind of the participants in a total war, not a war limited to a peninsula or to one country, and they typify the commitment developed by the combatants towards victory. If such words seem oddly out of place in war today, they at least serve to highlight to unique character of World War II as this country's only global, total war involvement. The LVT emerged from this war in almost its final form, yet modern wars require nuclear considerations and technology far in advance of that which confronted the LVT in World War II. Despite these changes, the LVT today remains basically similar in overall capabilities to the early Alligator conceived over forty years ago by Donald Roebling. A review of the further evolution of the vehicle from the end of World War II to the present will trace the trends that have developed to keep pace with the changes in war.

NOTES

[1] Benis M. Frank and Henry I. Shaw, Victory and Occupation, Vol. V of The History of the United States Marine Corps Operations in World War II (5 Vols.; Washington D.C.: Historical Branch, G-3 Division, Headquarters, United States Marine Corps, 1968), p. 13.

[2] Ibid., pp. 34-36.

[3] Charles S. Nichols, Jr. and Henry I. Shaw, Okinawa: Victory in the Pacific (Washington D.C.: Historical Branch, G-3 Division, Headquarters, United States Marine Corps, 1955), p. 50.

[4] Ibid., pp. 50-52.

[5] Frank and Shaw, Victory and Occupation, p. 40.

[6] Ibid., pp. 80-81.

[7] Nichols and Shaw, Okinawa, p. 304.

[8] Jeter A. Isely and Philip A. Crowl, The United States Marines and Amphibious War (Princeton: Princeton University Press, 1951), p. 535.

[9] Nichols and Shaw, Okinawa, p. 23.

[10] Borg-Warner, Model B Amphibian Cargo Carrier (Sales Pamphlet, undated with no location), p. 3.

[11] Ibid., p. 12.

[12] Ibid.

[13] Borg-Warner, Borg-Warner and You (Kalamazoo: Borg-Warner, 1945), p. 1.

[14] Bureau of Ships, Meet the LVT(3): Technical Publication No. 7 (Washington: Bureau of Ships, 1944), p. 3.

[15] Frank and Shaw, Victory and Occupation, p. 100.

[16] Nichols and Shaw, Okinawa, p. 260.

[17] Isely and Crowl, U.S. Marines and Amphibious War, p. 535.

[18] Nichols and Shaw, Okinawa, p. 260.

[19] Ibid., p. 45.

[20] Ibid., p. 64.

[21] Frank and Shaw, *Victory and Occupation*, p. 111.

[22] Nichols and Shaw, *Okinawa*, p. 118.

[23] Ibid., p. 154.

[24] Ibid., p. 215.

[25] Ibid., p. 218.

[26] Bureau of Ships, *Meet the LVT(3)*, p. 35.

PART IX

SUCCESSORS TO THE LEGEND

The war that developed the LVT was unique in history both in its size and unlimited character. It was a war that brought land, sea, and air into total play for the first time for a level of devastation never before equalled across the globe. These unique conditions forged the LVT into a form that has not changed substantially to this day. The amtrac provided a technological answer to a crucial tactical requirement that led to strategic victory.

The development of the LVT, however, hardly proceeded in a straight line. As evident in the early campaigns at Guadalcanal and Bougainville, the amtrac was not intended as the combat vehicle it later came to be, but rather was initially perceived as a logistical asset for hauling supplies until trucks could arrive or to move goods over terrain no wheeled vehicle could traverse. In the logistical role, the LVT was unarmored and basically lightly armed with only machine guns for self-defense. Curiously, before the war, the possible combat use of the vehicle had been outlined in the early editions of the NTP-167, the bible on amphibious war. That it was not initially so used is more a reflection of military conservatism than any early lack of capability for assault landings. The vehicle was radical and untried, and commanders were unlikely to risk a new product on the first waves of a new war. From the first, however, the LVT appears to have fully satisfied expectations as a cargo carrier because at Guadalcanal and more particularly at Bougainville, the LVT was the prime rough-terrain cargo carrier and all-purpose vehicle.

If the landings in the Pacific had met less opposition, and if the islands had no coral, the development of the LVT would have proceeded exclusively along cargo lines because the requirement for assault transport of troops might have been met by the trusty LCVP. Since the need for armor would have been minimized, the amtrac could have grown much larger to increase cargo capacity and the LVT(A) might never have been developed. In reality, the Pacific War was a part of a total war, and the LVT had to meet the test of combat as well as logistic use in the rear areas.

The need to use the LVT in the assault landing role introduced compromise into the design of a vehicle that was already a mass of compromises. Any amphibian must tread the thin line between use on land and employment in the water. To optimize the design for water travel would have given the vehicle a boat-like hull that would be very clumsy on land, yet a box-like hull with land treads would be too slow and dangerously unmanageable in water. The requirements of combat further complicated matters because armor then became an important addition and machine guns were no longer solely for self-defense but required considerable ammunition for suppressive fire as the vehicle approached the beach. The overall result was a loss in cargo space and capacity. Armor alone represented a thirty to forty-percent loss in cargo capacity, although, fortunately, much of it was the bolt-on type which could be dropped after the landing. Only the LVT(A)2 was developed as an armored cargo carrier for use by the Army; all others remained cargo types with only limited amounts of armor permanently mounted on the cab, bow, and sides protecting the gasoline tanks.

The armored LVT was brought in to the full assault role for the first time in the Marshalls. It would be misleading to assume that the use of the LVT at Tarawa to land troops inspired the creation of the armored amphibian because (as stated in Chapter 2) as early as 1941, prior to U.S. entry into the war, Marine Corps and Navy personnel had discussed the need to build an armed amphibian to blast its way ashore against defenses. Due to studies such as those performed by the brilliant Lieutenant Colonel Pete Ellis, the nature of combat in the Pacific had been glimpsed. Opposed landings were expected and an armored amtrac could play a key role in gaining an early foothold. Development of the armored amphibian had started before World War II, but the onset of the war initially interrupted this trend while total effort was directed towards providing enough LVT(1)s to meet the immediate needs of the Marine Corps. With the progress of the war up to the Solomons, the development of the armored amphibian resumed, but the LVT(A)1 did not enter production until July 1943, too late for Tarawa but in time for the long and complex campaign in the Marshalls.

Like the cargo amphibian, the development of the LVT(A) was not a sure process, and the first vehicle encountered problems in attempting to be something it was not --- a tank. The LVT(A)1 mounted a tank turret with a tank gun and this expedient tended to shape its tactical use on land. Unfortunately, the compromises of design for an amphibian were especially harmful to the armored amphibian. The vehicle could not be as heavily armored as a tank or it would not float; nor could it be as compact and low in silhouette as a tank since this would not displace enough water and, again, it would not float. The use of a tank gun represented a quick solution to the need for a tested and available gun mounting and was the initial direction of the research effort when the M5 tank turret was used in the Borg-Warner Model A and adopted in the final design manufactured by Food Machinery Corporation. The LVT(A)1 and the later (A)4 fulfilled its tactical design purpose in water admirably, blasting the shore with its main gun as it approached the beach to keep the enemy pinned down to the last second. Once out of the water, however, the compromises in design, such as a high silhouette and thin armor, made it an easy mark for anti-tank fire.

Arming the amtrac with a 75 mm howitzer was a practical solution for both effectiveness in water and survival on land. Although the LVT(A)4 was first used predominantly in direct fire roles, by the time it reached Okinawa it was recognized as a highly effective supplementary artillery piece on land, and this use maximized application of the gun, a howitzer, in the role for which it was designed and kept the vehicle in the rear, away from the deadly anti-tank fire that had caused so many casualties in the past.

The nature of World War II shaped the LVT into a water vehicle with many of the characteristics of the land tank including armor protection, firepower, and mobility. It became clear, however, that the tank's place in the order of battle was not threatened by the advent of the armored LVT but in fact was emphasized. The tank could not be compromised by thin armor for floatation and still be expected to survive in the battle field, and so it was stoutly built and could accept a heavier, more powerful gun, thus making it the logical vehicle to lead the troops, a function it still performs today.

The severity of World War II accelerated development of the LVT. A total of 18,616 LVTs of all types were produced during the conflict, and the LVT(1), (2), (3), and (4), plus three designs of armored amtracs, represent a hectic pace of development not matched by post-war years.[1]

The LVT(3) emerged from World War II as the standard cargo LVT of the Marine Corps with the LVT(A)5 as its companion amtrac. The main difference between the LVT(A)5 and the (A)4 was the installation in the (A)5 of a gyro-stabilization system to allow accurate shooting from the water. A significant modification was made to the LVT(3) during 1949 when its cargo compartment was covered by folding metal doors to block the entry of breaking waves and shield passengers from enemy grenades. A small turret mounting a machine gun was also added centered near the bow. The LVT(3)C (the "C" signifying it was covered) bore the brunt of the fighting in Korea, functioning more in the role of an armored personnel carrier on land than an amphibious vehicle in water-borne landings because the Korean struggle used the United States Marine Corps as much for its infantry fighting power as for its amphibious capability. Instead of short, sharp fights for islands, the Corps operated nearly continuously on land on the Korean Peninsula, requiring the LVT to assist more overland than over water. Along with the LVT(A)5, the LVT(3)C performed its duties with efficiency and greater reliability since more maintenance time was generally available than during the hectic days of a major World War II landing in the Pacific. The LVT(3)C remained standard with the Marine Corps until the introduction of the first major post-war design, the LVT(P)5, in 1953.

The introduction of the LVT(P)5 family of LVTs represented the fullest expansion of the role of the LVT. In addition to the basic personnel/cargo

Figure 46. The LVT(3)C. This view shows the caliber .30 machine gun cupola.

Figure 47. The LVT(3)C. This view shows the rear ramp. Vehicle is located at the LVT Museum, Camp Pendleton, California.

Figure 48. The LVT(P)5. This view shows the front ramp and rear engine design with the machine gun cupola forward in the center. The driver's hatch, surrounded by periscopes, is at the left front of the vehicle.

Figure 49. The rear view of the LVT(P)5. The track provided the water drive with its paddle-like cleats in the center section of the track. The command version, with the exception of additional antenna, looks identical on the outside.

Figure 50. The LVT(R)1. This retriever was highly effective. The boom apparatus is shown in its folded position for movement.

Figure 51. Rear view of the LVT(R)1.

Figure 52. The LVT(H)6 with its powerful 105mm howitzer. This vehicle remains the only armored amtrac available for service, despite its age.

Figure 53. Rear view of the LVT(H)6. This view shows the outline of the large turret that was specifically designed for this vehicle.

version, designated with the "P", other specialized variants were researched and construction at the factory to complement particular missions rather than modified later from the basic cargo vehicle. In addition to the cargo LVT, a specialized retriever vehicle was constructed with two winches, a welding rig, a crane, and other maintenance accessories to assist other LVTs needing repair or towing. It had a maximum winch capacity with a single line of 45,000 pounds.[2] A command vehicle, the LVT(C)5, "C"- for command, was produced to provide communications facilities to the unit commander in the mobile mode, a role first attempted on Saipan and one which has become very useful through the years. Communications operators in the command vehicle could send and receive on seven channels, and monitor four additional channels. By contrast, the cargo version of the LVT(P)5 had radio equipment sufficient to send and receive on one channel and listen on two channels. In addition, the LVT(C)5 had space for chairs, tables, and map boards and has been used not only for command during amphibious landings, but also during mobile operations on land.[3] The LVT family also expanded to include an engineer vehicle, fitted with an imposing V-shaped bulldozer blade with plow blades extending downwards to detonate mines, with the dual mission of clearing mines and breaching obstacles. It was also capable of firing a rocket-pulled, 350-foot line charge, resembling connected sausage, which would be detonated on the ground after being stretched to its full length by the rocket. The explosion cleared mines by sympathetic detonation in the area of the line charge and cleared a 350-foot lane for a vehicle to pass. In addition to the above array of vehicles, the new LVT family also included a redesigned armored LVT based on the new cargo vehicle's chassis, the LVT(H)6, "H" for howitzer, which mounted a standard 105 mm artillery piece used throughout the Marine Corps and the United States Army, with an effective range of 12,000 yards. The LVT(H)6 featured a fully enclosed turret designed specifically for the vehicle rather than an adaptation of an existing tank turret or self-propelled artillery motor carriage. With its standard artillery piece, the LVT(H)6 was routinely used to provide artillery fires once ashore, an outgrowth of the World War II experience with howitzer-equipped armored amtracs.

The LVT(P)5 family of vehicles were the largest and heaviest yet produced and represented the fullest range of LVT capabilities (command, cargo, armored amtrac, retriever), yet this advance in technology did not necessarily represent an overall increase in cargo capacity. The following is a table of comparison:

	LVT(3)	LVT(P)5
Length	24'6"	29'8"
Width	11'2"	11'8 1/2"
Height (top of vehicle)	9'11"	8'7 1/2"
(top of machine gun cupola)		10' 1/2"
Weight (empty)	26,600 lbs.	69,780 lbs.
Cargo capacity	12,000 lbs.	12,000 lbs. (water) 18,000 lbs. (land only)
Speed (land) (water)	17 mph 6 mph	30 mph 6.8 mph
Engine	Cadillac V-8(2) each at 220 HP	Continental V-12 (1) 810 HP

Source: Robert J. Icks, "Landing Vehicles Tracked," in <u>Armored Fighting Vehicles in Profile</u>, ed. Duncan Crow (New York: Doubleday & Company, Inc., 1972), p. 162, and United States Marine Corps, <u>Amphibian Vehicles: FMFM 9-2</u> (Washington, D.C.: United States Marine Corps, 1971), pp.94-96.

The LVT(P)5 family was used in combat in Viet Nam in a wide variety of roles from normal assault landing (although rarely against significant opposition) to resupply overland and employment in the swampy riverine environment of Viet Nam's rivers and delta regions. Although the vehicle was aging during the Viet Nam War, its availability remained high throughout most of the war with eighty percent or more remaining operational at any one time due to the complete maintenance facilities and personnel brought into Viet Nam for LVT support. LVT operations in Viet Nam were characterized by use of amtrac crewmen as infantry in addition to their duties with the vehicles and from this came the nickname "AmGrunts" ("Grunt" was the affectionate appellation given the hard-working infantryman). The armored amtrac, the LVT(H)6, supplied artillery fire for LVT operations and for mobile infantry operations and won high praise from the infantry for its versatility and staying power under sustained operations.

As with any complex vehicle, age eventually made repeated rebuilding of the same engines and vehicles uneconomical. Even during Viet Nam, persistent failures of some key parts and hydraulic and fuel leaks signaled the approach of the end of the useful life of the LVT(P)5. The Marine Corps, designated after World War II as the action agency for development of new LVTs, commenced design of a new family of LVTs, the LVT(P)7, which began phase-in during the early 1970s. (No LVT(P)6 design was ever developed.)

The design of the LVT(P)7 represents a response to the shortcoming of the LVT(P)5. The relative lack of maneuverability of the LVT(P)5 in water was corrected in the LVT(P)7 by a sophisticated water jet propulsion and steering system which allowed it to literally pivot on its own axis in the water. The ramp was in the rear of the vehicle, similar to the World War II position because the front placement was never popular with the hapless infantryman who must charge into the face of fire from a front ramp. The slow water speed of the LVT was always a major planning constraint and the LVT(P)7 design represents an attempt to optimize its hull shape for better water performance with the net result of an improvement in water speed from 6 mph in the LVT(P)5 to 8.4 mph in the LVT(P)7. In achieving this, however, the boxy and cargo-efficient design of the LVT(P)5 hull was discarded in favor of the new shape of the LVT(P)7 which does not allow as much troop or cargo capacity. The following comparison demonstrates the major differences:

	LVT(P)5	LVT(P)7
Length	29' 8"	26'
Width	11' 8 1/2"	10' 3 3/4"
Height (top of vehicle)	8' 7 1/2"	
(top of machine gun cupola)	10' 1/2"	9' 9"
Weight	69,780 lbs.	40,000 lbs.
Cargo	12,000 lbs. (water) 18,000 lbs. (land)	10,000 lbs.
Speed (land) (water)	30 mph 6 mph	40 mph 8.4 mph
Engine	Continental V-12 810 HP	Detroit Diesel 400 HP

Source: United States Marine Corps, *Amphibian Vehicles: FMFM 9-2* (Washington, D.C.: United States Marine Corps, 1971), pp. 94-96, 106-107.

Post-war LVTs have been rated in troop capacity based on the spaces provided by seating in contrast to the World War II practice of simply having the troops stand in the open-topped cargo compartments. With the advent of covered cargo compartments, troops could no longer comfortably stand and troop benches were provided. The LVT(P)7 seats only twenty-five

Figure 54. The LVT(P)7. This vehicle returned to the rear ramp and front engine design of the LVT(4), with the bow area modified for better water speed.

Figure 55. The LVT(C)7. The command version has seven antennae.

Figure 56. The LVT(R)7, rear view. The boom operator's seat is just visible with control levers in front of the seat.

Figure 57. The UH-1 Iroquois. Standard light helicopter flown by all services.

combat equipped troops versus the old LVT(P)5 which could seat thirty-four.

The LVT(P)7 family of vehicles has not reached the level of diversity of the older LVT(P)5. There are no new armored amtracs; the LVT(H)6 remains the only available armored amtrac and it is currently in preservative storage. There are no armored amtrac battalions active in the Marine Corps. The engineer vehicle, although developed, has not been fully introduced, primarily because of money. The passenger/cargo version, the command vehicle, LVT(C)7, and the retriever, LVT(R)7, constitute the new family of the LVT(P)7, and this shrinkage raises a fundamental question regarding the future of the vehicle. As in the past, it is a high-maintenance vehicle that wears rapidly and is costly to replace. With cost-effectiveness as a phrase permanently enshrined in the consciousness of the Defense Department planners since the McNamara Era, they are willing to invest only as many dollars as are justified and this justification involves looking at what other options are available in today's amphibious operations for delivering troops and supplies ashore. No discussion of the post-war LVT can be complete without mentioning the role of the greatest single tactical innovation in amphibious warfare since the LVT, the helicopter.

The helicopter was used during World War II, but only in the most limited roles such as messenger service and limited observation. In the post-war years the capabilities of this remarkable machine improved to the point where military applications were developed. The first uses were sea-air rescue and resupply but the last years of the Korean War saw some used for troop transport. As the study of helicopter employment continued, the concept of "vertical envelopment" was created. Essentially this concept viewed the helicopter as a means of delivering troops and supplies inland behind the beaches, either in concert with a surface assault or separately. Helicopter capability would force the enemy to consider a vast number of possible landing sites, a problem very difficult to solve because defenders cannot be everywhere at once with any significant strength. Helicopters in the vertical envelopment phase of an amphibious landing would be organized in waves much like the surface assault and designated helicopter landing zones would receive air strikes or naval gunfire just as surface assaults did prior to launching.

The workhorse of the Marine Corps in the early years of development was the H-19 Chickasaw, built by Sikorsky, with a crew of two and accommodations for ten combat-equipped troops. For heavy lift, the Sikorsky CH-37 Mojave was developed in the years immediately after the Korean War and could carry thirty-six troops.

Helicopters have generally followed the pattern of light, medium, and heavy types with the light helicopter used for observation, small lifts of personnel, and to provide commanders with an outstanding command vehicle for observation of the battle field. The medium helicopter primarily carries the assault waves of troops landing in the airborne portion of the amphibious operation. The heavy helicopter is used as a cargo lift vehicle but may be used for troop lift if available.

The current medium lift helicopter is the CH-46 Sea Knight which can lift twenty-five troops or carry a 6,600 pound cargo for a distance of 109 miles at sea level.[4] The current heavy lift helicopter is the CH-53 Sea Stallion, a fast helicopter capable of going 200 mph and lifting up to sixty-four combat-equipped troops or over 15,000 pounds of cargo.[5] From the above figures it can be seen that the CH-46 can carry as many

Figure 58. The CH-46 Sea Knight. This veteran helicopter is made by Boeing Vertol and is primarily for troop transport.

Figure 59. The CH-53 Sea Stallion, made by Sikorsky, is primarily for cargo. This is the first helicopter in the world to perform an aerial loop.

troops as the LVT(P)7, and the heavy lift helicopter can outlift the LVT by about 5,000 pounds. It is not surprising therefore that with these capabilities the helicopter was the chief vehicle for moving men and supplies in Viet Nam. The LVT was employed in a wide variety of tasks, but its operations were generally restricted to swamp or water areas best suited to its amphibious capability while the helicopter ranged over the entire countryside. Helicopter medical evacuation was a great morale boost to the troops in the field in Viet Nam because they knew the response time on an emergency evacuation call was as little as five minutes.

Although the CH-46 and the CH-53 were both used extensively in Viet Nam, no recommendation was ever made to replace Marine Corps surface assault capability in the LVT with the vertical envelopment of the helicopter. Replacing or eliminating the LVT is not a practical solution at this time because the helicopter has some definite shortcomings such as significant reliance on the weather. For example, if visibility is below a quarter mile, the helicopter becomes unusable. The helicopter also has maintenance problems similar in severity to the LVT, and availability of operational machines, even with sufficient servicing, can vary widely from one day to the next. The helicopter has a demonstrated vulnerability to ground fire from small arms as seen in Viet Nam, and the crash of a helicopter usually results in very high losses among the passengers.

The maintenance of the dual capability of landing on the beach against opposition and attacking inland with helicopters represents a desirable mix that will be maintained in the future. The all-weather capability of the LVT is a necessary back-up to the weather-sensitive helicopter, but the slow water speed of the LVT is causing significant concern among Marine Corps planners of future amphibious operations against enemies armed with sophisticated weapons. Modern missile artillery can deliver nuclear and heavy conventional explosives over very long distances and this long-range capability, plus the overall threat of nuclear war at any time, forces the amphibious attacker to resort to ever greater dispersion of his task forces to prevent too great a loss from artillery or nuclear strikes. One result of this necessary dispersion is the need to launch LVTs at a greater distance from shore and to lengthen the run into the beach. If ships launched the LVT at normal distances of less than 5,000 yards, they are too vulnerable to an array of hard-hitting enemy guided missiles that can be launched from shore or from patrol boats protecting the coast. Radar, the ever-present guardian of many coastlines in the world today, would have ample time to track the attackers and launch additional radar-guided rockets and aircraft, regardless of weather or time of day. The Navy desires to develop an over-the-horizon capability for launching amphibious assaults to defeat enemy radar, and while this is possible with the helicopter, such a launch at sea for the LVT (about twenty-five miles is considered distance to horizon) would necessitate over three hours in the water for the new LVT(P)7 traveling at 8 mph. This great length of time gives the enemy far too much time to bring his weapons to bear on this vulnerable target and tends to fix the amphibious task forces in place while they attempt to protect the LVTs as they move towards shore. In addition, the troops would be in poor condition after a three-hour ride in an LVT and many sea-sick men would be facing the crisis of their lives on the hostile beach at a time when they need absolutely clear heads. Something must be done to correct this situation, but the history of the development of the LVT offers little hope of improvement. In fact, the reader may recall that early test versions of the LVT(1) attained water speeds of over 9 mph, a figure not equalled to this day. The amtrac represents a compromise of many conflicting requirements and continuous development over thirty-five years has not created a break-through in this critical area, nor is any on the horizon. Many Marines agree that the present LVT(P)7 represents the last of its kind. A new vehicle for modern war must be developed to solve the problem of water speed to reduce the time spent in making long runs to the beach. Fortunately there are some alternative surface vehicles that may inherit the amtrac legend.

It is not widely known that the air cushion vehicle (ACV), which rides on a cushion of air forced out at the bottom, was combat tested in the Viet Nam War and has proven its ability to move at speeds up to 60 mph. Large versions of the ACV transport passengers across the English Channel, although ACVs used in Viet Nam carried no more than a squad of ten men and were used in the swamp and riverine environments to patrol large areas. To date, however, the ACV has poor lift capability and requires a great deal of power for lift and forward motion. It is also a relatively noisy machine that can be heard for quite a distance. Another alternative is the hydro-foil used on boats which is also capable of great speed, but has the serious drawback of being unable, in its present form, to move onto land. The ACV is capable of moving from water to land without even slowing down although its mobility on land is limited and it is unable to negotiate broken terrain. At this time, most of the Marine Corps' attention is focused on the ACV as the successor to the amtrac and its final combat design will incorporate many real constraints including the need to adapt the ACV to fit within available Navy transport ships. Currently, there is little real progress towards developing a practical ACV due to the lack of money for an extended research and development program. There is a real gap between the squad-carrying ACVs of Viet Nam and a vehicle that could carry a 10,000 pound cargo in an amphibious operation of the future. A comprehensive design effort is required to bring the ACV concept into the realm of practicality, but it appears it will be some time before such an effort can be funded.

The design of the ACV of the future for amphibious operations represents another round in the continuing interaction between war and technology. Given a set of conditions, if time permits, science and engineering will design a new answer to the problem of amphibious war in the 1970s and 1980s, essentially repeating the story of the LVT. World War II generated new amphibious requirements and the solution in the form of the LVT appeared just as radical as the ACV might appear to some today. Nevertheless, a solution must be achieved or this nation's military posture will be irretrievably degraded.

It is possible that the Central Pacific drive might have been successful without the LVT in World War II. Tremendous bombardment, in combination with something like parachute assault, a costly form of attack, or a landing using only the LCVP (also very costly if not prohibitive) might have succeeded. It would have been slower at best, possibly unsuccessful, and the net result would have been a longer war with many more lives lost. Today, the stakes are higher. The radar guidance systems and missiles of the modern battle field are far more accurate and have greater hitting power than anything else seen by man and unless the right vehicle is used, total failure is predictable. The present LVT is simply much too slow in the water for the job. The need is for a ten-fold increase in speed, or the gap will be too great in view of the modern weaponry that will be defending the beaches.

One can only hope that the future solution will work as well as the LVT did in World War II. The new vehicle will have a legend to follow, a legend that started in Guadalcanal and continued across the Pacific against beaches that were fanatically defended. Future defenders must be made to feel impending defeat as the Japanese, North Koreans, and North Vietnamese felt when they saw the LVTs climb over all obstacles and come at them, spitting fire from their machine guns and howitzers, on their way into the pages of history.

NOTES

[1] Robert J. Icks, "Landing Vehicle Tracked," in *Armored Fighting Vehicles in Profile*, ed. Duncan Crow (New York: Doubleday & Company, Inc., 1972), p. 161.

[2] United States Marine Corps, *Amphibious Vehicles: FMFM 9-2* (Washington, D.C.: United States Marine Corps, 1971), p. 105.

[3] Ibid., p. 173.

[4] John W. R. Taylor and Gordon Swanborough, *Military Aircraft of the World* (New York: Charles Scribner's and Sons, 1973), p. 23.

[5] Ibid., p. 123.

SELECTED BIBLIOGRAPHY

Books

Bartley, Whitman S. Iwo Jima: Amphibious Epic. Washington: Historical Branch, G-3 Division, Headquarters, United States Marine Corps, 1954.

Bauer, K. Jack. Surfboats and Horse Marines. Annapolis: United States Naval Institute, 1969.

Borg-Warner Corporation. Research, Investigation, and Experimentation in the Field of Amphibious Vehicles. Kalamazoo: Ingersoll Kalamazoo Division, 1957.

Chamberlin, Peter, and Ellis, Chris. Tanks of the World, 1915-1945. New York: Galahad Books, 1972.

Clifford, Kenneth J. Progress and Purpose: A Developmental History of the United States Marine Corps 1900-1970. Washington: History and Museum Division, Headquarters, United States Marine Corps, 1973.

De Jomini, Baron. The Art of War. Philadelphia: J. B. Kippincott, 1862: reprint ed., Westport: Greenwood Press, Publishers, 1973.

Esposito, Vincent J., ed. The West Point Atlas of American Wars. 2 vols. New York: Frederick A. Praeger, 1953.

Ford, Worthington Chauncey, ed. The Journals of the Continental Congress. 34 vols. Washington: Government Printing Office, 1904-37.

Frank, Benis M., and Shaw, Frank I. Victory and Occupation. Vol. V of History of United States Marine Operations in World War II. 5 vols. Historical Branch, G-3 Division, Headquarters, United States Marine Corps, 1968.

Fuller, J. F. C. The Second World War. New York: Duell, Sloan, and Pearce, 1949.

Garand, George W., and Strobridge, Truman R. Western Pacific Operations. Vol. IV of History of United States Marine Corps Operations in World War II. 5 vols. Washington: Historical Branch, G-3 Division, Headquarters, United States Marine Corps, 1971.

Heinl, Robert Debs, Jr. Soldiers of the Sea. Annapolis: United States Naval Institute, 1962.

Heinl, Robert D., and Crown, John A. *The Marshalls: Increasing the Tempo*. Washington: Historical Branch, G-3 Division, Headquarters, United States Marine Corps, 1954.

Henri, Raymond. "Logistics Afloat," in *The United States Marine Corps in World War II*. pp. 766-771. Edited by S. E. Smith. New York Random House, 1969.

Hoffman, Carl W. *Saipan: The Beginning of the End*. Washington: Historical Division, Headquarters, United States Marine Corps, 1950.

Hoffschmidt, E. J., and Tantum, W. H. *Tank Data 2*. Old Greenwich: WE Inc., 1969.

──────. *United States Military Vehicles, World War II*. Greenwich: WE Inc., 1970.

Hough, Frank O.; Ludwig, Verle E.; and Shaw, Henry I. *Pearl Harbor to Guadalcanal*. Vol. I of *History of the United States Marine Corps Operations in World War II*. 5 vols. Washington: Historical Branch, G-3 Division, Headquarters, United States Marine Corps, 1958.

Icks, Robert J. "Landing Vehicles Tracked." In *Armored Fighting Vehicles in Profile*. pp. 149-68. Edited by Duncan Crow. New York: Doubleday & Company, Inc., 1972.

Isely, Jeter A., and Crowl, Philip A. *The United States Marines and Amphibious War*. Princeton: Princeton University Press, 1951.

Kane, Douglas T., and Shaw, Henry I. *Isolation of Rabaul*. Vol. II of *History of United States Marine Corps Operations in World War II*. 5 vols. Washington: Historical Branch, G-3 Division, Headquarters, United States Marine Corps, 1958.

Keyes, Lord. *Amphibious Warfare and Combined Operations*. New York: Macmillan Company, 1943.

Miller, William M., and Johnstone, John H. *A Chronology of the United States Marine Corps, 1775-1934*. Washington: Historical Branch, Headquarters, United States Marine Corps, 1965.

Monks, John. *A Ribbon and A Star*. New York: Henry Holt and Company, 1945.

Nichols, Charles S., Jr., and Shaw, Henry I. *Okinawa: Victory in the Pacific*. Washington: Historical Branch, G-3 Division, Headquarters, United States Marine Corps, 1955.

Shaw, Henry I.; Nalty, Bernard C.; and Turnbladh, Edwin C. *Central Pacific Drive*. Vol. III of *History of United States Marine Corps Operations in World War II*. 5 vols. Washington: Historical Branch, G-3 Division, Headquarters, United States Marine Corps, 1966.

Sherrod, Robert. *History of Marine Aviation in World War II*. Washington: Combat Forces Press, 1952.

Sherwood, Robert E. *Roosevelt and Hopkins: An Intimate History*. New York: Harper Brothers, 1948.

Smith, Holland M. *Coral and Brass*. New York: Scribner's Sons, 1949.

Taylor, John W. R. *Combat Aircraft of the World*. New York: G. P. Putnam's Sons, 1969.

Taylor, John W. R., and Swanborough, Gordon. *Military Aircraft of the World*. New York: Charles Scribner's Sons, 1973.

Toland, John. *The Rising Sun*. 2 vols. New York: Random House, 1970.

Weigley, Russell F. *The American Way of War*. New York: Macmillan Publishing Co., 1973.

Zimmerman, John L. *The Guadalcanal Campaign*. Washington: Historical Division, Headquarters, United States Marine Corps, 1949.

Letters and Interviews

Director of War Plans, United States Navy. Letter of 23 August 1933 to Secretary of the Navy.

Grover, Master Gunnery Sergeant Thomas J. United States Marine Corps. 1st Tank Battalion, 1st Marine Division (Rein), FMF, Camp Pendleton, California. Interview, 15 June 1975.

Major General Commandant. Letter of 17 August 1933 to Secretary of the Navy.

Metzger, Lieutenant Colonel Louis B. Letter of 17 May 1948 to Special Marine Corps Amphibian Tractor Board.

Nutt, Harold. "Amphibian Tank Report." (Borg-Warner Memorandum) 1941.

Peterson, Master Sergeant C. J. United States Marine Corps. 1st Tank Battalion, 1st Marine Division (Rein), FMF, Camp Pendleton, California. Interview, 13 June 1975.

Williamson, Lieutenant J. I. Letter of 5 May 1948 to the Special Marine Corps Amphibian Tractor Board.

Official Publications

Bureau of Ships. *Meet the LVT(3): Technical Publication No.7*. Washington: Bureau of Ships, 1944.

Ellis, Earl H. "Advanced Base Defense During the Present War." (Unpublished and Undated report) Headquarters, United States Marine Corps.

Joint Board. Joint Overseas Expeditions. Washington: Government Printing Office, 1933.

Marine Corps Schools. Amphibious Operations, The LVT and LVT(A). Quantico: Marine Corps Schools, 1948.

United States Army. First Report on Amphibian Tractor (Roebling). Aberdeen: Aberdeen Proving Grounds, 1942.

United States Marine Corps. Amphibious Vehicles: FMFM 9-2. Washington: United States Marine Corps, 1971.

United States Marine Corps. Operations Plan 712H. Washington: Headquarters, United States Marine Corps, 1921.

United States Marine Corps. Tentative Manual for Landing Operations. Quantico: Marine Corps Schools, 1934.

United States Navy. Fleet Training Publication - 167, Change No. 1. Washington: United States Navy Department, 1941.

United States Navy. Navy Department General Order 241. Washington: Navy Department, 1933.

War Department. Instruction Book for Tracked Landing Vehicles. Washington: War Department, 1943.

War Department. TM 9-775, Landing Vehicle Tracked, MK I and MK II. Washington: War Department, 1944.

1st Amtrac Battalion. Muster Rolls. In the Field: 1st Amtrac Battalion, 1943.

2nd Amtrac Battalion. Operation Order No. 1, Forager. In the Field: 2nd Amtrac Battalion, 1944.

2nd Amtrac Battalion. Report of Galvanic Operations. In the Field: 2nd Amtrac Battalion, 1943.

2nd Amtrac Battalion. Special Action Report. In the Field: 2nd Amtrac Battalion, 1943.

2nd Amtrac Battalion. Special Action Report. In the Field: 2nd Amtrac Battalion, 1944.

5th Amtrac Battalion. Special Action Report. In the Field: 5th Amtrac Battalion, 1944.

VITA

Name	Alfred Dunlop Bailey
Birthplace	Washington D.C.
Birthdate	21 October 1937
High School	The Boyden School San Diego, California
College 1956-1960	United States Military Academy West Point, New York
Degree 1960	B.S., United States Military Academy West Point, New York
Professional Organizations	Marine Corps Association
Professional Positions	Platoon Commander, 1st Tank Battalion, 1st Marine Division, Camp Pendleton, California, 1961; Aide-de-Camp, Commanding General, 1st Marine Aircraft Wing, Iwakuni, Japan, 1962; Guard Officer and Range Officer, Marine Barracks, Vallejo, California, 1963-66; Executive Officer, Region II (Middle East-Africa), Marine Security Guard Battalion, Beirut, Lebanon, 1966-68; Commanding Officer, Company A, 1st Amtrac Battalion, Cua Viet, Viet Nam, 1959; Force Armor Officer, III Marine Amphibious Force Headquarters, G-3 Section, 1969; Marine Officer Instructor, NROTC Unit, University of Utah, Salt Lake City, Utah, 1970-73; Operations Officer, 1st Shore Party Battalion, 1st Marine Division, Camp Pendleton, California, 1974; Executive Officer, 1st Tank Battalion, 1st Marine Division, Camp Pendleton, California, 1974-76.
Publications	None

www.ingramcontent.com/pod-product-compliance
Lightning Source LLC
Chambersburg PA
CBHW081831170426
43199CB00017B/2703